RURAL POLITICS
IN COUNTY MEATH, IRELAND

Ethnographic and Historical Studies

RURAL POLITICS
IN COUNTY MEATH, IRELAND

Ethnographic and Historical Studies

Thomas M. Wilson

With a Preface by
Richard Jenkins

The Edwin Mellen Press
Lewiston•Queenston•Lampeter

Library of Congress Cataloging-in-Publication Data

Library of Congress Control Number: 2012955127

Wilson, Thomas, M.
  Rural politics in County Meath, Ireland : ethnographic and historical studies / with a foreword by Richard Jenkins.

1. Social science--Anthropology--general. 2. Social science--Cultural.
3. Political science--Government--Local.

      p cm.
  Includes bibliographical references and index.
  ISBN-13: 978-0-7734-3077-8 (hardcover)
  ISBN-10: 0-7734-3077-6 (hardcover)
  I. Title.

hors série.

A CIP catalog record for this book is available from the British Library.

Front cover: Hill of Slane, County Meath, Ireland, 2011
(photo by author)

The Edwin Mellen Press   The Edwin Mellen Press
Box 450   Box 67
Lewiston, New York   Queenston, Ontario
USA 14092-0450   CANADA L0S 1L0

The Edwin Mellen Press, Ltd.
Lampeter, Ceredigion, Wales
UNITED KINGDOM SA48 8LT

Printed in the United States of America

In loving memory of

Peter Paul Wilson and Anne Marie Downes Wilson

Table of Contents

Preface

This book has been a long time in the making. Tom Wilson began his doctoral research in Meath in 1976, and now, in 2012, three further field research trips later, here we have the considered fruits of a professional life-time's close anthropological attention to one small part of Ireland. A huge amount has changed in the course of that lifetime. After struggling as a developing nation on the rural periphery of the European Common Market, Ireland flexed its muscles as the Celtic Tiger, putting the economic fear of God into many of its fellow members of the European Union, before ruefully having to accept the stringencies and humiliation of a Eurozone rescue package, brought to its knees by a global banking crisis and the hubris of a generation of latter-day gombeen men. Although Wilson's gaze has remained constant throughout, he has changed, too. Had it been written in the early 1980s, Wilson the postdoc would have offered us a fairly typical graduate student's ethnography of rural Ireland (and I am sure that it would have been none the worse for that). Instead, what we now have is a magisterial synthesis of long-term case-study research, on the one hand, and a detailed knowledge of the last seventy years' anthropological literature on Ireland that few can rival, on the other.

Has the wait been worth it? Well, I would not be writing this if I didn't think so. Perhaps more of us should resist the 'publish or be damned' pressure of modern academic life, and take a little more time, particularly over our monographs. It is

i

not that Wilson has previously neglected to write about his field research, of course; a good deal of the present work has its origins in published papers. But there are two virtues to the long haul. The first is that Wilson has had the time to think and reflect on his final big work about Meath - which is what this is - in a way that short deadlines do not permit. The second virtue is that Wilson's careful analysis of political culture in Meath and Ireland, and its articulations with the European Union in particular, is an advertisement for the virtues of a case-study approach, and particularly a case-study approach that allows enough time to see things actually change. What singles this book out, as something *really* unusual, is its combination of fine-grained case-study research with a very long-term perspective (by ethnographic standards).

Thus this book offers more than a re-study - valuable as those are - could. It is an anthropological history of the last thirty-five years in Ireland, and in rural Meath in particular (although we should probably now be talking about semi-rural). The politics of academic life and research funding make this a very difficult thing to do, let alone pull off. That Wilson has been patient and dogged, and has been able to, is perhaps the great distinguishing virtue of this book. That it is so difficult for most of us to even contemplate is something to ponder: driven by the imperatives of contemporary academia, anthropology, in North America and Europe, has, if anything, been moving steadily towards shorter field work and more hermetically-sealed and topically-restricted projects. We need to find ways to make other kinds of anthropology possible.

Each reader must come to his or her own view about this book's qualities, of course: I will not presume to say too much more about that. I am simply glad that what I have been waiting for, for quite some time, has finally arrived. Nor will I attempt a summary of the contents: the tame chapter by chapter summary that all too often passes for an introduction or a preface has always seemed to me to be a redundant waste of paper, and something of an affront to the reader's intelligence into the bargain. Instead, in addition to its championing of long-term case-study research, there are several generic or meta themes about anthropology that this book explores or exemplifies, even if at times implicitly, about which a few words might be in order.

The first thing to note in this respect is that intellectually this is in many respects a very old-fashioned study. That, by the way, is intended as a major compliment; it is certainly not faint praise. The reader will search in vain for the kinds of self-absorbed reflexivity, or linguistically and conceptually opaque and complex theory, that have so disfigured the social sciences, and anthropology, since the various, fashionable 'post-turns' of the 1980s and 1990s. Wilson's study is, instead, an example of intellectual democracy at its best: accessible writing in the tradition of C Wright Mills and Howard Becker. It is, in fact, a fine example of what Mills called the 'sociological imagination': big public issues and everyday life brought into creative contact with each other. In emphasizing politics and political culture - of the kind that many political scientists are interested in - it is also, in strictly anthropological terms, a nudge in the direction of a return to the kind of political anthropology practiced by Max Gluckman, F. G. Bailey, Fredrik Barth and Joan Vincent.

These remarks lead me directly on to the next thought inspired by this work: it illustrates the impossibility of doing something called 'anthropology'. This may seem, in the light of the above remarks, a perverse thing to say. That is as may be, but what I mean is that anthropology has been fooling itself for years that it is an intellectually coherent and reasonably self-contained discipline; indeed as time goes on - and at least partly in response to the organizational and disciplinary politics of academic life - the boundary fences seem to have been built higher and made more formidable. Anthropology is no more coherent or self-contained than sociology or political science, for example, and they, thank goodness, are neither. The human world is not organized for the convenience of disciplines, so if we want to understand it we have to break out of the stockade. This Wilson does, again and again.

Finally there is the small matter of history. The relationship of anthropology to history has been vigorously debated, often to no useful end. I do not intend to enter or prolong those debates. My point is simple: anthropologists are not historians - although they may be, and they should work within a well-informed historical awareness - but ethnographers, be they anthropologists, sociologists or of whatever disciplinary persuasion, are writing history. We are always, necessarily, writing history, in the sense that our research is a contribution to the historical record (and it is to be hoped that it will be one which future historians will have the sense to use, and for which they will thank us). Ethnographers may occupy a peculiar place within the social sciences in this respect: statistics have been with us as long as there have been, for example, tax records, censuses and parish registers, and diarists and other observers of everyday life have been with us as long as writing has. However, the accounts of ethnographers, produced in the course of medium- to long-term, theoretically-sensitized engagements with everyday life, and shaped, ideally, by a well-primed sociological imagination, are, as historical data, probably a twentieth-century innovation. This book is just such an account, and a valuable contribution to what we know about contemporary Ireland. I commend it to you.

Richard Jenkins
Department of Sociological Studies
The University of Sheffield

Acknowledgements

This book is based on many years of ethnographic research in the Republic of Ireland and Northern Ireland. Most of the data and analyses that provide the historical dimensions to this particular examination of changes in political culture which had occurred by the 1980s in County Meath, Republic of Ireland, derive from 36 months of ethnographic field research which I conducted in Meath between 1976 and 1987.

In Meath so many people helped me in my initial doctoral and early post-doctoral research that I cannot list them all, and I apologize to those who are not named here, some of whom asked to remain anonymous. But I could not have completed my research at any stage if it were not for the help of Vincent and Kate O'Reilly, and their wider Clarke and O'Reilly families. Other families who provided vital and sustained help and support were the Brutons, the Clintons, the Coldricks, the Conways, the Dempseys, the Fitzsimons, the Gilsenans, and the O'Donoghues (of Ballsbridge). The late Willie O'Reilly and Johnny Mangan were my first mentors in local Navan history, complementing the erudition and inspiration of Fr. Gerry Rice, and Maurice Clarke gave me a tour of the political terrain of North Meath that still warms me to this day.

My many years of continued research in Navan could not have been possible without the continued support of William Cosgrave, who generously acted as my host in Castlerock for almost a decade and did so with unflagging patience, generosity and kindness. My time in Meath was also enhanced through the support and friendship of Eddie Farrell, Colum Geraghty, Sean Gilligan, Barney Reilly, Damian Usher, and the irrepressible Bud Kowalski. My entry into local public administration and politics would have been seriously impaired without the initial and continuing support of then Meath County Manager, Frank O'Brien. I have met and appreciated the political acumen of many elected representatives over the last thirty years, but I have never met a better scholar of politics than Frank. The staffs of the Meath County Council, the Central Statistics Office in Dublin, and the Navan County Library, particularly librarians Liam Smith and Andy Bennett, provided timely and generous aid whenever it was asked of them. So too did the party cadres, workers and supporters of all of the political parties in Meath. I hope this book in some small part their merits the faith they showed in me.

In those first years in Meath many other local government officers, elected officials, party workers, IFA members, and Tara Mines administrators encouraged me to embrace the complexity of local government and politics. Among these, some of whom are now gone but are always remembered and sorely missed, I thank Tom Cannon, Brendan Crinion, TD, Bill Dallas, Jim Dorgan, Gerry Foley, Pat Fullam, Willie Lynch, Fergus Muldoon, Johnny Murtagh, Austin Sharkey, Pat Traynor, and Jimmy Tully, TD. I want to thank sincerely the sitting members of the Meath County Council of 1976-1980 for their graciousness and patience. All welcomed me to office or home and sometimes both, for formal interviews but also for many informal briefing sessions. These allowed me to see both the organizational structure of local politics and the political substratum of history, economics, kinship and sentiment that was equally the stuff of local political life. Members of the urban councils of Navan, Kells and Trim, and many community councils elsewhere in Meath, were also invaluable sources of insight and hospitality.

In my later research, after moving from Navan to Slane, I was lucky to become the neighbor of the Dohertys. I owe a profound debt to the overall Doherty family of Gernonstown and Cruicetown, and in particular James, Phillip, Thomas and Anne Doherty, who truly have adopted my family to make us part of theirs. I am forever grateful too to my extended family in County Westmeath, Sean and Theresa Downes and the late Esther Downes and Hugh McCormack, for providing a haven for me in those early years.

My accomplishment in Ireland as researcher and academic owes a great deal to my teachers, friends and family in America. Over the years I have benefited from the intellectual and professional support of many academic friends and colleagues in Ireland, the USA, and elsewhere, whose expertise in matters related to the subject of this book provided the bedrock upon which I might build both research and career. In my dissertation years my doctoral supervisor, Edward C. Hansen, mentored me is so many aspects of anthropology and the politics of life that every section of this book reminds me of his sage advice. My graduate committee of Jane Schneider, John Cole and the late Mervyn Meggitt and Eric R. Wolf each contributed mightily, and they too have left their imprint on what I have written. In Ireland I was lucky, while doing fieldwork, to receive initial advice from Eileen Kane and Betty and John Messenger. I am also grateful to the many geographers, sociologists, historians and political scientists who advised me in the course of my doctoral research, including Peter Connel, Patrick Duffy, Jim Frawley, Tom Garvin, Jim Higgins, Peter Mair and Maurice Manning.

Over the years I have sought the knowledge and support of many other specialists in Irish society, culture and politics, and I am delighted that despite my incessant clamouring I was never turned away. James Anderson, Paul Arthur, Dominic Bryan, Chris Curtin, George and Sharon Gmelch, Richard Jenkins, Liam O'Dowd, Cathal McCall, Graham McFarlane, Maruska Svasek, Lawrence Taylor, Herve Varenne, and Joan Vincent were my principal targets, but the person who has borne the brunt of my academic curiosity has been Hastings Donnan. I thank them all sincerely, but add here in case they are quick to judge that I freely admit that any mistakes in the following book are entirely my own!

I also wish to acknowledge the financial support of the following agencies, without whom most of the research that forms the basis of this study would not have occurred: in the USA, the National Endowment for the Humanities, The National Science Foundation, The Social Science Research Council, The Wenner Gren Foundation for Anthropological Research, and Harpur College of Binghamton University, and, in Ireland, The British Academy, The British Council, The

Leverhulme Trust, and The Institute of Irish Studies and the School of Sociology, Social Policy and Social Work of The Queen's University of Belfast.

Finally, I wish to thank two good friends who encouraged and supported me as I approached critical crossroads of my life. Because of them I found and kept on the path that led to much that I have achieved professionally, including this book. John Finn helped to get me started in my original field work as we each searched for our Finn ancestors in a memorable Irish road trip, and Lisa Chapman was instrumental in reintegrating me into American life after I returned to New York to complete my dissertation. Although our paths have diverged, I would like them to know that I shall always cherish the friendship they showed me at what turned out to be crucial moments. So too do I lovingly acknowledge the debt I owe to Anahid Ordjanian Wilson and Peter Haig Wilson, who made so much of the effort that went into this book worthwhile. I close with the offering that both the PhD dissertation I wrote in the 1980s and this book are dedicated with love and longing to my parents, Peter and Anna Wilson, without whom I would never have had my love for scholarship, for Ireland, and for life.

Parts of this book are based on articles of mine that were published over the years, and although much of the analysis I offer here is a reconsideration, a revisiting, of my earlier writings, a great deal is original to this book. However, some chapters have clear connections to these earlier publications, and I wish to acknowledge the support I received from the editors and peer reviewers of the following publications: *Anthropological Quarterly* (1984. From Clare to the Common Market: Perspectives in Irish Ethnography. 57 (1): 1-15; the basis for Chapter 2 of my book); *American Ethnologist* (1988. Culture and Class Among The 'Large' Farmers of Eastern Ireland. 15 (4): 680-695; Chapter 3); *Ethnohistory* (1990. From Patronage to Brokerage in the Local Politics of Eastern Ireland. 37: 158-187; Chapter 4); *Human Organization* (1989. Large Farms, Local Politics, and the International Arena: The Irish Tax Dispute of 1979. 48 (1): 60-70; Chapter 6); *Ireland From Below: Social Change and Local Communities*. (1989. Chris Curtin and Thomas M. Wilson, eds. Galway: Galway University Press; Chapter 5).

Chapter 1

Ethnography, history and local politics in
County Meath, Ireland

In January 1973 the Republic of Ireland and the United Kingdom joined the European Economic Community, and in so doing changed the course of their histories. Both countries entered into new political and economic relations with the other European Economic Community (EEC) members, but also began a new relationship between the two neighboring nations, long associated over hundreds of years of colonialism, war, imperialism, and political union. In fact, accession to the EEC, today known as the European Union (EU), may be seen as an event unmatched in significance by any other in the establishment and subsequent history of each of these two neighboring nation-states. Along with Denmark, their fellow new member, Ireland and the UK embarked on a course of action in 1973 that would change the fundamental structures of their societies, polities, economies and cultures. As members of the European Community of the Nine, they were the first wave of expansion of what had up to then been primarily a Common Market set up by the original six EEC states.

This initial wave has become what some Euroskeptics and others in the Europe of the twenty-first century fear is a flood that will be difficult to stem, as the EU now has twenty-seven member states stretching from Ireland to Greece, and it is expected to expand more, perhaps to encompass Turkey. Whatever its future, the EU has changed the landscape of the European continent, and has done so particularly in its member states. These members daily contend with the forces of

1

Europeanization and European integration which emanate from the capitals of the EU, but which also have their sources in the cores and peripheries of each of the member nations.

It has been widely perceived that no country of the EU, and certainly no country in the expanded European Community which grew from the original six members of Belgium, France, Germany, Italy, Luxembourg and The Netherlands, has changed more due to the EU, or perhaps has benefited more from the EU, than has the Republic of Ireland.[1] In fact Ireland, towards the close of the century, had become the prime example of what a small nation can achieve as a member of the EU. This was due in large part to the Celtic Tiger economy which developed in the decades that followed accession to the EEC. But Ireland's new success, national confidence and economic independence were also owed to the social, economic and political forces which may be subsumed under the rubrics of European integration and Europeanization. These forces helped free Ireland from the restraints of post-colonial economics and politics, and succeed as a small nation within a confederation of larger ones that had dominated the realpolitik of Europe for centuries.

Thus, it is arguable, and in my view likely, that the decade following Ireland's entry into the EEC may come to be viewed as one of the most decisive in the history of the island, due to the converging forces of political and economic integration, Europeanization, secularism, modernization and globalization which were to affect all aspects of life on the island, sometimes in conjunction, sometimes sequentially. Some things in regard to the changes which befell Ireland in the 1970s are certain, however, despite any future debates about the relative importance of any of the forces at work and their

2

impact on locality and nation. Three of these, all central to the concerns of this book, are that the politics of agriculture, the roles of farmers and other agrarian sectors in the Irish political system, and Irish politics in general, were transformed over the 1970s. This occurred to a degree which might suggest, from our contemporary vantage point and with apologies to W. B. Yeats, that the cultures of politics and agriculture were changed utterly. To some of their participants, some of whom were beneficiaries and some victims, it is also clear that these changes were at times beautiful, and at times terrible. But what changed exactly, why were these changes so significant, and why do I tie the changes to Ireland's new membership in the EEC?

The year 1973, when Ireland joined the Common Market, ushered in what was to become the greatest period of socioeconomic growth in that country since the ending of the Irish government's protectionist policies in the 1950s. The EEC's community-wide agricultural policy, the Common Agricultural Policy (CAP), raised and guaranteed prices for farm produce, and guaranteed continental markets for Irish agricultural production. These economic safeguards and safety valves were enhanced by the loans, grants and subsidies which the EEC offered to Irish farmers, to help put their farms and businesses onto a more solid economic footing. Increased direct investment in agriculture through EEC programs, in conjunction with a national re-balancing of agricultural priorities that were effected through the processes of European integration, almost immediately began to disengage Irish agriculture's dependence on British markets. As a result of this economic upturn in Ireland, there was an influx of capital investment from private sources, mainly corporations from

3

outside Europe seeking a production or distribution base in the EEC. These corporate entities took advantage of lucrative tax breaks from the Irish government and a relatively well-educated and lower paid work force. The result was the highest growth rate in the EEC of the Nine, a growth rate that unhappily kept pace with Ireland's rising foreign debt, which by the end of the 1970s made her one of the greatest debtor nations per capita in Western Europe.

From the early days of European membership other changes also occurred rapidly. Not only did Irish governments have to manage the attendant effects of new markets, new production, and new consumption which were immediate after EEC accession, they also had to deal with the impact of EEC economic and political integration on many traditional political relationships within the state. One cause of political change for example was the redefinition of the relationships between and among the Irish economic sectors, including those of employers, labor, agriculture and other occupational and interest groups, all of whom recognized the opportunities and threats which the new Irish economy posed.

Another set of far-reaching changes, but one which at the time was largely under the radar of much public scrutiny, was the impact which European integration and other forces of change were having on political party organization and support. It was this transformation in local politics, in a county long dominated by agricultural interests and concerns, which brought me first to Meath to do my doctoral research. But the initial boom years were short-lived, and the relative decline which followed also brought new challenges to farming and politics throughout the nation. By the 1980s the Republic of Ireland was suffering up to 20 per cent unemployment, a

4

stagnating industrial base, breakdowns in the structure of agriculture, and the return of emigration as a panacea for the ills of the Irish economy and society.

To many Irish citizens of the day successive national governments had failed because they promised much but delivered less to an electorate reeling from economic blows from which their politicians seemed powerless to protect them (a situation which is sadly recurring in Ireland today, at the time of writing this book in 2011). Ironically, many of the politicians in Meath in the early 1980s were still motivated by what had transpired in the 1970s, when national politicians seemed to be able to achieve so much for their constituents in an Ireland liberated from many of its traditional economic restraints.

What was the economic base for so much change and initial confidence? In the first decade of EEC membership foreign capital, most notably from the United States, was attracted to Ireland. Because Irish farm produce was increasingly redirected to continental markets, there was a related diminishing of that sector's dependence on the British economy. Ireland received tremendous transfers of capital from the EC through the CAP and the Regional Fund (Hart 1985). Many of Ireland's policies, most notably foreign and agricultural, became Europeanized, for the first time giving Ireland a voice at the highest, supranational levels of European decision-making (Matthews 1983). Overall, in fact, the first five years of EEC membership were at the time the most lucrative in history for many sectors of the economy as well as for many traditional constituencies in Irish society and politics, among them political parties, interest groups and lobbies. While many in Ireland, including some farmers, miners, factory owners and political party cadres and supporters, had gone into Europe with some trepidation, by the end of the decade many of these same groups and individuals were relieved and pleased (O'Brien 1978; European Communities 1982; Matthews 1983; Finnegan 1983; Blackwell and O'Malley 1984).

The net gain in Ireland as a member of the EEC was substantial. In 1973 Ireland contributed a total of the equivalent of $6.1 million to the EEC but received $43.8 million. In 1981, its contribution was $112.2 million but its total payments from the EEC were $551.2 million (excluding $244.8 million in EEC loans). The best years of European membership for some sectors of the Irish economy came in 1978 and 1979, when Ireland contributed $42 million and $60 million respectively but received in turn from Europe $447 million and $550 million (European Communities 1982). And although those years are now long gone, when I was first living and researching in Ireland it was hard to find people involved in market economics who did not see the material benefits of Europe in Ireland in their everyday lives. So too politicians, whose bread and butter as local representatives was the supply and maintenance of services for their constituents, or at the least was the imaginative task of taking responsibility for the supplying of such services, were becoming committed Europeanists. Or at least some were, while others picked and chose which aspects of European membership were to be supported or opposed in the interests of their constituents, in a form-of variable geometry citizenship. And even as the boom years waned, later times did not see a major fall-off in Irish engagement with Europe. As the 1980s began, for example, Ireland continued to enjoy favored status within the EEC, due to deals negotiated to ensure Irish support for the membership bids of Spain, Portugal and Greece (Finnegan 1983). As that decade wore on Ireland still received sizeable economic support from Europe, culminating in the funding it was offered as the EEC prepared for the completion of the internal market in 1992.

Throughout all of these changes in Ireland in the 1970s it is clear that the sector of the Irish economy that benefited the most was agriculture. In 1978 farm incomes at then current values were over four times their levels in 1971, and real income levels in 1978 were 70 per cent higher than the levels farmers experienced in 1970 (Cox and Kearney 1983). Irish agriculture as an economic enterprise and as a way of life had been transformed. But such changes left many questions unanswered, especially for anthropologists interested in rural society and culture. It was clear that in the 1970s, in a country where agriculture had been the primary economic sector, and where the majority of the population lived in rural communities, the transformation of farming and the countryside were sure to change so much more in the manner in which Irish people lived and worked. And these changes were happening quickly. In 1980 farmers accounted for 20 per cent of the national work force, down from 25 per cent of the national labor force in 1971, but this had occurred while agriculture itself did not decline as an industry. In this period agriculture accounted for 40 per cent of total Irish exports and ten per cent of Irish GDP. By 1978 total Irish GNP increased by as much as 15 per cent above what it would have been without EC farm policy (Duchêne et al. 1985).

The CAP was a big part of this transformation in the Irish economy. It was widely welcomed from the first by Irish farmers because it guaranteed markets for unlimited agricultural production at high prices. This had the desired

7

effects of freeing Irish agriculture from its dependence on the cheap food policy of the United Kingdom, and shifted the burden of income support from Irish to EEC taxpayers (Cox and Kearney 1983). The economic causes of the transformation in Irish agriculture were relatively and rather quickly clear, but the social, political and cultural causes and effects of this transformation were not so clear at the time.

It was to try to understand this transformation of Irish farmers into Euro-farmers that I originally went to County Meath to do my doctoral research. But before I began that research, and all the while doing the research, I was aware I needed to understand the historical forces that shaped Irish rural society. I was unprepared, however, for the ways in which my ethnography would intersect with history in the making in Meath. Before turning to an examination of how Europe changed the domains of Meath culture and politics, I wish to consider some of the ways in which history, ethnography and anthropology came together in my research. For it was in the pursuit of this research that I became convinced that to understand the significance of this period in local and national Ireland, as a basis for the analysis of politics and culture in Ireland today, anthropologists and other scholars must approach history in practice and theory. Said differently, to know what Irish political culture is today, we shall need to know what it was, and how we got from there to here. Ethnographers, in their efforts to chronicle the intersections of past and present culture and politics, must themselves engage in historiography and the making of local and other histories.

8

History, ethnography, anthropology

History and anthropology have been in a love affair with each other since the academic disciplines associated with each were born. American anthropology early on in its formation accepted that one of its goals was the recording and reconstruction of Native American cultures, which were faced with assimilation and extinction. This time-framing encouraged the culture history approach which characterized many facets of academic cultural anthropology. British social anthropology was in the main synchronic in its steadfast application of ethnographic method, but this approach too was not as long-lived as its critics have charged, as it gave way in the late 1940s to more humanistic approaches, championed as we shall soon consider by one of the architects of structural-functionalism, E. E. Evans-Pritchard.

An analysis of the history of the ways in which history has been used and theorized in anthropology is beyond the scope of this book, but it is not coincidental that one of the best analyses of this history, and of the various ways in which anthropologists and historians converge and diverge in their scholarly practices, is that provided by Marilyn Silverman and P. H. Gulliver (1992a), in their introduction to a collection of essays on Irish case studies in historical anthropology (1992b). These scholars, struck by the seeming lack of involvement between the peoples in their research site in south-eastern Ireland with the major events of hundreds of years of Irish history, were even more stunned when historians of Ireland did not seem to think that this disengagement with the past was particularly significant. Silverman and Gulliver's subsequent analysis and publications offered a sophisticated examination of how this difference in approach highlighted many of the ways in which anthropology and history should be approached together, even if through the separate lenses of the two academic disciplines.

Anthropological approaches, however, have tended to fall into two main camps: historical ethnography and the anthropology of history (Silverman and Gulliver 1992a: 16-21), both of which have been attempts by anthropologists to link the past with the present, in order to understand present society and culture with reference to their pasts. The former approach, historical ethnography, seeks to reconstruct how things were in order to understand how they are now. Oral histories and archives provide much of the data for these reconstructions. An anthropology of history, on the other hand, is composed of various strategies to determine how constructions of the past are used to make the present meaningful, and how the past is created in the present and was created in past times. This latter approach involves the investigation of history as ideology and as the invention of tradition, important themes in much anthropology of nations and states over the last fifty years.

As important and as relevant as their analysis was and continues to be, it is in a footnote that they explicate that in the course of their fieldwork they had, in fact, 'made history'. They did this in two ways: in their historical anthropology they had in effect created a new version of the past of the town in which they lived and researched, and their work and presence in the community had become part of the history of the town after 1979 (Silverman and Gulliver 1992a: 11, 60). But this notion of making history serves too as my point of departure, and as one of the ways in which ethnography also is related to history. Ethnography itself provides a conceptualization of social and cultural life in space and time. Ethnographers' immersion

10

within local society demands attention to historicity as the by-product, the realization, and the subject of ethnographic research.

In this book I seek to contribute to the understanding of the relationships between ethnography and historicity, following Hirsch and Stewart (2005: 262), who conclude that historicity:

> describes a human situation in flow, where versions of the past and future (of persons, collectives or things) assume present form in relation to events, political needs, available cultural forms and emotional dispositions. . . Historicity in this sense is the manner in which persons operating under the constraints of social ideologies make sense of the past, while anticipating the future. Historicity is a dynamic social situation open to ethnographic investigation.

As presented in the following book, ethnography also acts as a process of historicity, wherein ethnographic research into the many historicities that are constructed and projected among the persons and groups encountered in field research offer insight into the ways in which people see how their past frames their present and future, and thus how 'historical situations affect historical descriptions' (Hirsch and Stewart 2005: 262). But in doing such research, where the ethnographer pushes the limits of how the past is present and utilized in the present in order to shape the future, anthropologists are simultaneously doing history as well. When they write their ethnography they write history. They offer chronicles of forces

11

at work in historical conjuncture and event, in the times and places of the field research.

In my view ethnography is in equal parts historicity and historiography, where while attending to ways in which people make their own history the ethnographer also makes their history too. When anthropologists do ethnography they also do history. But the histories they compile, narrate and interpret, while mostly local ones, i.e., of people, places and times that are often bypassed in other scholarly accounts, are also implicitly historical accounts of the anthropologist at work and of anthropology in practice. This has become especially apparent in recent years, as the reflexive turn in anthropology has increasingly encouraged ethnographers to consider themselves as subjects in their own research and writing.

The writing of history and ethnography are thus the recognition of the ways in which historicity and ethnicity converge in the lives of our hosts and informants. While ethnographers have always been interested in the many ways the events and institutions of the past are used, i.e., how they are constructed, interpreted, inherited, and made meaningful in the present, in today's forms of ethnography this is most often perceived in terms of the manner in which the social past is used for current political ends (Hirsch and Stewart 2005; see also Schapera 1962).

My perspectives on the craft, the art and the science of ethnography have been molded by the ideas of many scholars who before me have examined the changing nature of history and anthropology, but none has been more personally influential than E. E. Evans-Pritchard. In a series of groundbreaking lectures and published essays at the end of the 1940s and early 1950s, Evans-Pritchard redirected the course of social anthropology away from its pretensions of being a natural science towards the embrace of its role as both one of the humanities and one of the social sciences. The key to social anthropology's pivotal role as an interpretative science was its relationship to history, historicity and historiography. He famously concluded 'that while there are, of course, many differences between social anthropology and historiography they are differences of technique, of emphasis and of perspective, and not differences of method and aim (Evans-Pritchard 1962: 25). The differences in technique and emphasis did not deflect him from the conclusion that little separated the field of history and anthropology, precisely because of their common goals.

> The thesis I put before you, that social anthropology is a kind of historiography . . . implies that it studies societies as moral systems and not as natural systems, that it is interested in design rather than in process, and that it therefore seeks patterns and not scientific laws, and interprets rather than explains (Evans-Pritchard 1962: 26).

In this effort ethnographers, according to Evans-Pritchard, must translate from one culture to another, to make the ideas and values of one people understandable to others, thereby allowing others some opportunity at the level of consciousness and action to operate in that culture. But Evans-Pritchard makes us go farther in the crafting of an ethnographic study. In his view cultural intelligibility, at the heart of the ethnographic exercise, must also be matched by an understanding of a society's structural order, a set of

13

abstractions of course, but one that allows the observer to see the patterns of thought, action and practice which characterize social institutions. This establishment of patterns in turn allows greater abstractions, comparison, and model building in the social sciences. Thus cultural and sociological intelligibility are the goals of ethnography, and both of these are ways of knowing the present so that the past can be made clearer. These are also ways of engaging the past to make the present more intelligible.

Evans-Pritchard, in sum, agreed with Lévi-Strauss (1963) when he concluded that because people make their own history, both history and anthropology are thus justified and inseparable. Ethnography, like history, seeks patterns that make sense to the people who live in a society and daily recreate and reconstruct culture, but also looks for patterns that allow the specifics of the present and the past, particularly in everyday life, to be abstracted out in an effort to compare and generalize, perhaps even to understand cause and effect. And while I do not agree with all that Evans-Pritchard offered in his revisionist view of anthropology as one of the humanities—explanation would be one of the goals of social anthropology in my view— his assurance that social anthropology can be substituted for history in the following statement still guides me now and also guided me in the research that informs this book: 'History is not a succession of events, it is the links between them' (Evans-Pritchard 1962: 48). So too goes ethnography, which explicates the connections between people, their actions, and the meanings that construct their histories, their memories, and their social and cultural worlds.

In the analysis of local politics and government in Meath which follows, I agree with the now rather unfashionable conclusion of no less a luminary than Marshall Sahlins, when he asserted that historical and political events always occur within a system, and that such events must be interpreted with reference to that system (Sahlins 1985; see also Hirsch and Stewart 2005: 265). My historical portrait of Meath politics and government which I constructed in the 1970s and 1980s, in a portrait of the early years of the Irish Free State and later Republic in the 1920s to 1950s, and my analysis of what was then contemporary local Meath politics, but which we can now see from the vantage point of the twenty-first century as political and social history, all have been interpreted by me within the frame of a national political system of local government and politics.

This framework allows me to examine the intersection of culture and politics, at local and national levels of social integration and differentiation. If *all history is to be seen as ethnohistory*, since it is made according to cultural principles (Hirsch and Stewart 2005: 267), so too *all politics should be seen as ethnopolitics*, because they too are composed according to cultural principles. Both history and politics are thus not only accessible to ethnographic investigation, but their examination and interpretation seem impossible without the fine-grained humanistic, historiographical and comparative analysis which ethnographic research offers. As reported by Evans-Pritchard (1962: 64), the eminent British historian and jurist L. M Maitland almost a century before had asserted that 'social anthropology must choose between being history and being nothing'. My argument as set out here is one of agreement with this proposition, but I also concur with Evans-Pritchard's addendum: 'I accept this dictum, though only if it can also be

15

reversed – history must choose between being social anthropology and being nothing'.

But if history and historiography, and anthropology and ethnography, are all about context, what contexts are the crucial ones for investigation and explication, with an aim to offering some views on cultural and sociological intelligibility in regard to politics and history in Ireland? Here too I am guided by anthropologists who have charted a course between anthropology and history. As Eric R. Wolf concluded, in regard to the necessity for anthropologists to study history, economy and polity:

> In dealing with group relationships of a complex society, we cannot neglect to underline the fact that the exercise of power by some people over others enters into all of them, on all levels of integration. Certain economic and political relationships are crucial to the functioning of any complex society. . . . Finally we must be aware that a web of group relationships implies a historical dimension. Group relationships involve conflict and accommodation, integration and disintegration, processes which take place over time. . . . Local histories are important, as are the histories of national-level institutions, but they are not enough. They are local or institutional manifestations of group relations in continuous change (Wolf 1956: 1066).

The political history of local government in Meath, especially in regard to farmers and their changing roles in the political economy of Ireland at the end of the 1970s and in the early 1980s, is the subject for ethnographic examination

16

precisely because it allows the analysis of such relationships in the complex society that was and is Ireland. An anthropology that is sensitive to the issues raised by Wolf must seek out the histories that pertain to levels of power and their related relationships of social and cultural integration and differentiation. And it was with this intention that, in my field research over thirty years ago, I sought to identify the major transformations of the age in the everyday lives of wealthy and influential Irish farmers and their related cohorts in party politics in eastern Ireland. My goal was to understand the effects which all of the transformations in the fabric of Irish life were having on local society and culture in rural areas, so long dependent on the agricultural production of grass, meat, wheat and barley for markets at home and abroad. I set out to discover these effects, and to determine what relative impact they had in County Meath, the county best known in Ireland for commercial farmers with large estates. How were these farmers faring within this maelstrom of social, political and economic change?

This was the guiding question when I first went to Ireland in 1976 to scout a research site for my doctoral field research. How, I also wondered, would ethnographic research into the European dimensions of local agriculture and politics fit within an anthropology of Ireland, which had developed since the groundbreaking research which launched it in the 1930s?

The anthropology of Ireland[2]

Ireland's membership in the European Union is perhaps the single most important event in that country's history in the last sixty years. Yet before I began my research in Meath it had all but been ignored by anthropologists and other ethnographers. As the chapters that follow seek to demonstrate, in Meath in the late 1970s and early 1980s EEC[3] membership had already begun to radically alter large farmers' economic relationships. These changing conditions forced them to redefine their role in both local and national electoral politics so that they could influence and support either or both major political parties in a bloc within the Irish farmers' national organization. Thus, in the ethnographic environment in which I found myself in Meath, the Irish countryman, who had become the protagonist in most anthropological ethnographic research and writing on rural Ireland since the seminal work by Conrad Arensberg and Solon Kimball in County Clare in the West of Ireland in the 1930s, had become transformed into the Euro-farmer, the citizen and consumer of a new Europe of the EEC. But field research made it quickly apparent to me that a break with past ethnographic models was needed in order to understand aspects of local Irish society that were quickly passing from view in places such as Meath.

Moreover, it was also obvious to me then that, despite some powerful disciplinary and professional imperatives and constraints, I would need to rely on the data and analyses utilized by scholars in Ireland and elsewhere in political science, sociology, geography and economics. A study of community social structure, which in the 1970s was widely seen as de rigueur in terms of the principal feature of an ethnographic monograph, would have presented a distorted and incomplete view of the structures and processes in Meath life which *Meath people* saw as important, and which I had concluded were key features of a transformed local and regional political economy. A community study by me in Meath, along the lines of the model that at the time had been widely adopted in anthropology, might have been theoretically and methodologically acceptable if not laudable, but it also would have been ethnographically misleading. While I was only vaguely aware of it at the time, I now realize that my research was part of a transformation in ethnographic research in Ireland, one that helped to break molds that had long fashioned ethnographies in the image of that done by Arensberg and Kimball a generation and more before.

The nature of the ethnographic research which Arensberg and Kimball conducted in the West of Ireland in the 1930s is examined in chapter two. Here it should be noted that because their work was a conscious effort to combine the theoretical and methodological models of ethnography as developed in both the British and American worlds of anthropology, they established ethnography as the principal methodology in the sociology and anthropology of Ireland for generations to come. Their rural and urban studies in County Clare were structural and functional in intent and realization. They were in the main less interested in history and social change than in the ways in which social organization maintained patterns of culture in Ireland, which to them was a modern nation experiencing the beginnings of national industrialization and independence. But their focus, as lasting and influential as it became in Ireland, was on social and cultural theory as they related to the practices of anthropological research rather than on Ireland itself. This was because they were part of a revolution in modern social science, one that championed the idea that long-term ethnographic research would yield the best data possible on

19

how communities were structured and reproduced. And they had begun their studies in ethnography before ever arriving in Ireland.

Arensberg and Kimball were in fact undergraduate researchers in the famous Yankee City study, the path-breaking sociological study of an industrial city in the Northeast of the USA. Arensberg and Kimball had been recruited to that study by W. Lloyd Warner who at that time was an instructor at Harvard University. When Warner was brought in to design the social anthropological component of a Harvard-led three-field anthropological analysis of modern Ireland he asked his young colleagues, who had participated in the initial stages of the Yankee City research, in Newburyport, Massachusetts, to be the principal investigators in a social anthropological study of representative communities in a representative county in Ireland. However, in ways they could not have predicted, their wonderful study of social stability and change in the West of Ireland became a template in the sociology and anthropology of town and country in Ireland. The Americans in essence had kick-started generations of scholarly debate over theory and method in rural Irish research. The result was that they were widely praised worldwide as groundbreakers in the comparative study of community, and almost equally widely attacked for their lack of attention to history, power, politics, religion, and economic class. These criticisms arose despite the fact that Arensberg and Kimball had not intended their case study to stand for any part of Ireland except for those areas in County Clare in which it had occurred. In the end, criticisms aside, they became founding figures in the social science of modern Ireland.

However, even with this iconic status, it seemed odd to me, as I began my preparations for anthropological fieldwork in the political economy of culture and government in rural Ireland, that a key category of Arensberg and Kimball's analysis had not become a focus of subsequent scholarship in Ireland. The group in question were the farmers with land, wealth and social status, the *large farmers* of Ireland, who while found throughout the island were most famous for the roles they played in local and national agriculture from their bases in farms and estates in the East of Ireland. These large farmers, who were also called *big farmers, big men, strong farmers* and occasionally *ranchers*, were often the successors to the Anglo-Irish gentry who established the great Irish cattle 'ranches' of the late eighteenth and nineteenth centuries, which were the result of the clearances which followed the deprivations of the great famines of Irish history, but were also the result of capitalist transformation in Irish agriculture from a largely grain producing island to a beef producer.

I was both surprised and secretly delighted that these men of wealth and power, who had functioned as elites in Ireland for at least a century (and longer if one saw them as the inheritors of aristocratic privilege), had not been featured in any major sociological or political study at the time of my doctoral research planning. Of particular importance to me was that since the original fieldwork of Arensberg and Kimball had pointed to large farmers as a population worthy of ethnographic study, little if anything had been written on their social organization. There was a noticeable lack of data on the life styles of these large farmers, who had been approached by Arensberg and Kimball as one of the two 'classes' of farmers that were to be so often alluded to in the social science

21

literature that followed. And even though the gap between the two types of farmers had widened by the 1970s, there had still not been any systematic sociological analysis of the characteristics of small and large farmers (Peillon 1982). My research design, which I set out to employ in County Meath[4] in the East of Ireland in 1977, and the analyses of the resulting data which I have published over the years, sought to rectify this lack of knowledge about large farmers in their social, cultural and political contexts. As may be seen in the chapters that follow, I intended in my years of field research among the big farmers of Meath to introduce them anthropologically through an overview of large farmers' perceptions of their own culture and class, of their roles in local politics and government, and of the ways in which their local practices and organizations had been transformed in the years after Ireland had joined the European Economic Community in 1973.

But my intentions then, and to some degree over the intervening years, were often out of synch with other anthropological and sociological perspectives on Ireland, precisely because that while I took a social group identified by Arensberg and Kimball as my ethnographic starting point, my interest in government and politics, at regional, national and supranational levels of political economy diverged considerably from the interests and accomplishments of those early Masters. In fact, the themes that motivated so much of the anthropology of Ireland up to the 1970s clearly continued to owe much to the letter and spirit of Arensberg and Kimball's work. Anthropologists had researched kinship and social structure (Gibbon and Curtin 1978; Fox 1978, 1979), rural-urban relations (Taylor 1980a, 1980b), rural decline and modernization (Scheper Hughes 1979), kinship, class and

22

religion (McFarlane 1979), and urbanization (Messenger 1975; Gmelch 1977). But many of these publications, mine among them, also demonstrated interests in other aspects of social and cultural life, mirroring the evolution of anthropology world-wide. All in all, these works presented models and sets of data which offered a new framework to the anthropology of Ireland, and one which helped to keep it in the mainstream of global anthropology throughout the twentieth century.

Making waves

In line with this New Wave in the anthropology of Ireland in the 1970s, my research project was planned by me to be a reflection of new models in political anthropology. It was, at least in part, also my attempt to answer the clarion calls for new directions in Irish ethnography which had begun to be made in that period (Leyton 1975; Messenger 1978). For example, besides noting the dearth of research in towns and cities, Leyton identified the need for more research on religion, class and elite behavior in the North, Midlands, and East of the country. In a similar vein, Messenger advocated more anthropological attention in Ireland to an applied anthropology of acculturation, emigration, folklore and the pervasive power of religion and church in Irish life. But while both authors implicitly supported community studies, they were reluctant to suggest how best to analyze the complexities of the above topics within the community level of social organization.

One solution to this problem was, at least as far as I was concerned, to focus on local and national connections at the level of the region, through a focus on networks, quasi-groups and the politics of the interstitial. This was far from my solution

23

alone; in fact, I was part of a new wave of ethnographers, scattered across Europe and Latin America in the late 1970s, who investigated regional political economy. Influenced by a Marxist-based turn in social anthropology, these young ethnographers had concluded, with the inspiration of people like Eric Wolf and his colleagues and students, that

> Communities which form parts of complex society can . . . be viewed no longer as self-contained and integrated systems in their own right. It is more appropriate to view them as the local termini of a web of group relations which extend through intermediate levels from the level of the community to that of the nation (Wolf 1956, quoted in Silverman and Gulliver 1992a).

Anthropologists interested in delineating the nature of political and economic processes beyond the village and neighborhood had begun to theorize the nature of space, place and territory, particularly as they related to local, regional and national cultures. As John Cole summarized in his 1977 assessment of the state of the anthropology of Europe, the variety of forces in which localities found themselves to be both agents and pawns led anthropologists to see the region as a unit of analysis (1977: 365). Many of these anthropologists had done research in relatively peripheral regions of nation-states, but ones with strong historical and continuing identities, such as Sicily (Schneider and Schneider 1976), Catalonia (Hansen 1977), and Trentino (Cole and Wolf 1974). The thread that ran through most of this regional anthropology in the 1960s and 1970s, and which has continued to some extent to the present, was that a region was 'a unit of political ecology, where local resources and people are organized by an elite which is interposed between community and nation—and which may even bypass the nation in its relations with the world system' (Cole 1977: 365). Cole and his contemporaries, and many anthropologists who have done regional research since (see, for example, Grillo 1980; Kockel 1991; Cole 1997; Stacul 2003; Jenkins 2008), sought to see the ways in which institutions and agents of power external to localities frame if not direct aspects of local life. Much theorizing today in fact is about how localities bypass the nation and state in their relations with the global, and although the study of elites has not been fashionable in trans-Atlantic anthropology lately, the study of those who have and wield power has been at the center of the anthropological profession for some time, and is in no danger of abetting.

The complexity of socioeconomic life which I encountered in Meath was much different from other Irish communities found in the scholarly literature. The cleavages of class, religion, residence, and political affiliation militated against establishing arbitrary local community boundaries in a study which by definition was of a regional elite. Furthermore, the communities of eastern Ireland could in no sense be considered isolated or peripheral. The centralization of government and politics, new communication and entertainment media, tourism, returned emigrants, and the proximity of Dublin had made many if not most of the people of eastern Ireland part of mainstream and cosmopolitan Irish life. They had also become more subject to international forces, in the forms of European integration and Europeanization among others, than they had been for a generation or more,

25

making anachronistic any notion that they were in any way trustees of traditional society and culture.

Thus my research turned into the first long-term ethnography of rural life in the agricultural areas of eastern Ireland, and the first anthropological study of an Irish agricultural elite, in this case the large farmers of Meath. Its focus on regional political economy within an EEC context also introduced new data and models to the ethnographic literature of Ireland, and to the wider social anthropology of Europe. In this regard my research and writing contributed to new currents in the anthropology of Ireland.

By the late 1980s, anthropologists researching in Ireland had become concerned with issues of urban unemployment (Blacking et al. 1989; Howe 1989a, 1989b, 1990; McLaughlin 1989); rituals and religion (Crozier 1989; Szuchewycz 1989; Taylor 1989a, 1989b; McFarlane 1989, 1994); international frontiers and sovereignty (Vincent 1993; Wilson 1993b); women's roles and rights (Gaetz 1993; LeMaster 1993; McCann 1994); nation and nationalism (Shanks 1994; Wilson 1994b); political violence and the state (Vincent 1989; Sluka 1989; 1992; Feldman 1991); political rituals and symbolism (Cecil 1993; Wilson 1994b); suburban life and globalized culture (Varenne 1993); tourism and rural development (Curtin and Varley 1989); ethnicity and minority rights (Vincent 1993; Donnan 1994); intellectuals and national culture (Sheehan 1993); consumer culture (Curtin and Ryan 1989; Wilson 1993c); and local and national history and historiography (Silverman 1989; Wilson 1990; Silverman and Gulliver 1992a; Vincent 1992). Besides these varied approaches to theoretical and methodological matters, all of which quickly modernized the anthropology of Ireland, there were shifts in geographic

26

focus too. The overall tendency for anthropologists to do field research in more peripheral areas of the West, North and South of the country slowly became balanced by studies in the East. For example, Gulliver (1989), Silverman (1989) and Conway (1989) all worked on history, class, local politics, and urbanization in southern Leinster Province around the same time I was in the north of Leinster.

Perhaps the ways in which ethnographers in Ireland had begun to share the concerns that motivated a more global anthropology elsewhere were best seen in how anthropologists had turned to the comparative study and theorization of urban Ireland (Curtin et al. 1993). In Irish towns and cities a variety of forces had brought the problems of poverty, homelessness, disease, racism, sexism, the environment, urban sprawl, and increased levels of violence to the forefront of public culture. While anthropologists in Ireland might have been accused of being slow to react to the ways in which people had been affected and responded to these social problems, they took to their new perspectives and interests with alacrity, vigor and enthusiasm.

The growing movement among anthropologists in Ireland to do research on social and economic problems, in order to provide a more applied focus to academic anthropology, inevitably impelled ethnographers to the investigation of public policy. Although it was clear that anthropologists in Northern Ireland had been focused longer on issues of social disintegration, conflict, ethnicity and class, as well as their relationships to public policy formation (for a review of this, see Donnan and McFarlane 1989), the anthropological examination of policy in city and countryside became all-island by the end of the 1980s. Hence the interest in everyday life in cities and the ways in which culture and politics converged in policy became twin focuses of much of this new anthropology in Ireland. One of the longest studied issues in urban life, and still one of the most serious problems in Irish towns and cities today, has been the pressures young people face because of the rapidly changing political economy of Ireland. Jenkins (1983), Bell (1990) and Gaetz (1993) have chronicled youth culture Ireland, where young adults have to face the day to day dilemmas of unemployment, peer pressure, poverty, the ups and downs of economic development, and the transformations in urban landscape.

Other problems in the social fabric of Ireland were also drawing the attention of ethnographers in the 1980s and 1990s, in ways that seemed to break with past traditions in academic anthropology because of scholars' wish to apply their research findings in order to help alleviate the conditions of the poor and dispossessed. Ethnographic methods, in particular participant observation, allowed anthropologists to describe the experiences of travelling people (Helleiner 1993) and homeless men (O'Sullivan 1993) in their efforts to survive in the face of remarkable discrimination. And while Irish social environments suffer from a variety of human forces, so too did the physical environment, on an island that is increasingly becoming one of the tourist havens for the people of the European Union precisely because of its traditional ways and relatively unspoilt environment. Urban planners, government leaders, industrial developers and environmental lobbies increasingly argued over the future of the Irish landscape, in a debate in which anthropologists have been active (Peace 1993; Milton 1993, 1994). These anthropologists, like many of their colleagues, were contributing to a scholarly movement which is also simultaneously a social movement of concerned citizens in Ireland. They have sought to use their research in ways that matter to the quality of the lives of the people among whom they live and work, whereby scholarship is put to political use rather than solely having politics put to scholarly use.

This growing notion in scholarly circles that social science may actually have a role to play in direct social and political action In Ireland also reflects the late twentieth century interest in marrying the political with the cultural in all forms of public discourse. Thus it is far from surprising that the increasing relevance and contemporary value of anthropological research for Ireland, and perhaps beyond Ireland, has to a great extent come through the ethnographic analysis of social and political problems and policy. This focus on policy has led sociologists and anthropologists to greater interest in government and politics, and the ways in which policy formation and implementation intersect with the perceptions, organization and needs of local society and culture. This has been especially apparent in anthropological attention to European integration, which has been a major theme in much of the anthropology of Ireland in the last quarter of the twentieth century.

In fact, anthropological research in Ireland has demonstrated how often the realities of local social and cultural life do not match the ideal constructions of national societies as seen from the spectrum of European 'centres', be they national capitals, core regions in states, or the key institutions and bodies of the European Union in Brussels. This mismatch between localities, national centres and European capitals is one cause of the perceived 'democratic deficit' which seemingly marks the powerful apparatuses of the European

Union. And while the anthropology of European integration has been more concerned with local material issues, like grants and subsidies that come from Europe, the assessment of the impact of Europeanization in Ireland has grown in importance due to the escalating role of supranational bodies in the everyday lives of the EU's citizens.

While the anthropology and sociology of the European Union, in Ireland and elsewhere in the continent, are small in scale and influence when compared with the voluminous literature in political science and economics on the European Union and integration, most of what concerns the scholars of other scholarly disciplines is focused on top-down and centre-out perspectives on national trends. Despite its size, however, the anthropological lens is a valuable one. Policies determined in metropolises distant from the localities of Ireland often have a variety of effects on Irish everyday life that are both unintended and unnoticed by policy-makers. To many Irish people, for example, national and European Union economic policies provide a variety of changing contexts for local initiatives. This is especially apparent in the informal and black economies, wherein any amount of statistical analysis cannot fail to omit a wide range of productive economic activities which define many local communities' notions of work, wealth and class. For example, Howe (1989a, 1989b, 1990) has documented the many ways in which the Belfast unemployed make a living through a variety of legal and illegal actions. Their 'doing the double' is an apt term for claiming social welfare benefits, sometimes in more than one location, while at the same time working in such occupations as laborers, taxi drivers, thieves, baby-sitters and bouncers.

The cities have not been the only places where European policy and practice have created new opportunities and new hindrances in local political economy. People in Northern Ireland at the land border between the Republic of Ireland and the United Kingdom have made veritable fortunes through smuggling, especially in agricultural goods, tobacco, alcohol and consumer durables. The many large bungalows and holiday homes which were constructed along the Irish border in the 1990s not only reflected the wealth which had been made, allegedly illicitly, by some locals reputed to be large-scale smugglers, but they also indicated the thriving construction trade and the opportunities for construction workers in the borderlands. There locals collected the dole (unemployment benefits) in both the Republic of Ireland and Northern Ireland, while sometimes working a full week off the books at construction. And while smuggling and welfare fraud are often difficult for social scientists to document, they are often so instrumental to local community life that they may be inescapable aspects to any ethnographic study of a community in Ireland, North and South. Because of the nature of participant observation, still the mainstay of anthropological research, it is all but impossible for ethnographers to avoid recognizing the importance of the local informal economy, which intersects so many forms of political and governmental practice.

As such, the economics of everyday life are inseparable from the politics of everyday life. Together, they are part of the forces that impel ethnographers to increasingly dedicate themselves to filling in the gaps in the social science of public policy in Europe, particularly from an ethnographic perspective which privileges that of the 'ground up'. These intentions were evident in the strong record that had developed in the ethnographic study of government and politics at the time I was beginning my doctoral field research.

Anthropology and local politics

The political anthropology of the Republic of Ireland has concentrated for much of its history on the analysis of political patronage, brokerage, and clientelism in rural areas. This attention to informal politics resulted in portraits of local and national politicians as public servants who provided needed goods and services to constituents and who relayed information up and down within the hierarchies of local and national government and politics. These politicians were seen to use their personal attributes and political networks to sustain their nation's democratic political system, thereby making government more responsive to the needs of local communities. Some less flattering analyses suggested too that cajolery and deception were also part and parcel of the stereotypical charm and clever word games of Irish politicians, and that secrecy and factionalism were endemic aspects of Irish politics at all levels of society. Perhaps the most salient deceit of all was the self-promotion by local politicians who contended, in spite of generations of party and government centralization, that they still had the influence to provide material rewards to their constituents. As we shall see in later chapters, this was a power that had all but been lost to local politicians by the 1970s, but they continued to traffic on the premise that they still had the power and influence which had certainly been theirs in the halcyon days of local government in the years after independence from the United Kingdom.

The two most detailed ethnographic analyses of local politics in Ireland were conducted in the 1970s, and they viewed politicians and their party structures as political machines which, with some brief interludes excepted, were built up in the years following the creation of the Irish Free State in 1922 and which lasted at the very least up to the early 1970s. These studies of electoral constituencies in County Cork (Bax 1976) and County Donegal (Sacks 1976) ended with the 1969 and 1973 general elections respectively. A keystone in each of these analyses was constituents' persistence in believing that politicians could provide fundamental political, economic, and social goods and services, because of politicians' special access to local and national bureaucracies and government leaders (Sacks 1976: 224-225). Political parties cultivated the misconception that politicians supplied crucial and instrumental aid to their constituents when in fact their ability to do so was extremely limited, or nonexistent. This 'imaginary patronage' (Sacks 1976: 7) was fundamental to local Irish politics, and was an essential aspect of the workings of all political networks and machines in the 1970s.

Over the last forty years political ethnographers have not progressed much beyond this view of local Irish politics, which is surprising given developments in political anthropology and sociology elsewhere in Europe and the Americas. Much of the scholarly debate in anthropology about the politics of the Republic of Ireland continued to be focused on circular definitions of patrons and clients, which, although important in the context of Irish politics, seemingly distracted ethnographers, among others, from the political issues of class, ethnicity, sectarianism and sexism (areas anthropologists have increasingly investigated in Ireland, North and South, as may be seen in the range of ethnographic cases offered in Curtin and Wilson 1989; Donnan and McFarlane 1989; Curtin et al. 1993). This partial stagnation of political ethnography was also surprising because the ground breaking analyses of these two political machines provided so many stimulating avenues for further research.

Perhaps most surprising of all is that, despite the richness of the two studies mentioned, and the wide range of problematic issues which they identified in local political culture, few social scientists have attempted an ethnographic or historical study of another local political machine, or of a local political elite, in either the Republic of Ireland or Northern Ireland. This lack of attention to local politics by ethnographers could not have been because of a general or specific lack of interest on the part of Irish people in politics. After all, they had exported the idea and practices of the political machine to places like New York and Chicago, and anyone who has spent any time at all in Ireland will recognize the Irish private love and public disdain for all things political. Perhaps it was due to the general anthropological reticence to get entangled in party politics and local government, domains sometimes perceived to be best left to political scientists. But whatever was the cause for such avoidance, it did not deter me from my own investigation into the government and politics of rural life in County Meath.

What forces drove me on? In my preliminary field research which was conducted in the summer of 1976 I was continually struck by how local Irish people, and especially local farmers, looked to the EEC as a major factor in social and economic change to their daily lives. This attention to Europe was apparent everywhere on the island I looked (I was

34

especially interested in possible field sites in Counties Mayo, Westmeath and Meath), but this notion of a new Ireland in a new Europe was best and most forcefully expressed by large farmers in Meath. As a result of this awareness, and given the focus on large farmers offered in the original Arensberg and Kimball research, I was determined to return to Meath the following year for my doctoral field research.

What did I intend? The transformations in Irish agriculture, and other changes to Irish society and economy within the EEC, I hypothesized, were sure to make other changes in Irish agricultural politics. Up to the 1970s Irish politicians and farmers had enjoyed a relatively stable relationship in which the farmers' support of parties and politicians depended in part on reciprocated institutionalized agricultural subsidies. For over a generation of government protectionism, farmers had competed for national funds and selective protectionist policies through their traditional avenues of political brokerage. The system had seemed to work seamlessly. But as I prepared for my doctoral research I discovered the aforementioned studies of Cork and Donegal, along with others of local urban politics. These studies portrayed more unstable Irish politics at the local level that revolved around various forms of changing patron-client relationships (Bax 1976; Sacks 1976; Higgins 1982; Komito 1984), wherein local and national politicians mediated between individual and group constituents, on the one hand, and public and private agencies at the local and national levels on the other. Many scholars had begun to investigate how this type of politics fitted in well with the evolving political system of the new state (Garvin 1981), which had resulted in clearly defined cleavages in agricultural dimensions to local and national politics. In fact, in the years after the creation of the Irish Free State (later the Republic of Ireland) in the 1920s, large farmers had in the main supported Fine Gael (FG), the second largest party of Ireland, while small farmers had been a mainstay of Fianna Fáil (FF) since the late 1920s (Rumpf and Hepburn 1977; Gallagher 1985).

This was a major fact of political life in what was then, and continued to be in the 1970s, a rural society. National agricultural policy in the short term and over long periods had been decided by politicians who in most cases depended on farmers, their families and those whose businesses were tied to the financial success of a rural economy. In short, in a country where the majority of people lived in rural constituencies, politicians needed the farm vote to get and to keep being elected. The rules of the game were clear-cut: politicians used their influence at national and local levels to solve problems and to do favors for their political clients. This patron-client relationship was based on the assumption that a local politician had networks that stretched to the capital of Ireland, and reached into political and administrative decision-making circles, and that these networks could be utilized to help constituents through the intercession of the local politician.

This system was in operation in Ireland in the 1970s, and it seemed to thrive despite the general recognition that not all politicians had the networks to deliver goods and services equally, nor did they all have the political acumen and social skills to sustain such networks over some pretty fair distances and time. Thus much of the patron-client system that was at work in that period was based on little more than 'imaginary patronage' (Sacks 1976; Laver 1986a, 1986b), wherein politicians claimed credit for services that were received by constituents. This claim was made despite the fact that the provision of such services was a citizen's right and they were often received in the normal course of government activity. In other words, what constituents received often had little and sometimes nothing to do with what a politician claimed they had done to get that result.

'Traditional' rural politics in this form had lasted at least since the creation of the Irish state in the 1920s. But in the 1970s, and due in great part to the overall effects of EEC membership, Irish farmers had frequently voted against type, and had begun to baffle those who had come to rely on relatively stable, regional and class-based support for their parties at election time. One of the key pieces of this new puzzle was that farmers did not seem to be voting their interests in ways they once had. It had become increasingly clear that farmers' interests had begun to change in ways that they seemed to appreciate long before their political representatives had. It had in fact become difficult to ascertain how farmers as a group voted in national and local elections, or for that matter to gauge how large and small farmers voted as blocs—voting statistics by ballot box are not kept with this precision. But it was clear that rural constituencies had experienced major shifts in voting patterns in the 1970s, and had done so from one election to the next.

In fact, there was a growing consensus at the time that since the 1973 general election farmers' traditional support for political parties had become volatile, i.e., politicians had to win votes from those whose support they had come to expect over the years, and they had to win them from voters who seemed to jump party from election to election. Others saw the new voting patterns as 'secular', i.e., after the 1977 general election it was becoming clear that there had been an attenuation of traditional political loyalties due to voters' newly perceived self-interests (Farrell and Manning 1978: 164). In Meath, as in Ireland on the whole, elections thus had begun to change as party cadres, who themselves had used campaign promises to help fashion the current generation of farmers into instrumental voters eager to safeguard their livelihood, at the least tried to get that instrumental vote for their candidates at each election (for perspectives on the social bases of Irish party support up to that time see Gallagher 1985; Laver 1986a, 1986b).

In the 1970s, Meath farmers, whose numbers had been slowly decreasing over the years due to declining birth rates, emigration, structural agricultural reform, and the lure of wage labor, had started to vote according to the issues rather than by party lines or family loyalties, in a series of elections that had been contested almost exclusively on economic grounds. In County Meath, renowned for its good land, large farms, and influential and wealthy farmers, in Leinster, the eastern province of Ireland which served as the end point in a national network of pastoral farm production and distribution, this transformation in economy and polity had a major impact. The consensus among local politicians in Meath at the end of the 1970s was that in both local and national elections farmers had become unpredictable and volatile. Of the twenty-nine sitting Meath County Councillors whom I interviewed before the June 1979 local government elections, for example, all concluded that the two major parties could no longer depend on traditional loyalties and farmers' political support. These politicians, many with over twenty years experience as public representatives at the county and national levels of government, were particularly mindful of the shift in large farmer support in Meath from Fine

Gael to Fianna Fáil in the 1977 general election. The general consensus at the time was that farmers had switched parties in the election due to the twin forces of their opposition to the tax measures introduced by the Fine Gael-led coalition government in Dáil Éireann (the Irish parliament) and their support for Fianna Fáil's proposal to remove a number of long-standing taxes if they were able to form the next national government.

This appreciation of the sea change in local political practice and culture was widespread. Among the more than fifty farmers I interviewed in the Navan Electoral Area of Meath (one of five political subdivisions in the Meath constituency), none disputed these notions which I had learned from their elected representatives. Most farmers believed that they faced a new political and economic world, one in which their businesses would have to come before other values and actions, and despite past loyalties and sentiments. Although many of these farmers claimed they still voted for their family's traditional political choice, just as many had admitted to me that they had voted for the party that they perceived would not take as much of their profits away through taxes or poor policy-making. And they often argued that they needed firm representation to safeguard their interests both at home and in Europe. By the end of the 1970s, in fact, the perception among Meath farmers themselves was that they had become volatile voters, and this was in the main welcomed as a source for new influence in Irish life. It seemed to me then that if this perception was shared by farmers elsewhere in the country, and I had no reason to doubt it was at least in part so shared, judging by national media, political scholars and the opinion of politicians whose networks stretched much further than mine, then the partisanship of large and small farmers was clearly becoming problematical in Irish politics nationwide.

Farmer party independence and electoral volatility continued in Meath for some time too. In the 1985 local elections in Meath, farmer opposition to the Fine Gael land tax plan helped give the county council to Fianna Fáil. In the 1987 general election, Meath farmers again switched their vote according to their own perceived interests, in an election that seriously threatened any views that farmers might return to being traditional loyal party supporters, who in the past had been more interested in the Irish Civil War issues which many politicians hoped would still frame electoral support for the two main parties, rather than more immediate meat and potato issues.

But the 1970s and 1980s had seemed to suggest otherwise, at least for farming communities in County Meath, who appeared to be firmly on a different and new path of political relationships. In the 1987 election (Gallagher 1988), Meath farmers helped to elect three Fianna Fáil TDs (MPs), with one of them out-polling a Meath TD who was not only a national leader of the Fine Gael party but also a farmer who was being groomed by some to be the party's leader (he went on to become prime minister). The local Member of the European Parliament (James Fitzsimons, MEP), who at the time represented rural Leinster Province in the European Parliament, had predicted (in an earlier interview with me, August 1986) Fianna Fáil's 1987 Meath success, which he at the time attributed to farmers' continuing need to give Irish political parties a clear message: farmers will fight all governments' moves to tax farmers and they will demand and support a strong farmers' lobby in Europe.

In 1977 when I eagerly arrived on the scene in County Meath, local politics greatly resembled the studies of rural politics from elsewhere in Ireland. When I began my doctoral field research I immediately sought to recognize the role of the local agricultural community in state and international politics. Because Meath was renowned in Ireland as the county with the largest farms and the wealthiest farmers, I particularly wanted to analyze how the county's farming elite functioned in the political realm. But not long into the study it became apparent that a once strong and flourishing Meath political machine was in sharp decline. Local, national, and international forces had left the Meath machine vulnerable and, at times, disorganized. But the goal of this book is not to chronicle this decline. Rather I wish to explore what I have come to recognize as clear indications of how the transformations in local agriculture and politics were indicative of social and political forces at work throughout Ireland, many of which were due to the increasing importance of European integration.

Then in its first decade, but now in its thirty-eighth year, the European Union, which at the time of my initial fieldwork was still known principally as the European Economic Community, has been a crucial factor in the internationalization of capital and power in Ireland, and as such has also been a dominant element in the organization of local, regional, and national society. No group, economic sector, occupation or way of life has been more affected by European integration than Ireland's agriculture and farmers.

From Irish countryman to Euro-farmer

Membership in the EEC ushered in an era of tremendous changes in the lives of all Irish communities. The impact in the countryside was almost immediate. Growing towns and cities, greater domestic demand for food, the decline in emigration, assured access to continental markets, guaranteed high prices for agricultural produce, and the expansion of public and private sources of credit all helped turn many Irish farms into successful businesses. Farm profits and subsidies within the EEC made the Irish agricultural community aware of their new role as European citizens and farmers, a situation which, with few exceptions, made the relative absence of an EEC-dimension in anthropological and sociological studies of local communities at the time all the more remarkable. At least that was the premise of my doctoral research design,[5] with which I came equipped in the autumn of 1977 when I arrived first in Dublin to do my field research.

My research in agropolitics in County Meath, in the fertile agricultural zone of eastern Ireland in Leinster province, highlighted for me the benefits attendant upon both my utilization of models drawn from political economy approaches in anthropology, models different from many used previously in Irish ethnography, and my comprehensive reading in other Irish disciplines. The population I sought to study in Meath, where I was resident from 1977 to 1979, and in follow-up trips in the summers of 1980 and 1982, was representative of the large farmers of Ireland so often referred to in the anthropological literature but who had never been the subject of ethnographic or any other form of intensive sociological research. For almost a century these farmers, owners of the largest and richest agricultural holdings in the country, had been at the receiving end of an internal Irish market in cattle. Calves dropped on small farms in the West, South, and Northwest of the country (areas which before the 1970s had been the traditional locations of anthropological field research) were sold as store cattle to be fattened on farms in the Midlands, whose owners, in turn, sold them to the large farmers of the East for final fattening for the Dublin or British markets.

These large farmers had long been considered the most influential agricultural interest group in the social, political, and economic life of the modern Irish nation, yet before my research began little was known of them sociologically. Preliminary research in 1976 made clear to me that an anthropological study of this agricultural elite demanded that I abandon a narrow community study and that I concentrate on the regional (i.e., Leinster) role these farmers play in Irish political economy.

The large farmers of Meath of the 1970s and today have much in common both with each other and with other commercial farmers across the province and the nation. Acreage, high costs and high incomes, specialization of farm enterprise, similar roles in party politics and in newly powerful lobbies, and significant rates of investment and spending have been some of the shared features of large farmers' lives. And while the subsidies and guarantees are not as high or prevalent today as they once were, and in post-Celtic Tiger Ireland the value of land and buildings has begun to fall in line with the curtailment of credit and finance, in the time of my fieldwork the money flowed even more smoothly than the influence which farmers still enjoyed.

Meath large farmers also demonstrated a convergence of values and ideas in such things as education, social mobility,

43

conspicuous consumption and leisure. Despite these similarities, they also perceived themselves as clearly belonging to separate categories of 'large farmers,' as types of farmer defined by much more than their commercial roles or acreages. The remnants of the 'county families' had a number of religious and political attitudes and traditions in common with other Anglo-Irish and Protestant farmers, but these aspects of culture often differed to some degree, in turn, from those farmers who were the descendants of nineteenth-century tenants who were both Catholic and Protestant. But in the years after EEC entry, large farmers had become an ever-shrinking but more articulate minority within the state. Sectarianism and political beliefs had proved poor barriers to farmer organization in the face of increasing state threats to their livelihood. Overriding many of the relationships among Meath large farmers was their growing consciousness as members of the rural middle class, a class that increasingly relied on itself within the diminishing farm communities of Ireland.

As we shall see in the chapters which follow, large farmers of the 1970s and 1980s mobilized themselves as an interest group within the state precisely because of their consciousness as part of the dominant class of Ireland (Hazelkorn 1986). The rise of the Irish Farmers' Association as a national farming political lobby was a predictable step by farmers who one scholar had concluded 'reaped a higher return from investment in politics than investment in agriculture' (Lee 1982: 10). Certainly then-current trends in voter volatility suggested that many supporters of the major political parties had voted instrumentally in elections, that is, had broken with political traditions in order to support the party that promised the most in material incentives. Farmers' electoral support for

44

Fine Gael, the nation's second party and the one most often in opposition in parliament, was at the time also singled out as an important example of this volatility (Farrell and Manning 1978: 156-157; Garvin 1982: 36).

As my field research began it was clear to me that the roles of the strong farmers of Ireland in the transformations of modern Irish society had been significant but remained largely unexplored in social science scholarship. This book is one attempt to set that record straight. It seeks to serve as a start in the creation of a more detailed historical picture of Irish rural life since the country entered the Europe of the EEC, today's EU. The 'large farmers' of Arensberg and Kimball's time had become the 'big men' of modern Meath. They were farmers whose cultural traditions both unite and divide them but whose businesses, politics, and social roles had made them prominent members of an increasingly important Irish middle class.

Social and economic distinctions among large farmers in Meath are recognized not only by large farmers but by all the people of Meath's rural communities. Yet commercial farmers' perceptions about themselves do not figure prominently, if at all, in the meager literature on inequities in wealth, power, and status in Ireland. Nevertheless, studies of the structure of national social classes highlight the role of farmers, along with other employers and businessmen, in the bourgeoisie (Rottman et al. 1982). Such studies also call attention to their mutual class interests, reflecting the fact that people in Ireland with wealth and power will seek to preserve their elite status within the national class hierarchy and will do so through organizations established by those same class interests (Rottman and O'Connell 1982: 75). Large farmers today, and over the last century, have been forces of tradition and change

45

that have shaped Irish society (Peillon 1986: 113). Their changing perceptions of their own traditions and values are keys to the understanding of the dynamics of class formation in Ireland, and, by extension, to the changing patterns of class relations wherever commercial family farmers have experienced the processes of European integration and Europeanization within the EEC. These processes are also forces of globalization, like many that have shaped commercial agriculture worldwide.

In fact, in the 1980s the number of family farms had declined worldwide and part-time farming had increased due, in part, to national and international agricultural policies that favored agribusiness, the development of new technologies, the consolidation of land, and the concentration and centralization of capital. These forces for capitalization and consolidation had, in turn, resulted in farmer marginalization and proletarianization (Friedmann 1978, 1980; Buttel and Newby 1980; Newby 1980a). Although the need for studies of farmers and their roles in state policy-making in Europe had been clear for some time (Franklin 1973; Newby 1983), when I began my own field studies little research had been conducted on family farmers and their political and economic strategies in those times of crisis (Flinn 1982; Havens and Newby 1983).

By the end of the 1970s the transformations in the structure of global agriculture in general and farming in Europe in particular, combined with the changing relationships between the state and farmers in advanced industrial societies, had forced farmers to adapt to conditions which made them into national minorities eager to influence the formation of policies vital to their businesses and way of life (Feld 1966, 1974; Averyt 1977; Neville-Rolfe 1984). Ironically the processes of

46

agricultural policy-making often resulted in laws that were perceived by farmers to be contrary to their interests, thereby threatening the very people the state proposed to protect, the commercial family farmer (Mann and Dickinson 1980; Sinclair 1980).

Irish family farmers were experiencing a crisis which was threatening the very foundations of commercial family farming throughout Western Europe and North America (Newby and Buttel 1980; Buttel 1982). Pressured into political and economic positions that were to them precarious, family farmers were beginning to see themselves as one of many interest groups battling for power in national and international arenas. In Western Europe the processes of internationalization and Europeanization had occurred so rapidly that farmers across the continent could no longer rely on their traditional political alliances to safeguard their businesses. As agricultural, social and financial policies eroded their way of life, farmers had become as interested in the determination of policy as they were in its impact. Ironically, social scientists who were eager to analyze the effects of policy decisions on local populations were slow to recognize the importance of studying those same populations' role in policy formation and determination (Newby 1983; Rogers 1987). The policy role that commercial family farmers have played and will continue to play in advanced industrial societies has been a crucial one for themselves. It must also be a critical area of study by political and historical anthropologists.

New social and political actors were changing the configurations of policy making in Ireland and Northern Ireland, where in the 1970s top-down decision making was being challenged by a wide range of interest groups, lobbies, concerned community associations, and new issue-oriented political parties. Traditional forms of politics were being transformed in Ireland precisely because many local communities and groups of citizens were aware of alternatives to the construction of the social policies which directly affected them. There were many reasons for this relatively recent awareness of the issues and roles of public policy in the daily lives of Ireland's citizens, and in the research agendas of Ireland's anthropologists, but one of the most important agents for change in this regard has been the European Union.

At the time when I began my doctoral research the EEC's impact on the institutions and values of people and communities at local level had seldom been investigated by social scientists. This relative lack of interest also was true of ethnographers, who in the main failed to recognize the implications of EEC and EU policies. The irony was that ethnographers had as an essential aspect of their research their participation in community life, often for a year or more, and were therefore well placed to chronicle these changes. As a result of this myopia, relative to other research and publishing, and despite the importance of the European Union, there had been very little contemporary research done by anthropologists throughout Europe on the institutions and policies of the European Union. This was partly due to the ethnographer's emphasis on local communities and to the methodological difficulties of conducting field research from a locality up and out to the centres of political and economic decision-making, which are external to the community being studied.

It was in Ireland where things first began to change in a major way in terms of anthropology's interest in European integration. By the end of the 1980s, in fact, the anthropological investigation of various aspects of the European Union, in terms of the ways its policies were experienced at local levels, and in the ways it was defining and transforming a wide range of identities, had become a strong theme in anthropological research in Ireland. This interest yielded a growing literature on both 'Europe' in Ireland and on an anthropology of the European Union in general (see, for example, Dilley 1989; Sheehan 1991; Shutes 1991, 1993; Wilson 1993a, 1993b, 1993c). This attention had much to do with contesting notions of 'being' or 'becoming' European in Ireland. 'Europe' in the guise of the European Union was then and continues to be very important to many Irish people, and thus became important in anthropology because of the discipline's goal of chronicling and understanding the social and cultural formations to everyday life. It is far from an exaggeration to say that the European Union has become an integral factor in everybody's daily life in Ireland, and in my experience it is widely perceived as such by Irish people. This is due to a number of factors which, although not peculiar to Ireland, have given it a unique configuration of 'Europeanness'.

There are many elements in the 'European' identities which Irish people evidence. Some Irish people in an economy which has long been dominated by farming and the food industries have benefited from the Common Agricultural Policy. There is a rich history of many ties to what is perceived to be the best of European culture. Among these ties are the connections fostered by emigration in the modern era, political republicanism, the traditions of Christianity, colonialism and post-colonialism, and a shared Celtic past. Many Irish have looked to the European Union as a possible arena within which to solve the problems of nationalism and sectarianism in

49

Northern Ireland. Many others deny a European identity precisely because the European Union has influenced changes to the constitutional character of both the Republic of Ireland and Northern Ireland.

Whatever may be the cause, Irish people today are aware of the moves, which originate at local, national, and European levels, to one day have them acknowledge their European identity, if they have not already done so. Some welcome this, others oppose it. But debates over European identity in Ireland continue in part because for decades Irish people have also been European citizens, with rights and privileges that extend to their expanded role in all twenty-seven member states. These rights, in voting, employment and political representation, also create new pressures at home as the same rights are extended to new European immigrants. In consequence, such developments as more competition for Irish agriculture, the end of special subsidies for Irish goods, bailouts for the poorer countries of the EU which affect the help needed by Ireland in its current post-Celtic Tiger depression, and the new European multiculturalism, which has engendered at least for a minority a new Irish racism, are all forces which will continue to fuel anthropological chronicles of cultural change in Ireland.

It was cultural change that brought me to Ireland in the first place, change framed by Ireland's recent admission to the EEC, but also change impelled by so much more that was internally and externally generated. Global capitalism necessitated drastic alterations to the business and way of life of commercial farming. The patronage politics that had characterized the new Irish state were giving way to new forms of local and national government, with new elites emerging in the cities to compete with the more traditional political forces that were associated with rural Ireland (an image that persisted despite the many socialist and other movements on the left which had originated in the Irish countryside over the previous century). The Catholic Church, though still stalwart, was contested increasingly by new forms of secularism and popular and consumer culture. And in County Meath, these changes converged to transform local political culture, class relations, social values and practices, and political institutions. In the chapters that follow, I examine first how large farmers' lives fared in the 1970s and 1980s within the changing dimensions of an Ireland new to Europe. These changes both eroded and bolstered many aspects of culture and class among the peoples of rural and urban Meath. The influence which farmers had enjoyed in Meath public culture up to that time was due to some extent to their roles in local government, and I review many of the historical forces at work in the new Irish state which made this so, before exploring how political culture and the cultures of government began to alter, in ways still being experienced in Meath today.

Notes

1. It has been a sore point in much scholarship on Ireland in the twentieth century that despite so much in Irish life to the contrary, many scholars do not include Northern Ireland in their assessments of 'Ireland'. This has been a shame not only because of the many historical, cultural, political, economic and social ties that bind so many people on the island to each other, but also because it has tended to reflect biases in academic disciplines, where a state's society and polity have been in the main viewed as coterminous with the nation-state. In this book, which is principally about changes to government and politics in a rural constituency in the Republic

of Ireland, I shall run the risk of inviting similar criticism: in the main in this book when reference is made to Ireland I refer to the Republic of Ireland and its twenty-six counties. I also at times refer to Northern Ireland when discussing Ireland, and have attempted to make the distinctions in emphasis clear in the text.

2. For a more comprehensive review of the history and contemporary dimensions of the social and cultural anthropology of Ireland, see Wilson and Donnan 2006.

3. In this book the European Economic Community or EEC is used to refer to the various institutional manifestations of European Integration which evolved from the Common Market since 1973 when Ireland and the United Kingdom became members. I do this to simplify both the writing and reading of the text, with full knowledge that EEC here stands for multiple European communities at any one time and over time, including today's European Union.

4. County Meath is bound on the east by County Dublin and the Irish Sea, on the north by Counties Louth, Monaghan, and Cavan, on the west by County Westmeath, and on the south by Counties Offaly, Kildare and Dublin. In 1979 it had an area of 577,800 acres (903 square miles), 95 per cent of which was under farmed. In 1981, the population was 95,419.

5. In my doctoral research, besides the ethnographic methodological mainstay of 'participant observation', I utilized a number of methods and relied on many sources for my data. Among them were county and national newspapers, County Council minutes and records, formal and informal interviews with all active and retired members of the County Council and Dáil Éireann, and formal and informal interviews with literally hundreds of farmers in over thirty years of living and working in Meath.

Chapter 2

Ethnography and Anthropology in Ireland

The anthropology of politics in Ireland was in its infancy when I arrived there in the summer of 1976 to search for a field site for the doctoral research I planned for the following year. I knew then that my interests in politics and government might set me apart from other anthropologists working in Ireland, since the vast majority of ethnographic work done in Ireland up to then was on social organization in mostly rural local communities. And while my studies in history, economics and politics had led me to the complex world of Irish political culture, I knew too that I would have to master published Irish ethnography in order to persuade my doctoral committee and others that anthropologists should do research on national and local government and politics. But first and foremost I had to master the past and present of the anthropology of Ireland, which continues to shape research in local politics and history today.

Anthropology in Ireland: The early years

Modern anthropological research in Ireland began with the field research conducted from 1932 to 1934 by Conrad Arensberg and Solon Kimball in a rural and peripheral area of County Clare, in the West of Ireland. The publications which resulted from this anthropological research (Arensberg 1937; Arensberg and Kimball 1940, 1968), focused on social and cultural stability and change in the lives of poor farmers and their neighboring townspeople. They were part of a wider study which was initiated by a team of anthropologists from Harvard

University in order to chronicle the state of Irish culture from the perspectives of three fields of anthropology, i.e., archaeology, biology and ethnology.[1] But it was Arensberg and Kimball's research which became the most widely known and the most influential, on both sides of the Atlantic.

Arensberg and Kimball's perspectives on the lives of the Irish countryman and Irish townsman set the standard by which much of the anthropology of Ireland was judged up to the 1980s. The template for rural ethnographic research became their community-based model wherein kinship and social structure were examined as a means of testing the theoretical dimensions of structural-functionalism (Wilson 1984). This theoretical paradigm, which up to then had mainly been applied and tested by scholars in the far-flung and exotic areas of the early twentieth-century empires, had also at the time been utilized in a few community studies in North America. In bringing this new perspective to Europe, Arensberg and Kimball clearly sought to bring an anthropological perspective to a modern nation which, if not as fully industrialized or modernized as other locations in 1930s Europe, was clearly one of the civilized societies at the fringe of Europe.

Their theoretical intentions notwithstanding, it was their field study and its portraits of the Irish farm family and rural way of life that seemed to impel Irish local sociological studies for the decades that followed. Arensberg and Kimball made Clare so famous in the ethnographic literature that subsequent researchers viewed the Clare case as a microcosm of Irish rural society as a whole. However, at no point in either Arensberg's series of lectures on the subject (1937) or in their later ethnographic account (1968) did Arensberg and Kimball argue that their analysis and conclusions held for anything except for

Clare (although their liberal use of "Irish' instead of 'Clare' as an adjective did not help clarify matters. And although Arensberg and Kimball chose their study-site as a 'representative mean among the major social and economic conditions in Ireland' (Arensberg and Kimball 1968: xxvii), so that their study would have as large an application or relevance as possible, it is clear that their study was only of three small rural communities and the town of Ennis. It was only meant to be suggestive of cultural relationships among small farmers and town dwellers elsewhere in Ireland. Clare offered Arensberg and Kimball a sample field situation which enabled them to observe the form of the range of relations among small farmers (i.e., those with holdings of very small acreage), who represented the largest percentage of the rural population of Ireland. They sought to delineate the relationships of small farm folk with each other, and also with large farmers, shopkeepers, marriage middlemen, and cattle dealers, community members with whom the men and women of small farms came into regular contact.

To Arensberg and Kimball the content of these relations, i.e. the social webs in which all countrymen found themselves, was, until further research proved otherwise, specific to county Clare. Focusing on relationships organized through blood and marriage, their fieldwork was a descriptive account of the connection between 'several aspects of community life among the small farmers of County Clare and their system of ordering family relationships (Arensberg and Kimball 1968: xxvi). Thus their data provided a starting point for subsequent ethnographic investigation into Irish rural society and a point of departure for comparative research. Arensberg and Kimball's study was 'offered to the Irish people as a merest beginning in a task' which they expected the Irish themselves to complete (Arensberg and Kimball 1968: xxvi). They sought to identify the social forces at work in Clare that might facilitate the transition to a modern Irish society. Thus, they were also provoking anthropologists to ethnographically study modern societies and to show the value of anthropological methods and theories for the sociological understanding of modern society and culture.

Their interest in applying anthropological theory to Ireland was in aid of advancing what was to them an innovation in ethnographic methodology. Outside of Ireland, the benefits of anthropological community studies in modern industrialized societies had been shown already, in two recent major field studies done in the USA (those of Yankee City and Middletown). The leaders of the Harvard research team were keen to use Ireland as the locus of the first such study in Europe.[2] In 1931, when Arensberg and his mentor, Lloyd Warner, first surveyed Ireland for a research site, a consensus had hardly been reached in anthropology as a whole on the necessity for extended fieldwork, let alone within structural-functionalism. Arensberg and Kimball's study was of course interested in explaining aspects of Irish society. But there is also much to suggest that the Clare case study was equally dedicated to the format of the study, which was never intended as a definitive statement on Irish society. The Clare data enabled Arensberg and Kimball to argue for a functionalist theory and a methodology for extended field community studies.

Ironically, this attempt by Arensberg and Kimball to modernize the fields of social and cultural anthropology, i.e., British and American anthropology respectively, resulted in a long period of theoretical and methodological dormancy, in which the majority of anthropologists researching in Ireland 'felt the need to explain their research as an extension, validation, contradiction or variation of the work of Arensberg and Kimball' (Kane et al. 1988: 97). This adherence to the intentions and achievements of the two Americans was simultaneously beneficial and detrimental. Their explicit and implicit research results led to a number of healthy if also at times heated scholarly debates (on the nature of the Irish family, for example, or on the resilience of rural social structure in urban Ireland) which in large part not only infused Irish social science but brought many Irish scholars to the attention of a more global audience. At the same time, however, the template became restrictive as well.

Up to the late 1970s, with a few exceptions, most anthropologists and sociologists in Ireland, and most elsewhere who studied Ireland, chose or were directed to test the theory, methods, and empirical findings of the original path breaking research in Clare, despite the facts that Ireland, the scholarship of Ireland, and anthropological notions of community studies had moved decidedly on. When a revisionist conference of social sciences published their report on the state of play in local sociological studies in Ireland in 1988, they concluded that

> Far from being coherent, the follow-up to Arensberg and Kimball has simply been repetitive, or fitfully genuflective. Rather than examining their theoretical approach and ethnography, researchers interested in Ireland have experienced the classic work initially as a centripetal force;

57

their own findings are then presented as centrifugal extensions of the touchstone (Kane et al. 1988: 98).

The impact of the Arensberg and Kimball works has today been diminished, due partly to critiques of the anthropology and sociology of Ireland that have tried to set new research agendas (see for example; Coulter 1999; Conway 2006; Wilson and Donnan 2006). Nevertheless, the importance of Arensberg and Kimball in the received wisdom of anthropologists with some knowledge of Ireland persists. For example, in 1992 an American doctoral candidate who was doing field work in Belfast told me how influential my own work had been to her in the preparation of her doctoral research on politics and culture in Northern Ireland. But she also pointed out the irony of how her doctoral committee at her eminent university in the USA had insisted that she talk less about Wilson and other contemporary ethnographers working in Ireland and more about the classic texts that needed to be engaged. The message she received at her doctoral qualifying exams, and which she relayed to me after a colloquium in the social anthropology department at Queens University, was: 'enough talk about these others, now where are Arensberg and Kimball in your research design?'

The hegemony of scholarly and academic ideas and models aside (for a consideration of how they have played a part in the anthropology of Ireland, see Wilson and Donnan 2006), this anecdote is suggestive of the lingering relevance of the early Clare study to some perspectives on Ireland today. In fact, the continuing importance of their work to contemporary social science in Ireland may be seen in the Irish-produced third edition of their jointly-authored analysis of the town of Ennis and its rural environs, *Family and Community in Ireland* (Arensberg and Kimball 2001). And while their theoretical models of cultural change and social stability are now long out of favor among anthropologists and sociologists, their ethnographic research is still seen in many scholarly quarters as being at the least a relatively accurate historical view of County Clare that continues to yield 'insights into a way of life of which many fragments persist still, some remain vivid in memory, and others would have been forgotten without their book to recall them' (Byrne et al. 2001: ii).

The impact of the Arensberg and Kimball study on research and scholarship in Ireland was not immediate. It took fifteen years until another ethnographer did a rural community study in Ireland (Rosemary Harris in County Tyrone [Harris 1972]). But when ethnographic research began to be pursued in earnest, and in many locations in Ireland, the influence of that earlier research became apparent. For over a generation after the publication of the results of the Clare study, ethnographic research in Ireland was dominated by the analysis of family roles, generational relations, inheritance, marriage patterns, and formal and informal kinship and social structure. This research was almost entirely done in rural settings. Up to the early 1970s most ethnographers had kinship and community solidarity or division as their initial if not major focuses. The publications that resulted from most of this research demonstrated implicit or explicit acceptance of both the model and ethnographic accuracy of the original Clare study.

Thus each ethnography (i.e., the book or other writing that derive from ethnographic research) tended to identify similarities and differences between the selected field site and that of Arensberg and Kimball. This should be expected, given the ground breaking early research and its role in putting local Irish society onto a global scholarly stage. But due to this specifically Irish case it appears that ethnographers went into the field expecting to find a homogeneous rural culture, and their studies seemed to proceed from that assumed state of social life. When their data did not match that of Arensberg and Kimball, they had two directions in which to go. Some attempted to account for the factors in local society that changed it from the ethnographic 'facts' originally found in Clare. This most often entailed an analysis of the demoralization, decline and anomie of local society as a result of modernization (Cresswell 1969; Brody 1973; McNabb 1964). Other ethnographers saw the differences in their data to be representative of conditions endemic to the particular locale or region of the field study. In the latter case local society and culture were proffered to anthropological audiences as being just as traditional and enduring as those found in Clare. This was especially noticeable in studies done in Northern Ireland (see for example Harris 1972; Leyton 1975) which unlike work done in the Republic engaged the divisive factors of sectarianism and class.

Despite these relatively minor digressions from the original model, the ethnographic work of Arensberg and Kimball must surely rival any other in the world as the most significant anthropological scholarship in the development of one nation's intellectual traditions. In fact it is difficult if not impossible for me to think of an ethnography from another country which has so profoundly affected the dimensions of that country's society to be found in subsequent research.

As a result, up to the end of the 1960s, as in most ethnographic studies done around the world at the time, the

60

analysis of kinship and its role in local social and economic cooperation became the principal theme of anthropological research in Ireland. Most of this research took place in the west and south of the island. A review of the research focuses of those studies can give an inkling as to how the political ethnography which concerns us in this book represented a radical departure from the mainstream of the time.

Cresswell (1969) investigated the effects of modernization on a community in Clare just south of Arensberg and Kimball's original field site. Brody (1973) offered a composite view of communities in the West of Ireland in order to depict the decline of local culture and the disintegration of society in the face of forces external to the locality and region, themes which Scheper-Hughes (1979) echoed later. Humphreys (1966) traced the progress of rural families who had moved to Dublin, and he analyzed the effects of urbanization on the fabric of rural kinship. In the first complete study of an Irish-speaking area, Messenger (1964, 1968, 1969) identified historical and contemporary political, economic, religious, and social influences in the everyday lives of Aran islanders (in what proved to be a controversial analysis due to the reaction by islanders to what he wrote, a theme that can also be seen in the subsequent local Irish reception of Scheper Hughes' book (see Messenger 1988, 1989; Scheper Hughes 2000 for their versions of these events). McNabb (1964) investigated community change in another southern county, Limerick. But none of these studies questioned directly the accuracy of Arensberg and Kimball's ethnographic account. On the contrary, they each in their own ways used the Clare study as their model. When the data on social structure or community relations were different from the Clare case, reference was often made to the curiousness of such findings (Messenger 1969: 73, 79).

Early ethnography in Northern Ireland also modeled itself partly on the Arensberg and Kimball study (Mogey 1947), but when faced with the reality of the political partition of Ireland into a twenty-six county Free State (later Republic) and a six-county Northern Ireland, one of the constituent territories of the UK, social structure became only one facet of ethnographic community studies. The political, economic, social and cultural integration and contest associated with divergent national identifications, class conflict and religious affiliation cross-cut all levels of Northern Ireland. As a result even the most narrowly focused ethnographic analysis had to account for an ethnographic situation which was radically different from that of Clare.

Harris (1972) examined structured group friction and competition in her study of a predominantly Catholic community in County Tyrone. Leyton (1966, 1970, 1974, 1975) focused on the web of kinship institutions in a community in County Down which was divided by religion, class, and history. These were new concepts to the wider anthropology of Ireland but for some time they remained particular to ethnographic studies done in Northern Ireland. But even in these studies kinship was the major focus of community study: when Leyton found a wide variation in the significance of kinship throughout the population of Ireland, rather than questioning why this was so he proposed 'to make the analysis of social class a more explicit and integral part of kinship studies' (1975: 1). The concept of class, which might have served as a point of departure for a new wave of ethnographic studies in Ireland, taking anthropology a long way from the

62

structural functionalism of Arensberg and Kimball, became instead a means whereby the kinship system, interdependent with the class system, became more easily understandable (Leyton 1975: 3).

Kinship also provided the focus for ethnographies done in those parts of Ulster outside of Northern Ireland.[3] Fox (1963, 1968, 1978, 1979) studied the social structure of small communities on Tory Island off the coast of Donegal. Shanklin (1980, 1982) had a more geo-economic focus when she examined how local social life declined in rural Donegal after their market town was separated from them by the imposition of the international border in the 1920s, a shock still being felt in the 1970s. Kane (1968), an Irish-American anthropologist who helped found the first department of anthropology in a university in the Republic of Ireland (in what is today known as National University of Ireland-Maynooth; the Department of Social Anthropology in Queens University in Belfast, Northern Ireland, pre-dated its southern neighbor), compared the kin differences in Donegal with nearby Tory and more distant Clare, and made some tentative explanations about such diversity being due to variations in geography, rural-urban relations, and class, but this initial step into what might later be seen to be political and geographical analysis was not carried through in any systematic way by her or others (Kane 1968).

This widespread interest in the data and theoretical models of the Arensberg and Kimball study was not without its critics, some of whom were from outside of the field of anthropology. From the early 1970s, critiques of the methods and theory of the Arensberg and Kimball type of community study began to appear. Their common theme was the notion that anthropologists should not generalize to any great extent

63

from the Clare study, which in their shared view was rooted in the time and place of Clare in the 1930s. The simple departure point for this soft but growing criticism was that the Clare case did not account for behavioral and social structural variations throughout Ireland.

For example, Gibbon (1973) criticized Arensberg and Kimball's historical methods, Messenger (1964, 1968, 1969, 1983) identified a host of cultural values and political factors which were to be found on the Aran Islands off the west coast of Ireland, but which were not mentioned or were not emphasized in the Clare research, and Brody (1973) reviewed the many ways that traditional farm life and rural community values were breaking down in the face of modernization and economic marginalization in the West of Ireland. However, these critics were not necessarily in agreement, and some of their criticisms, such as those of Messenger, were offered reverently. The same cannot be said of the critique of Peter Gibbon, which not only challenged much that Arensberg and Kimball wrote but indicted anthropologists and their approaches to Irish history, economics and politics.

Gibbon's (1973) analysis of the state of anthropological analyses of local Irish society pointed out the inconsistencies at play in the anthropological use of Arensberg and Kimball's work, which overall viewed Irish rural society as traditional, stable, and either flourishing or declining. Gibbon lamented that Arensberg and Kimball's principally theoretical writing had rural Ireland as its subject because the impact of the theory led people to uncritically accept the ethnography (Gibbon 1973: 496). Gibbon did not stop there. He used the more recent ethnographic data found in Brody's (1973) analysis of rural demoralization in the West of Ireland to make a simple but telling point: anthropologists cannot trace decline from a traditional or stable society (Clare of the 1930s) when that society was neither traditional or stable. Gibbon showed how rural Clare in the 1930s had been caught up in major forces of social structural, agricultural and urban change which had existed since at least as far back as the Great Famine of the 1840s. Gibbon further contended that Clare of the 1930s was not representative of a traditional and stable rural order, which did not exist in the ways suggested by Arensberg and Kimball anywhere in Ireland. On the contrary, Clare was an example of structures and processes that had been in flux for almost a century. Gibbon concluded that Arensberg and Kimball's study was not a 'repository of revealed truth.' Rather, because of their insistence on supporting a theoretical model based on the family, the mutual aid system among farmers, the economic and cultural stability of local society, and its attendant politics, 'their account ranges from the inaccurate to the fictive' (Gibbon 1973: 491). Although targeted at Brody's work, Gibbon's barbs were perhaps meant to pierce other anthropological skins, for his criticism seemed to be aimed at other ethnographic research in Ireland that had been published before the 1970s.

Before turning to the changes in anthropology in Ireland in the 1970s, it should be noted that although many later scholars, reporters and other Irish social critics assailed most of the anthropological writings up to then as relatively simple portraits of an unchanging and traditional Ireland, it is clear that Arensberg and Kimball intended no such portrait. They were drawn to Clare as a place, and to Ireland on the whole, because of the latter's ongoing transition from the traditional to the modern. They were well aware that the historical, geographical

65

and cultural dimensions of this transition were by no means simple or complete. Although principally an agricultural land, many parts of the island had been industrialized for some time. The major cities of Ireland had been part of wider global commercial networks for centuries, at the least as nodes in the British Empire. Arensberg and Kimball were in Ireland to witness and chronicle Ireland's modernization, but from the perspective of rural and urban localities. They sought to observe stability and change in a period that was in dramatic flux, which was precisely why they were there. It was in fact because of the clash of tradition and internally and externally produced social change that made this relatively but never entirely isolated corner of Ireland so attractive. They were not alone, for this was also a region which attracted national political leaders, filmmakers, cultural nationalists and many other intellectuals of Ireland and beyond because of its association with traditional Ireland (Wilson 1987).

Debates over what was intended by Arensberg and Kimball and their successors in the anthropology and ethnography of Ireland excepted, one thing was eminently clear to newly trained anthropology students in the 1960s and 1970s: traditions then were different from those of the 1930s, there had been a generation's worth of political and economic change since then, Ireland was about to join the Common Market, conflict had erupted in Northern Ireland, and so much seemed to be happening so quickly in some Irish quarters that any attempt to understand Ireland from an anthropological perspective would need new ideas and approaches.

Ethnographic departures: The 1970s

The contradictions that were emerging in the anthropology of Ireland in this period perhaps can best be illustrated by ethnographic research which began to be conducted in Northern Ireland in the years after 'the Troubles'[4] returned in 1969. Although the initial community studies of Northern Irish villages and cityscapes focused on networks of kinship and social organization, different results were obtained in part because of the perceived differences between the cultural values and social structure of Northern Ireland and those of the Republic, societies which at that point had been separated by geopolitics for almost fifty years. The ethnographers of Northern Ireland could not ignore the facts of social class, nationalism and sectarianism. Thus the community studies of Harris (1961, 1972), Leyton (1966, 1970, 1974, 1975), McFarlane (1979), Buckley (1982) and Bufwack (1982), among others, attempted to describe local village life in Northern Ireland, but also account for the cleavages which cross-cut all levels of Northern Irish society.

In the anthropology of Northern Ireland it has been all but impossible to understand local rural and urban communities without understanding ethnicity, sectarianism, national identities, class, and the overall importance of history in everyday life. This was apparent in the first ethnographies published on Northern Ireland. Indeed, it was in the earlier anthropology of Northern Ireland that the origins of much of the applied anthropological focus of today's ethnographic research across the whole of Ireland can be found (Donnan and McFarlane 1989, 1997). However, this turn to applied and policy anthropology took a while to come to fruition in both the Republic and in Northern Ireland, in part due to the durability of many older anthropological models, even in the heady times of the 1970s when there was a sharp rise in the numbers of local and foreign ethnographers who embarked on new field research in Ireland.

Much of this newly vitalized ethnographic research of the 1970s began to appear in print near the end of that decade and into the first years of the next (but as often happens some research took even longer to see print). In fact, in their efforts to establish anthropology more firmly as an academic subject in Irish universities, concerns were expressed that the majority of anthropological research projects conducted in Ireland took too long to publish (Kane et al. 1988). The research and publications of these two decades thus clearly saw the continuation of trends that had been established earlier, but also the birth of some new ones. The 1980s was not only a time which ushered in a number of new developments in the anthropology of Ireland, to be found in new interests in politics, power, policy, gender, history and economics, but was also a time when the strong traditions in methods and theories begun by Arensberg and Kimball continued apace.

The themes of these publications represented major departures from the 'sacred texts' of Arensberg and Kimball. However, because of the traditional nature of anthropology itself, where key ideas are tested, contested and attested in the dialectics of scholarly debate and publishing, affording certain theories and methods their own shelf lives, much research and writing continued to focus on the same type of questions and analysis as had been outlined in Clare. While it was clear to most anthropologists that the small farming communities of the West of Ireland were unlike those of Arensberg and Kimball's day, and might no longer even qualify as peasants as they had

68

in so much of the literature, nevertheless a great deal of influential anthropological production continued to characterize rural Ireland as declining or dying (see, for example, Brody 1973; Scheper-Hughes 1979; Messenger 1983). Others continued to look at the structures and functions of kinship, social organization, marriage, the family, and the conditions of work and production which kept villages stable, peaceful, and relatively traditional in their concerns (see, for example, Kane 1979; Taylor 1981; Buckley 1982; Bufwack 1982; Shanklin 1982).

Lively exchange and discordant voices appeared in the midst of this new anthropology. A debate developed in print in the anthropology of Ireland in this period which revolved around issues of family form and function (see, for example, Gibbon and Curtin 1978, 1983a, 1983b; Harris 1988) and rural social and political patrons and clients (see, for example, Gibbon and Higgins 1974; Shanklin 1980). Much of this latter interest not only reflected some innovative approaches in anthropology which were developed elsewhere, where maverick anthropologists were pushing ethnographers to look for power and influence in the informal interstices between social and political institutions (the most important such call to me was in Wolf 1966), but also showed that much mainstream anthropology, which was embracing historical sources and new methodological and theoretical innovations, such as networks and network theory, was finding an audience in Ireland.

The 1970s and early 1980s also witnessed the beginnings of research agendas which paralleled those of scholars in North America, Britain, and the rest of Europe. A series of ethnographic critiques, overviews, and scholarly calls to arms appeared which were to reset the research agenda for

69

Ireland, North and South (see, for example, Wilson 1984; Donnan and McFarlane 1986, 1997; Jenkins 1986; Kane et al. 1988; Curtin and Wilson 1989; Peace 1989). The changes in anthropological interests and research designs which were evidenced in these publications were a reaction to two sets of transformations. The first was in the changes that had occurred to anthropology globally, where history, politics, and economics had each become subfields in anthropology, and where feminist, anti-imperialist, and anti-racist perspectives, among many other forms of politics, had transformed the ways in which anthropology was taught and researched.

The second set of transformations involved those which both Northern Ireland and the Republic were undergoing. Ireland had become much more urbanized and suburbanized. While a war raged in Northern Ireland over the constitutional issue, Northern Ireland, as part of the UK, and the Republic of Ireland, had joined the EEC. Economic recession had led to greater emigration. National media grew in influence, as did new forms of popular culture: every night the images and events of Europe and beyond were brought into the kitchens and sitting rooms of Irish households, encouraging processes of secularization, modernization, and internationalization. National educational reforms, access to new markets in continental Europe, and advances in information and communication technologies weakened the traditional ties of church and politics, encouraging new forms of engagement with others in Europe and more globally.

As a result of all of these real-world changes, it was obvious to all but the most traditional of ethnographers that Irish rural villages could no longer be perceived as social and cultural isolates. Revisionist trends in the anthropology of

70

Ireland had begun to focus on the ways in which rural communities were tied to social, economic and political formations external to the locality. Anthropologists set out to investigate the ways in which the people of Ireland's farms, villages, towns and cities were linked to local, national and European institutions, and they began to examine the regional and national processes of social change (in a manner that was being adopted elsewhere in Europe, where new approaches to regions, nations and the state were being developed; see Boissevain 1975; Cole 1977).

These transformations in intellectual frames, professional anthropology and Irish society and culture were the spark to a veritable explosion in ethnographic research and writing.[5] The break that was being made at the time with many past interests and approaches in anthropology was made clear in two collections of ethnographic case studies. These books, which dealt with change at local levels in the countryside (Curtin and Wilson 1989) and in towns and cities (Curtin et al. 1993) across the island of Ireland, included essays from anthropologists from Ireland, the United Kingdom, Canada, and the United States, were intended as textbooks, and were adopted in Irish universities as what might be seen as new models for anthropological research and writing. Their chapters offered what the editors and many of their authors hoped would be at least a partial response to the questions which had been surfacing among anthropologists regarding the relevance and applicability of anthropology to contemporary Ireland (as found, for example, in Wilson 1984; Kane et al. 1988). Many of these questions about future directions to research in Ireland were based on the community studies that were then being seen to be deficient in terms of method and research design.

71

The upshot of all of this turn to new research agendas in Ireland was that it placed the anthropology of Ireland squarely within a variety of mainstream concerns of the field elsewhere, but principally within many of the themes which were emerging in the development of anthropology in Britain, North America and continental Europe. These new research interests branched off in diverse ways, many of which were aimed at applying anthropology to various forms of public culture in Ireland, and not exclusively within the academy. Ireland in fact became the site and the focus of some of the first anthropological analyses anywhere in Europe of the impact of European integration at local levels, and of local peoples' responses as well (see, for example, Dilley 1989; Sheehan 1991; Shutes 1991, 1993; Wilson 1989a).

But one of the more significant breaks with past models of anthropology in Ireland came with the 1960s and 1970s turn by ethnographers to the study of local government and politics as cornerstones of Irish culture and society. This turn to the study of political institutions, relations and processes, which reflected new approaches in anthropology that were gaining momentum elsewhere,[6] was based on research done on the political machines of national electoral constituencies in Counties Cork (Bax 1976) and Donegal (Sacks 1976).

These field studies, done independently of each other but in parliamentary constituencies with important histories of national prominence in the affairs of the nation, had remarkably similar goals. Both Bax and Sacks sought to examine the formal institutional and organizational aspects of local and national politics as they played out in a rural constituency, but they also wanted to identify the roles such politics play in the lives of a number of communities across whole counties. Bax, a

Dutch anthropologist, borrowing from models developed in both southern European and southern Asian ethnography, delineated and analyzed the many political, economic, and social components of political brokerage in rural communities in Cork (Bax 1975, 1976). Sacks, an American political sociologist, though his analysis of a constituency in Donegal, ended up with what is the most comprehensive extended case study in the history of Irish political scholarship. In so doing, Sacks also brought our collective attention to the formal and informal bases of social and political power in local communities in Donegal, power with sources that were both internal and external to those communities, and were constructed through local, regional and national political networks.

These studies utilized models which were not developed within or dependent on prior Irish ethnographic research. Moreover, they used models and theories, largely designed and applied to politics and culture in other parts of the world, to study aspects of local Irish life which had not previously been seen in the ethnographic literature, precisely because ethnographers before them simply did not consider politics and politicians as subjects of ethnographic enquiry. By the 1970s, when a good number of new ethnographic projects were started in Ireland, including my own, these studies of local politics and government had helped to break the mould of social structure in Irish ethnography, and the hold which theoretical models of stability had on the imaginations of Irish ethnographers.

Politics and a theoretical frame

In 1975, just before my initial doctoral research began, Tony Fahey, an Irish sociologist, concluded that 'No attempt, good or bad, has been made to construct a theoretical framework for the analysis of Irish society' (Fahey 1975: 95). In his view, Irish sociology had developed as a response to local and national problems in Irish society, such as emigration, poverty, unequal economic development, family disintegration, secularization, and the lack of employment and educational opportunities. But none of the resultant national problem-orientated sociology was developed within wider historical or methodological contexts, for, as far as Fahey was concerned, sociology never went beyond the commonsense view of society, or identified any problems which could not have been discovered by a good journalist (Fahey 1975: 95).

In characterizing the sociology of Ireland in the 1970s, Fahey concluded that the lack of theory in sociology was the result of those who defined what was problematical in society in his discipline. In his view, and it is one difficult to dispute, 'problems' do not just emerge fully formed from the head of some superior being. They have to be defined by scholars in response to social conditions which exist around them. But Fahey was asking for something more: a commitment to sociological theory in the face of the surrounding real-world problems. According to him, in the years up to the 1970s in Ireland, sociological problems had been defined by politicians, clergymen, and pressure groups of all kinds, but not by sociologists (Fahey 1975: 96).

The opposite situation had developed in the social and cultural anthropology of Ireland, wherein what had been defined as problematical had almost exclusively been

74

determined by scholars who followed the paradigms of community study and structural functionalism which had been espoused by Arensberg and Kimball. In most of this anthropological scholarship the problems of everyday life in Ireland, and certainly the problems of groups of people in society which were the lifeblood of sociology at the time, were seldom seen as problematical for anthropological research and theorizing.

It would be foolish to suggest that Irish sociology was or is now anti-theory or non-theoretical. Nor is it my intention to suggest that social anthropology and sociology in Ireland years ago were developing in completely different and unrelated ways. In fact, the Arensberg and Kimball research became an important part of Irish sociology, but due much more to its data, and to a lesser extent to its methodology and theory. The rural farm family and its relations with other community institutions became a principal focus of many sociological studies, which in turn were tied by university and government researchers to the practical problems of Ireland. When I began my own field research in rural Leinster province the sociologists of the Irish semi-state bodies were the most helpful to me in ascertaining the relevant academic literature about Irish agriculture as well as the real life problems that would be most relevant to Irish farmers. Irish sociologists had published in the period up to the 1970s a great deal on the changing nature of rural social organization as it related to major forces in Irish life such as migration, education, class mobility, and the disintegration of community structures (as may be seen in the works of Hannan 1970, 1972, 1979, 1982).

Of special concern to sociologists who were trying to contribute to the solution of Irish social and economic problems

75

was the quality of life of a farming population that in large part subsisted on uneconomic holdings which they owned and were unwilling or unlikely to leave (Commins and Kelleher 1973; Frawley 1975). In much of this work, and in approaches which really did set sociology apart from anthropological work being done in rural areas at the same time, social relations were viewed as factors that enhanced or retarded social change. And at that time and even since in Ireland, in the academic discipline of sociology, such change is seen as being within the purview of government policy. Not surprisingly, local community life in Ireland was and is still often studied in aid of contributing to the policy processes related to the solving of social ills, and in the spirit of academic collaboration with government in mutually agreed public goals.

Thus, a great deal of socio-economic research was conducted in the 1960s and 1970s in both government and university circles in Ireland on the problems of community and regional development, with emphases on matters such as the maintenance of income and lifestyle among small farmers (Scully 1971), the push and pull factors of migration (Hannan 1970), and local industrialization (Kane 1978, 1979). This policy dimension to Irish sociology, though perhaps based a bit on the Arensberg and Kimball research, showed too some of the divergence from anthropology in Ireland at the time.

It is clear that despite their partially shared origins in the work or Arensberg and Kimball in the 1930s, the sociology and anthropology of Ireland developed along different lines. Social anthropology overall in the twentieth century has focused on method and theory, evading in large measure the 'common-sense' view for which sociology was criticized. For at least forty years after the research in Clare, anthropological

76

ethnographers, with few exceptions, utilized the same unit of analysis (the community), the same focus for the analysis of social life (kinship and social structure), and the same theoretical model of local society (structural-functionalism) as did the two Americans. While in the period up to the 1970s some anthropologists criticized Arensberg and Kimball's model of society, by attempting to describe and account for social and cultural changes, or attacked their data, very few conducted research which was not framed by either if not both.

This had two results. Up to then, the anthropology of Ireland, to consider it at its best, had contributed to the theorizing of structural functionalism and the community study method through its many kinship-based studies of social stability and change. Seen perhaps at its worst, however, the anthropology of Ireland had been stuck in a bit of a rut by steadfastly testing and re-testing a theoretical model that hardly needed such attention. And this was done for at least a generation of research. Obviously, this was the exact opposite to that for which Fahey had indicted Irish sociology.

Anthropology's strength then, and still, was its adherence to the extended case study method, with its core method and motif: participant observation. In most if not all of the ethnographic studies done in Ireland up to the 1970s, the period that most concerns us in this book, but also, I wager, up to the present (although what passes for ethnography in many recent versions of anthropology is not much more than data-light culturally-sensitive interviewing in pursuit of culture as biography) data were consistently identified, collected, and compared in a methodical fashion, in aid of supporting anthropology as a social science. As a result, the ethnographic literature on Ireland is one of the strongest and most coherent in anthropology in Europe, and might usefully serve as a model for national anthropologies elsewhere (Wilson and Donnan 2006).

The rigor and coherence of a century of Irish ethnography is due in great measure to the pioneering work of Arensberg and Kimball. It is lamentable to me that more young anthropologists today do not seem to find particular worth in Arensberg's notions of ethnographic research (here quoted from a letter he wrote in 1961 to one of his original Irish research assistants, in which he discussed his activities since leaving Clare):

> I'm still advocate and developer of 'field-work,' participant observation or other methods of community study which require an active immersion, with much observation and interviewing in the ongoing life of place being studied, in the social and economic activities of the region where a problem is being studied. Our researchers must know all the statistical and historical background data to be got, but they must also live and work on the ground, interviewing and questioning the people concerned and attempting to understand the fit of the problem being studied to their lives and the life of their region and country. Over the years such intensive methods have been sharpened, their rationale worked out better, their justification further advanced (Arensberg, as quoted in Meghen 1961: 62).

At the time of my doctoral research, and even when I first made note of this sentiment of Arensberg in a publication (Wilson 1984), it was clear that his theoretical and methodological models had not only been adopted by a generation of ethnographers, but had helped to frame a global anthropological attention to the value of, as well as the means to do, an ethnographic community study. Today, in 2011 as I write this book, I am just as sure that most new ethnographers who have been university trained in Anglophone anthropology have little faith and little interest in such methods and fieldwork. But in the 1970s at least, and in what one day may be judged as the historical highpoint of ethnography in Ireland, Arensberg and Kimball's most notable achievement was in the establishment of a paradigm for ethnographic research. Any ethnographic design faults of the later twentieth century should not be laid at the feet of the masters themselves. That must fall to those of their successors who had difficulty separating out Arensberg and Kimball's ethnographic data from their theoretical and methodological constructions.

However, as we have seen, since the 1970s, as Ireland and Northern Ireland became more involved in the processes of globalization, Europeanization, internationalization and transnationalization, as part of their role in the European Union but due to many other forces of global politics and capitalism, the ethnographers of Ireland have increasingly adopted new models, theories and methodologies in their effort to be more relevant and applicable to the needs of contemporary Ireland. They have recognized and in most part have transcended the limits of past models, data, and theory. They now in the main offer a more common sense perspective on Irish society and culture. Many of these turns to more practical and applied research began in the 1970s with particular attention to local Irish politics and political culture. It was with the goal to investigate the political roles of relatively wealthy and influential farmers in the East of Ireland that I first went to Navan, the capital town of County Meath.

Notes

1. The overall Harvard Irish Study (1931-1936) was led by Professor Earnest Hooton of Harvard University (to whom Arensberg and Kimball dedicated *Family and Community in Ireland*). The project involved biological, archaeological and ethnological research throughout Ireland in what was planned as the first comprehensive anthropological study of a small modern nation (for an overview of the project, see Byrne et al. 2001). Arensberg and Kimball used their Irish research as the basis for their doctoral degrees at Harvard.

2. Arensberg's research began in 1932, and he was later joined by Kimball, his colleague from the USA. They are still widely considered in social science circles to have done the first great social anthropological study of a European community (for a brief history of the origins of the anthropology of Europe, see Cole 1977).

3. The traditional Irish province of Ulster, the northern most province of the four in Ireland, had nine counties historically. In the partition of Ireland in 1921, six of those counties remained in the United Kingdom, and since that time they have constituted Northern Ireland. The three remaining counties are in the Republic of Ireland, a separate nation-state. Many Irish people still refer to Ulster in terms of the north of the island of Ireland (and to the related histories, cultures, way of life etc) and in so doing include all nine counties, but many other people in Ireland, most notably many Unionists in Northern Ireland, use 'Ulster' as the referent to the six counties of Northern Ireland. Ireland traditionally was composed of four provinces: Connaught in the west of the island, Munster in the south, Leinster in the east and Ulster in the north. References in this book to 'West' and 'South' reflect mainstream Irish usage and are relative to the whole island.

4. 'The Troubles' is the Irish term for the conflict that raged in Northern Ireland from 1969 to 1998. While there is still ethnic tension, nationalist dispute, and terrorism in Northern Ireland at the time of writing this book, open warfare has all but ceased.

5. Anthropologists had begun to study government and politics (Bax 1975; Komito 1984; Wilson 1989a, 1989b), religion and the Church (Eipper 1986; Taylor 1995); colonialism (Taylor 1980a, b); urbanization (Gmelch 1977); migration (Gmelch and Gmelch 1985; Gmelch 1986); rural industrialization and development (Kane 1978; Ruane 1989); ethnicity (Gmelch 1989); and class (Vincent 1983; Silverman 1989; Cohen 1993).

6. See the magisterial work by Vincent (1990) for a review of this revisionist period in political anthropology; as she indicates however, political anthropology seldom involved comprehensive analyses of local or national governments and politics. The Irish case studies reviewed here, and their successors' research into Irish political culture (such as Peace 1997), demonstrated that when anthropologists conduct research in the halls of power, the inescapable logic of the importance of analyzing the interactions of culture and politics in institutional settings such as in parliaments, courts, and bureaucratic committee rooms is apparent.

Chapter 3

Culture and Class in Meath

Most ethnographic accounts of rural life in Ireland before the 1970s focused on the lives of relatively poor, powerless and marginalized people. The majority of these anthropological studies were of post-peasant small farmers in the West and South of Ireland. As late as the 1970s, and to a great extent still today, commercial farmers with land, wealth and power have not been a major subject of anthropological and sociological investigation, despite their roles as local and national elites, and their obvious influence in social and political circles in Ireland and in the wider Europe. This chapter looks at some ways in which these commercial and influential farmers, known in Ireland as 'large' or 'big' farmers, played significant roles in Meath society and culture in the 1970s, and how that role was hindered and enhanced by forces of modernization and internationalization that continued into the 1980s, and which in many ways continue today, for example, as part of the processes of Europeanization.

In fact, while the forces of change that had an impact on the lives and livelihood of Irish farmers everywhere in the country in the 1970s were many, none were more important or more far-reaching than those that accompanied Ireland's membership in the European Economic Community. In this chapter we review first some of the general aspects of the impact of the EEC on Irish farmers, before we turn to an overview of class, culture and politics among the large farmers of County Meath. These farmers played an influential role in local government and politics for a century, and were the subject of my doctoral research on agricultural politics.

Farmers and policy

Meath farmers in this period had become increasingly sophisticated in their roles as Euro-farmers and businessmen. They were acutely aware of their small voice in Europe, a voice that they were convinced must be heard because of their interests in the success of the CAP. Although they welcomed wholeheartedly the price and market policies within the EEC, they knew that their interests placed them in opposition to other aims of European farm policy. Because increased production of most commodities was unprofitable at the EEC level, other member nations opposed many price supports for agricultural products. Ireland, however, benefited from expansion in such areas as dairy and beef production, and the ever-growing milk lake and meat mountains which were being sustained by the EEC, because the whole EEC must pay the costs of the disposal of the surplus. This tension was exacerbated by the essential contradiction in the CAP as a whole: the achievement of two seemingly mutually exclusive goals of an improved standard of living for all EEC farmers and the rationalization of agriculture through the elimination of wasteful and inefficient farm practices and farmers.

The 'equity' versus 'efficiency' issue had not caused conflict in Ireland between large and small farmers up to that time, and little since if truth be told, but tensions had begun to rise between farmers and other sectors of the economy. Irish consumers and taxpayers in the 1970s and 1980s had increasingly and clearly held that they were paying the real costs of higher prices and subsidized agriculture (Sheehy and O'Connor 1985). In the same period political parties were also attempting to adapt to their changed role within the EEC, not only with their constituents and lobbies, but also with their new partner political parties in Europe. Elections in Ireland had become media events on a national scale in which the party that promised the most to an increasingly skeptical electorate seemingly won new voters and even elections.

As a result of this changed playing field, every national election from 1973 to 1987 saw the opposition party forming the new government. Irish farmers were being molded—or perhaps it is better said that they were molding themselves-- into stronger and more united interest groups under the aegis of their occupational societies. The Irish Farmers' Association (IFA) and the Irish Creamery Milk Suppliers Association (ICMSA) consistently advanced the interests of farmers at all levels of policymaking in Ireland, and did the same more and more at European levels of lobbying. The changed attitude of farmers, as members of a revitalized farm interest group, had been demonstrated in the continuing struggle between farmers and government over taxes. Since 1979, when the government introduced a 2 per cent levy on agricultural production, farmers had waged a running battle with each political party that had been in power.

Meath farmers were at the forefront in this struggle. From the mid-1970s to mid-1980s five successive Irish governments attempted to catch more farmers in the tax net, but with only mixed success. Their efforts to get more tax revenue from farmers, whose wealth overall had clearly risen over the same period, despite the equally clear evidence that many small farmers had suffered due to their inability to compete with agribusinesses and their large farmer neighbors, was also a reaction to other interests in Irish society. Inflation, unemployment, higher prices, and EEC curbs on production had made the incomes of farmers a contentious point for many small business owners and wage-earning employees who had tax deducted from their incomes at the point of payment. Increasingly powerless local and national politicians were caught in the middle in rural constituencies.

Politicians in many cases wanted to court the rural voter whose economic well-being was tied to such farmers. But they, in government or outside of power, were caught in a delicate position, both in regard to the welfare of the nation and in regard to their political futures. In the mid-1980s the Irish government was faced with a budget deficit of 8.5 per cent of GNP, and there were calls to cut government spending by £1,000 million (Wren 1987). At the same time there had been a drop in farmers' incomes, by 40 per cent in aggregate real farm income between 1978 and 1980 alone (Sheehy 1984). Spiraling inflation, unemployment, and massive foreign debt threatened both the Irish economy and the futures of the politicians entrusted with the public welfare. Politicians had to make some moves to pry the recently gained wealth from farmers, but farmers too saw the good times fading. EEC limits on production, high real interest rates, and new government initiatives in taxing farmers were again influencing the nature of farmer support for government and party programs. Some expert observers of the time concluded that Ireland's cattle and beef industries, agricultural income and land structure were little better off than before EEC entry (Cox and Kearney 1983; Drudy and McAleese 1984).

Politicians were also mindful of how all of these pressures in the Irish economy were affecting constituents who were not so directly tied to the farmer electorate. They also had constituents who were paying more for food, were getting less in their pay packet due to rising taxes, and who were daily reminded of the wealth of farmers who were being accused in some circles of getting preferential treatment from the government. The IFA had become the principal representative of farmers in this fight and had usurped much of the power of the politicians in the IFA's efforts to make the shrinking farming electorate into an effective national and international lobby. The internationalization of Irish agricultural policymaking had thus helped to redefine Irish farmers' roles within national politics and to a lesser extent, but one which is still being played out in the 21st century, within European politics.

Thus, in the first decades of EEC membership it was clear that the large farmers in counties such as Meath had seen their lives changed, but many other Irish populations more frequently encountered in the ethnographic literature had also been affected. Shopkeepers, small farmers, and the proletarians of the towns and cities also needed to protect their own common interests against the state and other member nations. Things heated up considerably while I was doing my doctoral field research when, in 1979, 5000 farmers demonstrated in Dublin against the government's new farm tax, in what was the largest public show of farmer strength and opposition to the government in decades. When the government decided to amend its tax plan in what was seen as a response to the farmer demonstration, 150,000 workers took to the streets of Dublin to protest their tax burden in the largest demonstration of its kind in Irish history. The message from all sides in the disputes was clear: no one wants to lose their share of the pie, especially when that pie was shrinking markedly in comparison with other economies within a united Europe, and in comparison with the boom years that had ended just a short while before.

The complex changes that occurred in Ireland in those early years of an Ireland newly admitted to the EEC were not just significant for national political development but also had a direct impact on the political culture of one rural Irish parliamentary constituency in Meath. However, the Meath constituency in its own way had an impact on the national changes taking place. It certainly played a part in farmer politics both within local and national government but also in terms of the leaders which Meath supplied at the time to the IFA. My ethnographic case study of Meath and other Leinster farmers allowed me to place these changes in a number of historical, political and sociological contexts, in ways which would have been difficult if not impossible just using aggregate and survey data. The large farmers of Meath had been widely seen nationally as traditional supporters of Fine Gael. They were leaders in the farmers' interest group, the IFA, which has an increasingly important role in national and international policy negotiations for Ireland. Their voting patterns over twenty years of local and national elections had demonstrated changing aspects of Irish politics such as electoral volatility, the importance of identity and culture in new European politics, and the role of European capitalism in the loosening up of past social and political ties.

Most of these changes took time for me to discover ethnographically over the course of what became twenty-four months of fieldwork while I was resident in Navan, County

Meath. During that time I learned a great deal about the dimensions of local class and culture which underpinned the roles of large farmers in Meath society. In order to understand how their networks operated politically, and how politicians were linked to farmers in so many ways, my ethnographic research had to reach beyond politics, government and policy, to examine Meath society and culture, in order, in turn, to provide a fuller picture of the manner in which culture and politics intersected in rural Meath in the late 1970s and early 1980s.

Culture, class and large farmers

It was obvious to me while living in Meath that in word and deed the big farmers of County Meath saw themselves as members of various groups of influential farmers. This was not universally so of course. Many I met who had large landholdings and many acres filled with tillage, beef, dairy herds and/or sheep were quiet, even reclusive. But class and culture are aspects of life that are not just found in the consciousness of individuals and groups. They are also to be found in the ebb and flow of everyday community life, where influence, authority and power do not always map neatly onto wealth and conspicuous consumption, or onto other matrices related to such things as family pedigree, education, and social networks. But all of these play roles in local societal notions of who ranks higher, who should be listened to, who has a say, or even more of a say, in public and private decision-making. If I was to understand farmers' roles in politics I had to also understand the politics of their roles in family, church, sport, leisure and work.

It was also clear to me after just a short time in Meath in those early days of my field work that modernization and internationalization (I later grew to see some of these processes as Europeanization) in Irish society had made large farmers increasingly part of a growing national rural middle class. My initial portrait of the important changes which occurred in the culture and class relations of large farmers in Meath, which at the time also served to me as a possible reflection of changes elsewhere among similar farmers in the rest of Leinster, was clearly a departure in the ethnography of the political economy of Ireland, as well as an addition to the study of the Europeanization of commercial family farmers within the EEC.

When I began this research there had been remarkably little ethnographic analysis of social and economic class in rural Ireland. Excluding a number of studies that investigated rural society in Northern Ireland (see, for example, Harris 1972; Leyton 1975) such concepts as class and social stratification had taken a back seat to more descriptive and structural-functional studies of communities of farmers, villagers, shopkeepers and townspeople. This is especially surprising in regard to farmers, who were identified in the pioneering research of Arensberg and Kimball as living in a world that was complex and multifaceted. Nonetheless, in the subsequent ethnographic literature farmers had often been treated as a relatively homogeneous group who seemingly shared a culture and social structure that made them the most recognizable and influential group of people in what was then a predominantly agricultural nation. This, too, is ironic because Arensberg and Kimball also noted the principal Irish distinction regarding Irish farmers: there are two types, 'large' and 'small,' that is, those with wealth, land and influence and those without

(Arensberg and Kimball 1940: 3-30). But the farmers who had been consistently investigated in anthropological research, and who were seemingly the veritable 'stuff' of rural community studies, were principally the poor and relatively powerless small farmers.

Prior to my research in Meath, there had been no description of the groups who make up the socially recognized Irish subculture of large farmers in the ethnographic literature. Even when they were identified as being worthy of critical investigation, which in Ireland had been most often in sociology and political science (Manning 1971, 1979; Peillon 1982), they were seldom treated as anything other than one half of the dichotomy of 'the farmers.' As one scholar has concluded in his overview of Irish society, there may in fact be two separate 'classes' of Irish farmers, divided between what are popularly called the 'large' and the 'small' (Peillon 1982: 17-18). But even here Peillon's treatment of farmers as being in two 'classes' clearly refers to their social class statuses; in a later essay (1986) Peillon widens his view to tentatively suggest some of the ways farmers are tied to other social groups in Ireland through their economic class relations.

While it is useful to use indicators such as farm enterprise, acreages, political affiliations, rates of emigration, and favorite newspapers (Arensberg and Kimball 1940; Peillon 1982) to describe divisions in the ways of life of Irish farmers, these only serve as initial classificatory tools in the analysis of the realities of farmers and their political and economic influence, social rankings and cultural traditions. In this chapter I seek to examine large farmers' perceptions of their social statuses and heritages as a necessary step in the investigation of

91

Irish commercial farmers' roles in political and class relations in Ireland.

In this and in the original research upon which this chapter is based my analysis was influenced by the growing anthropological interest in Europe, particularly in the ways in which people as members of classes lived their lives and dealt in cultural terms with the complexities of the productive relations in which they were engaged. In the course of my field study in Meath it became apparent to me that the group known as 'large farmers' saw themselves as divided into a number of subgroups, each defined principally through cultural, social and political histories, farm enterprises, and wealth. These perceptions suggested that Irish farmers overall may not have constituted one or two classes but as individuals and groups they acted within increasingly fluid class relations, relations that had been affected by the many changes Ireland had experienced over the previous generation.

One of the most important of these changes in farmers' lives was Ireland's membership in the EEC. From the early 1970s the social processes that yielded a number of fractions or types of large farmers had given way to new processes of class formation. Entry into the EEC had altered rural class relations, helping to create a more 'urbanized' (if not suburbanized in the counties around Dublin, such as Meath) rural middle class, which had become much more culturally integrated and politically pragmatic. This occurred despite large farmer insistence at the time that the differences that made up the separate types of large farmer were still important and relevant. The fact that these farmers perceived these differences, and, in some cases, exaggerated them, while increasingly behaving in very similar ways, indicated the changing cultural definition of class in rural Ireland.

Processes such as these may very well have had parallels in other EEC member states then and now. But it was true then and still the case today that although there has been great ethnographic interest in the cultural dimensions to social class, there have been relatively few analyses of the relationship between culture and class in the nations of the EEC overall, and almost none that relate class and culture to the processes of Europeanization and European integration. This was so when there was the original Community of six nations, and it remains the case, at least in anthropological terms, in the EU of twenty-seven members today.

Although there were some notable exceptions to this sad state of affairs in the anthropology of Europe—such as may be found in my own professors' work (for example, in Cole and Wolf 1974; Schneider and Schneider 1976)—the ethnographic investigation of the great changes brought by the EEC which were, by definition, intended to modernize and internationalize the nations and cultures of its constituent members was in its infancy in 1976. It was clear to a number of newly trained anthropologists who were beginning field research about that time that they were in excellent position to document (see, for example, Giordano 1987) and, perhaps, affect the changes being made by Europe at the local level. But the overall numbers of those anthropologists who saw this need, and were willing to respond to it, were small then and have only grown slowly over the years. This is lamentable, for ethnographers may be the best body of scholars with the theoretical questions and research methods to carry out long-term case studies on EEC-induced social change in local communities.

However, despite years of research on the EEC and EU by anthropologists, a great deal of this work has been done in the centers of political power, and has focused on culture and power as seen from above so to speak. To a much lesser extent has there been anthropological research on European integration as seen or experienced from below, in local and regional society (for reviews of some of the history of the anthropology of the EU, see Wilson 1998; Bellier and Wilson 2000a, 2000b). Ethnographic and anthropological scholars are not alone in this: across the social sciences there has been a great deal of theorizing the nature of Europeanization in political and economic institutions and programs, but much less so in terms of the analysis of the qualitative effects of the EEC on its people.

My study in County Meath, of the ways in which the lives of the large farmers of Ireland have changed since Ireland's accession to the EEC, showed that the analyses of class and culture are inextricably related, and that farmers' perceptions of either or both are significant aspects of their adaptations to the processes of modernization and Europeanization that have affected all farmers of Europe.

The 'big men' of Meath

Arensberg and Kimball designated 'large' and 'small' farmers as groups of people who were 'widely different' and who 'belong to ways of life which are quite opposed' (Arensberg and Kimball 1940: 3). These two groups of farmers of 1930s Clare differed in their agricultural techniques, products, land use, farm organization, labor, farm activities, and their relations with other community members. And although Arensberg and

Kimball used this dichotomy to introduce their own research on the family and communities of small farmers, the distinctions that they were making were also those made by their hosts. Their statistical introduction to the West of Ireland offered a 'factual base to the divisions the Irish reckon in the countryside themselves' (Arensberg and Kimball 1940: 3). The place they identified as being a 'typical' one for large farmers and their farms was Meath, in Leinster Province, in the east of Ireland.

County Meath, north and west of County Dublin, was still considered in 1980s Ireland to be a county of large farmers, who were then and are still today known as 'strong farmers,' 'big farmers,' or, among farmers themselves, the 'big men'. In the popular culture of Ireland in the 1970s, and especially among the nation's farmers, Meath was rightly considered to be the county with the greatest number of cattle, the most fertile land, the largest farms, and the richest farmers. In its area of 577,000 acres (903 square miles) there lived over 100,000 people, 5000 of whom were farmers. They enjoyed the highest ratio of land devoted to agriculture in Ireland (95 percent of the county's land was devoted to tillage and grass in the early 1980s) (ACOT-Meath 1982; Central Statistics Office-Ireland 1982).

These overall farmer numbers, and the relative proportion of large farmers, depended of course on the criteria being used. When I was conducting research there was a problem in Ireland using official census figures for landholdings and farmers' numbers because of the difficult relationship between farmers and the state over taxes. The 1982 figures used by the Meath agricultural advisory service, a branch of the national semi-state body set up to advise and train farmers, listed 5364 farmers, 3916 of them being full-time.

Because the agricultural advisory service was not interested in highlighting differences in wealth among farmers, they simply pointed out in their background information for Meath that 15.2 percent of the county's farmers own farms of over 100 acres, and these farmers occupied 53 percent of the farmland.

Meath's fame as a farming county was due in part to its role as the terminus in Ireland's internal cattle trade, a role it had played since the eighteenth century. In this trade calves born in the West of Ireland were sold to farms in the midlands of Ireland as store cattle, which, in turn, were sold at two years of age to farms in the East where they were fattened for national consumption or export. Meath had long been a supplier of fattened beef for both Dublin and Britain and in the 1970s had redirected a good deal of its trade in order to sell beef and beef products throughout the EEC. Although Meath farms were known nationwide as beef farms, after 1973 many of the largest farms in the county had turned to dairying because of EEC grants, guaranteed milk prices, and the increased demand in nearby Dublin. This shift in large farm enterprise from beef to dairying mirrored the national trend (Commins 1986: 55).

Meath was also becoming an urban and urbane county. It had been a national center for furniture and carpet manufacturing; it was home to the largest lead and zinc mines in Europe; and it enjoyed a reputation as one of the finest counties for the breeding and training of bloodstock horses. Apart from the small 'horsey set,' however, most Meath farmers were solidly middle class and Catholic, the descendants of the strong tenants of the nineteenth century, who by tradition, education, foresight, wealth, and good luck were at the center of local, regional and national politics and agriculture. In fact, the wealth and power of the farmers of

96

Meath over the years were linked to the development of the state of the Republic of Ireland. In the last century they have functioned as local elite in most aspects of Meath life. They owned or rented the best land, controlled the cattle trade, served as merchants and cattle agents, set up agricultural cooperatives and livestock marts, helped form and then dominate farmers' organizations, and controlled much of local government for most of the first half of the twentieth century.

In the 1980s, the holdings of the large farmers of Meath were, on average, not only the largest in Ireland but are also among the largest in the EEC. In the European Community of the Ten, before Spain and Portugal joined, Ireland's average holding was 22.7 hectares, a figure surpassed only by the UK (68.7ha), Luxembourg (27.6ha), France (25.4ha), and Denmark (24.9ha). Significantly, only 9 percent of the utilized agricultural area in Ireland was rented, the lowest percentage in the EEC (Sheehy and O'Connor 1985: 34). The percentage of farms of over 50 hectares in Ireland was 16.8, fourth highest in the EEC of the Ten, accounting for almost 10 percent of these holdings throughout the EEC. The three countries with greater percentages of large farms (over 50ha) were the UK (52.1 percent; 28.2 percent of EC10 total), Luxembourg (23.9 percent; 0.2 percent), and France (17.4 percent; 38.6 percent) (Duchêne et al. 1985: 278).

In an Irish system of reckoning, in which the term 'large' or 'small' is very much determined by social constructions of size and importance, these landholdings were very large indeed. In Meath in the 1980s 'large' farms were considered by most Meath farmers to be about 200 acres and above, 'medium' farms were 100 acres and above, and 'small' were below that mark. In the Midlands of Ireland at the time

150 acres were often considered a large holding, while in the poorer areas of the West 100 acres might have constituted a big farm. In a county of 103,000 people, with a little less than 4000 full-time farmers, over 10 percent of the farmers owned 200 acres or more. The fact that Meath is home to more large farmers than any other Irish county was proved by the Irish government's 1986 Land Tax lists in which the 2000 largest farmers in the nation were identified. Of that number 379 were in Meath and they owned 91,470 'adjusted' tax acres (their actual county gross acreage was 122,537).

These Meath large farmers did not see themselves as a homogeneous group, however. They came from diverse social, political and religious backgrounds. Together they formed an elite that had dominated local society up to the 1970s, when both Meath and Ireland had changed around them. Since that time their status as large farmers remained, but their roles in Meath life changed.

Large farming stays, but farmers' identities and how the land is used do not remain the same. From the start of the twentieth century the great landlords of Leinster had been under considerable pressure. Their land was demanded by their former tenants. The British government was no longer able to protect their interests, and many of their family members had died in the Great War. Foreign agricultural competition ate into their profits. Irish republicanism seemed to threaten their very lives. Although some were determined to stay, most of the remnant of the gentry left and their land was purchased by their former tenants.

But these people alone did not constitute the category of the beef farmers of Meath so famous in the last century. Protestant farmers, many from the North of Ireland, took advantage of their own skills to work Meath land, developing farms similar in size and enterprise to those of their Catholic neighbors. It made little difference if their holdings were 200 acres instead of 2000, for these were the largest farms that most men of some means could expect to inherit or to buy in the depression days of the first quarter of the century. And there were social, economic, and political compensations as well for the hard-working man of means. By the 1960s their sons, with educations undreamed of a generation before, were ready to turn their farms into successful businesses. It was these businessmen who were the large farmers of my study in Meath.

Types of Meath farmers

The 'big men' of Meath in the first decades of EEC membership were much more than businessmen. As Arensberg and Kimball and many anthropologists since have demonstrated for the world of small farmers, the observable material conditions of their lives were but a starting place for the analysis of the structure and organization of their communities, their businesses, their social networks and their way of life overall. Although Irish people reckoned then, and perhaps still do, that there are distinct cultural differences between large and small farmers, few country people reduced these divisions to perceived sets of behavioral characteristics (a trap that some ethnographers of the time were less successful in avoiding). Meath people knew that they were residents in the county of the largest farmers, but few were ready to proffer to me in interviews any characterizations of what 'large' meant, or to indicate to me to which farms the adjective applied. The consensus was, among people in and out of farming in Meath,

99

that influence, prestige, wealth and power were the social consequences of holding sizable farms.

Using acreage as a guide in identifying the largest farmers in Meath, I thus constructed the following scheme of types of large farmers, a scheme that delineates some of the aspects of culture and class that were associated with the various groups that large farmers described to me over the years. This scheme is based on the descriptions given me by farmers themselves as well as the impressions of non-farming Meath people. This sort of ethnographic introduction aims at presenting a fuller profile of commercial farmers whose lives had been transformed because of the many changes in Irish life which they had experienced, including a growing secularization, economic independence from the UK, the continuing national question regarding Northern Ireland, and the internationalization and Europeanization of agricultural policy-making after 1973.

County Families

The largest individual landowners in Meath were the few descendants of the Anglo-Norman and British families that dominated first the Pale (the area around Dublin longest under British control) and then all of the island. These families, whose names are still linked to the seats of their past glory such as Slane, Dunsany and Headfort, were at the social pinnacle of the old Ascendancy class in Meath. This group was known as the *county families*, the last of the great Protestant families who flourished in the eighteenth and nineteenth centuries. Much of the life of this minority (slightly less than 3 percent of the county's inhabitants at the time were Protestant) was culturally

100

distinct from the majority. They were the descendants of landlords who ruled very large estates, usually from the 'Big House' at the end of a tree-lined lane. This Georgian mansion was often still the residence of the family, although farm sheds and assorted out-buildings stood nearby, and sometimes the descendants of these county families were the farmers themselves, i.e., they did the managing and a great deal of the labor. If not in a Georgian house, these county families often resided in a two-story stone house of historical or their own design, height being of some significance in claims to prestige within local society.

The farms that these families owned, and actually worked in many cases, were in the 1970s and early 1980s principally beef farms, although tradition, investments, inheritance and social prestige often demanded that they also keep horses for show jumping, hunting, breeding and/or racing. Almost all county families were members of the Church of Ireland. Although some Catholic families with land, wealth and long-standing residence mimicked them culturally, in the main they were only partially accepted by the county families and were often derided by other Catholic farming families for their attempts to be socially mobile. The social life of the county families reinforced their religious separateness. Most children went to private schools in the county, in Dublin or in Britain and then to British universities or to Trinity College, Dublin. They were most likely to marry people of the same religion, socioeconomic background and education from outside the county. Attendance at Gaelic football matches and public support of Fianna Fáil (a political party dedicated to Republicanism) were scrupulously avoided.

The old county families continued to make a lasting impression on the character of Meath society during my research. Needless to say, some people still looked on them with resentment. I recall one small farmer, in a conversation we had in mid-1978, talking about a local big farmer 'taking a whip' to one of his workers, and warning me about what to expect when I visited the farm. It took me five minutes to ascertain that the event took place in the eighteenth century! The tale-teller did not share my amusement at the seriousness of his warning.

In my experience, most Meath residents looked on the descendants of the old landlords with respect sometimes mixed with deference or apathy. Since their social networks did not often intersect, it was easy to be affable, tolerant and at the same time pleased by the knowledge that the day of the county families and the hegemony of their class had passed. Although there were occasional spirited outbursts by small farmers, who evoked a past republican cause in order to demand more land from the 'gentry,' there was no real threat in Meath to either their livelihoods or their lives. Among the county families themselves, I observed no regrets at the exclusiveness of their position. Meath was their home. Ireland was their country. Many continued to see Britain in a benign light and they often wished their neighbors would do so as well. In general, they were not happy with the Irish government, but overall I concluded that, at least in Meath, they lived apart from Irish politics, and not within them (although there were exceptions, such as the Conynghams of Slane). The county families I knew then had long since given up hope of having any real political choice in Ireland. Most had supported the Fine Gael party since its founding, but even that sort of traditional support had waned since the early 1970s.

The county families' lives in Meath revolved around their farms, their horses, their outside investments in business, and a social life that took them out of the county much more so than their Catholic neighbors. Their economic importance in the county was considerable, given the land they owned, the people they employed, the valuable link they provided in the internal cattle trade, the professions their families brought to the county, and the capital investment they made in the county, for example in the business of horse breeding. Their political role had been minimized over the last three generations. But these county families had been instrumental in making the Home Rule movement possible in the nineteenth century and they had helped to establish the local government system of 1899, which took over from the landlord-run Grand Juries (institutions which, admittedly, many other county families fought to preserve). They remained a force in the secularization of both Meath and the nation as a whole, in the process by which the state must distance itself from the Roman Catholic Church.

Strong Protestants

A number of other Protestant farmers with sizable holdings were also large farmers, but most of these had not held their land for nearly as long as had the county families. They were the farmers whose ancestors had worked as agents and overseers on the great estates and who took advantage of the Land Acts of the last century. Many were immigrants from the north of Ireland who came from as far away as Donegal in the internal migrations of cattlemen who followed their animals to the market towns of the east coast. There were many of these self-made Protestant farmers in east Meath because their ancestors had migrated south from Ulster in the nineteenth century to work in cotton and linen mills in Slane and Drogheda and in shipping cattle and corn to Scotland and England. Some came to Meath to use their knowledge of beef production to seek tenant holdings from the ranches established after the Great Famine of 1845-48. A few British people who retired to Meath on sizable holdings to pursue 'gentleman farming' also belonged to this group, although in my experience they preferred to be associated with the long-standing county families than with their Catholic neighbors.

At first glance, most of the self-made Protestant farmers seemed little different from their Catholic neighbors. They dressed, spoke and participated in community functions in ways that made it difficult for an outsider to distinguish their cultural or religious backgrounds. Although their residence in Meath had been perceived as relatively brief -- I often overheard a version of the term 'back-door Protestants' to refer to their relatively late arrival in the county -- they seemed to participate fully in most community activities. The principal aspect of local society in which they were set apart, however, was in their religion, which was most often Church of Ireland or Presbyterian. But materially and politically they were very like their Catholic neighbors. Because of their immigrant past and their present religion, however, they were sometimes singled out by their neighbors as having less claim on the land than others had. Legally this was preposterous, but culturally it presented an interesting view of the social cleavages that existed among large farmers, a group that was often perceived by outsiders to be socially homogeneous.

Strong Catholics

The majority of large farmers in Meath are members of the Roman Catholic Church in Ireland, descendants of the 'strong' tenants of the gentry of old. Although many of them arrived in Meath in the last century for the same reasons that motivated the strong Protestant farmers, most large farmers with whom I talked took pride in their Meath heritage. Over the 1970s many of these strong self-made Catholic farmers increasingly saw themselves as members of a rural middle-class, as did their neighbors in the towns. When I pushed the subject further class was most often associated by my informants with income and wealth, but it was also clear to me that there were many social and cultural components to local class structures and relations.

Some of these middle-class Catholic farmers in Meath were descended from skilled agricultural workers who had left the North and West of Ireland to meet the nineteenth-century demand for skilled agricultural and pastoral labor. In the main they had been managers, stewards, cattle dealers, and herdsmen. Some had also been required to work with both draught and thoroughbred horses. Still other forebears of Meath strong farmers were the tenants of pre-Famine landlords, most of whom had been able to purchase their holdings during and after the Land Wars of the nineteenth century. These strong middle class Catholic and Protestant farmers are the real big men of Meath today. Outside of their own circles there was little known about their way of life. Often in the 1970s I encountered people elsewhere in Ireland who had some notions of large farmers in Meath, and many of these notions referred to the great estates of the mansion-dwelling grazier gentry of the past. But the real wealth and decision making in Irish agriculture was in the collective hands of the large farmers of Ireland. In Meath, these farmers were middle class businessmen whose inheritance, sense of tradition and way of life made them leaders in their county and in their nation.

During the normal work day the self-made farmers looked remarkably like Irish farmers everywhere in the country, whatever the size of their holding. Although they might have paid more attention to some tonsorial details, they were still dressed in cap, collared shirt, old trousers, Wellington boots and the ever-present jacket (which was often an old suit jacket relegated to the chores of manual labor). Differences in class position were seldom apparent when toiling in the fields or out counting cattle. Similarities in dress and speech between large and small farmers during the work day obscured class distinctions, at least until the work was over. When the large farmer cleaned himself up at night in preparation for a political or farmers' meeting the differences in wealth and other class characteristics became much more apparent. The new suit, tweed cap and shiny brogues signified wealth and social standing that were unlikely to be based on the income from a small farm. Even the old cars farmers drove around their farms were deceptive. The new car was out back in the garage, or the wife was using it at her job or on her errands (that is, if she did not have her own car).

One theme that emerged in my research, that was common to most of these middle-class families, whether Catholic or Protestant, young or old, was the central role of women in creating, maintaining, and invigorating both homes and families. Sometimes women played dual roles as worker or professional outside of the home, and caregiver and homemaker in it. The wives of young big farmers were fashion conscious and educated (at least to the completion of secondary school), they were usually employed in local service jobs or in the city, and they were in almost complete control of the daily activities in the home. Older wives stayed more at home, the result as much of the lack of opportunities for education and employment when they were young as of the demands of caring for their children. Although it was not a key focus of my research, I was struck by the attitude of many male farmers to their families. They often acted as strangers or guests in their own homes and among their own families, in the sense that their domain was clearly thought to be that of business, politics, and external community relations. The house and the complexities of domestic relations were presumed by both farm men and women to be the domain of the woman of the house. Many Meath people were quick to point out that these attitudes were also changing, and had shifted remarkably over the last generation.

Big farmers, like farmers throughout Ireland, did not live in nucleated settlements. The family home was at the end of a tarmacadam drive, surrounded by trees and farm buildings, on the largest single holding of the farm (or, in Meath terms, on the largest 'farm'). Both the building and the family's original farm fields were called the 'home place.' Most homes were two-story and made of stone, and they had a number of rooms added to accommodate new kitchens, toilets and bedrooms. The fields or farms of a holding were usually scattered, sometimes ranging five to twenty miles away from each other, and many fields and farms were in other counties. But most large farms in

Meath were then and are today centralized, that is, most of a farmer's holdings are in the same townland, where the home place also is situated.

In rural Ireland the postal address outside of towns is the townland, which has been the basic unit of land census division in the Irish countryside since the seventeenth century. The townland distinguishes all locations in Ireland and is the country's smallest administrative division. The townland also acts as the referent for home, wherein farmers did not say that they were going 'home' in the evenings after work or leisure but rather used the metonym of the townland to indicate the location of home, house, family and farm, that together constituted places with names like Hayestown, Painestown, Alexandereid or Rathnaree.

The physical layout of the homes of the Meath strong farmers of the time also set them apart from other farmers and often too from townspeople. The wealth of the farmer yielded appliances and other consumer goods that certainly made the farmhouse something much grander than that name suggests. Most of the large farmer households I visited had various types of washing machine, clothes dryer, color TV, dishwasher, stereo, hair dryer, video recorder and central heating. Families spent most of their time indoors in the kitchen and sitting room (parlors and dining rooms were reserved for guests and formal occasions), except when sleeping; most young children doubled up in bedrooms but the older ones often got their own rooms, in buildings that were often equipped with many such sleeping quarters.

The children of these middle-class farmers usually attended the local Catholic national primary and the Catholic secondary schools (such as the Navan 'classical' school for boys or the convent schools for the girls), although some more secular technical schools were available for the less academically minded. A few farmers' sons attended the local agricultural college for secondary and third level education. Most children of the Meath strong farmers were encouraged to complete their secondary education and many went on to technical college or to university.

The wife and mother of the household went to her own job, or did the shopping, cleaning and organization for dinner, at which she had all those 'belonging to her' on the farm for a meal. This seldom included farm laborers, who were in the main hired from neighboring farms, as the days when the woman of the house fed the farm's workers were over, except perhaps in hay-making season when long, hard hours were kept. At the afternoon dinner, meat, potatoes and vegetables were served after soup and before sweet and tea.

Most adult women on a big farm are either the wife or unmarried siblings of the farmer. Few farms at the time were run by women, and the term 'farmer' was reserved for males; this practice is no longer sanctioned in public forums, but is largely adhered to in everyday language in Meath today. Parents might also be present, but in Ireland the practice of one child inheriting the family farm was usually triggered when the father had passed away or retired. If the farmer's wife was employed and thus away from the home during the day, a daughter or hired housekeeper (a farmer's wife or daughter from a small farm in the townland or nearby, or a female member of the husband or wife's kindred) stayed for the day. The family was reunited at tea time, i.e., for the evening meal, at approximately 6:00 p.m. and after the Angelus, before or after which the cows were milked (they were first milked at breakfast time by either a laborer or household member). During the day the farmer attended to the chores associated with being the 'boss,' a common term used by sons and workers in reference to the farmer on his own farm. A quiet pint at the local pub, an evening of cards at home, a football match as player or spectator at the Gaelic Athletic Association pitch, a meeting of the Irish Farmers' Association (IFA) or Irish Countrywomen's Association, or a visit to a neighbor on business or pleasure rounded out a normal day.

The Horsey Set

The last group of large farmers who are worth noting because of their social, economic and political significance were the new owners of stud farms, many of whom were not native to the county and some of whom were not from farming families. Most, however, among those I met and interviewed while doing my research in Meath, were Catholics who were raised in the beef trade but who were using bloodstock as a new investment. But I came across a few who were ex-urbanites who had adopted a horsey way of life after making their money elsewhere. Although difficult to categorize because they overlapped all the groups mentioned above, these bloodstock farmers formed a recognizable subgroup in Meath, especially in the areas near Kildare and Dublin, and one which promised to increase in size and importance in the future due to the importance of horse breeding and racing in the Irish economy and way of life, but also due to the influx of capital and expatriate investors from Europe. These bloodstock farmers were the group of large farmers who were the most difficult for me to get information on through participant observation, primarily because the demands of their work schedules and the clear boundaries between a great deal of their lives and those of their neighbors tended to keep me circulating in different social circles to them. This and other difficulties of doing political research in Meath reflect the many forms of social and political differentiation which were at work in Meath in the 1970s.

Social and political differentiation

Anthropologists have long been identified with studies of the local, but my research in Meath reflected new interests in anthropology in theorizing local, regional and national relations within a much wider political economy than the village or local community. The large farmers of Meath were part of regional networks and associations that made them a social and political elite in their own villages and towns. They had played this role for some time, since at least an independent Ireland was established in the 1920s. But local societies can look remarkably homogeneous from the outside. The preceding description of types of large farmer in Meath shows that there were, and I expect still very much are, many social and cultural differences within the category of large farmer. At least, this is the way it was explained to me by just about anybody I talked this over with in Meath then, and this is the way I saw it as well, as ethnographic field research cannot just take the opinions of informants as self-evident facts.

The mistaken notion that all wealthy farmers must be alike is understandable. Many things in their lives made large farmers similar to each other. After all they owned or worked large tracts of land, that alone might lead to lumping such farmers together into a separate social class. But large farmers also enjoyed the related social standing in local and regional life that was associated with their own and their families' income, education, and social networks. It was clear in Meath of the 1970s that large farmers were members of networks of relationships that connected them to each other, to small farmers, and to others in Irish society in a variety of ways.

However, there were things that separated them too. The above review of the types of large farmer shows that the cultural identity associated with being Irish or British in origin, one's religion, the years and generations in which one had resided in Meath, and the social connections associated with the farm enterprise in which one was engaged, were all factors that brought large farmers into many different networks. Of course sometimes these networks overlapped and intersected, but they also diverged a great deal of the time. Some of the principal means by which these strong farmers differed from each other in terms of their networks were in regard to the historical and political traditions they followed, their current and recent political party affiliations, their religions and the social relations attendant on their church communities, and the ways they spent their time and money in leisure activities.

Roman Catholic and Church of Ireland farmers traditionally belonged, for the most part, to largely separate social circles. Beyond the relationships necessary for business these farmers tended to interact with each other only rarely, and then usually at political or farmers' events, at the tennis and golf clubs, or at race meetings. One subject that was avoided in most public discussions was politics. In Meath in the 1970s and 1980s this meant that unless these men were meeting at a political function or in the act of doing something political (at the county council or in electioneering, for example), certain subjects were not mentioned publicly. Past political feuds (for example, from elections or from the 1920s Civil War), present party affiliation and electoral preferences, and the 'Troubles' in the north of Ireland were not the subject for polite discussion. This of course made ethnographic field research in political anthropology particularly difficult.

Early in my research I learned to publicly avoid certain political topics. I adopted a strategy that simply followed the advice offered me by one farmer, as we walked his fields and he pointed out the boundaries of his farm and identified his neighbors' lands and animals. He advised me to avoid asking direct questions about politics: 'they can only lead to trouble,' for most people already know where 'the other fellow stands' on these issues. The Protestant big farmers, both county families and self-made businessmen, were invariably members of families who were on the pro-Treaty side in the Civil War of 1922 and who had supported the Fine Gael party up to the 1970s. The Catholic farmers often shared a different image of Britain and its role in Northern Ireland and were likelier to be members of the Fianna Fáil party. And while there is much to suggest that in the Republic of Ireland farmers have tended to support Fine Gael since the 1930s (Rumpf and Hepburn 1977), in Meath, a county of large farmers, there was still sizable support for Fianna Fáil and other republican-oriented parties.

One thing was clear: before the late 1970s it was almost impossible to find a Protestant farmer supporting Fianna Fáil. This separation of political interests was mirrored in other aspects of their social lives. Besides the obvious activities of church attendance and membership, which might include such activities as novenas, prayer meetings, teas and fund-raisers, Catholics and Protestants tended to socialize more with those with whom they shared these activities and the values associated with them. Self-made middle-class Catholic farmers would be as surprised to receive an invitation to tea at the neighboring 'Big House' as descendants of the gentry would be if they were asked to the local parish's Gaelic football match. However, there were forces at work in the late 1970s which were chipping away at these old political loyalties among these strong commercial farmers. In fact, large farmers in Meath had increasingly become a 'volatile' electorate, that is, one that voted according to their perceived material interests, a fact that perplexed local party cadres who were almost always in a state of preparation for the next election.

Many Meath farmers had other notions of traditional values and loyalties. For example, most Meath large farmers believed in the preservation and conservation of national monuments and resources, but many believed that the local branch of the national preservation society was dominated by the county families. The Meath Archaeological and Historical Society, though ably led during much of my research time in Meath by a Catholic cleric, was widely perceived to be made up of people who were Protestant. Although the membership lists of these local bodies contradicted these widely held views, local farmers clearly believed that such separate interests on the part of Catholics and Protestants were to be recognized and upheld.

In this vein Protestants were held to be football (soccer) and rugby supporters and players, while Catholics joined the Gaelic Athletic Association and played Gaelic football and hurling. The facts that the major county rugby team was almost entirely Catholic and that other sports such as golf, show jumping and horse racing were clearly integrated did not seem to dispel these widely held notions that the two sides, the two religions, pursued remarkably different social pastimes. Beliefs such as these helped to either create or to reinforce aspects of 'otherness' in regard to fellow large farmers. Thus, it is clear that large farmers' acreages did not account for cultural, social or political homogeneity. Their diverse ideologies and practices differentiated large farmers, and highlighted their lack of cohesion if the definition of them as a group depended on assessments of their agricultural holdings or enterprises.

Meath Euro-farmers

Ireland's entrance into the EEC in 1973 began one of the greatest periods of socioeconomic growth in the country's history. Irish farmers were among the principal recipients of the capital which flowed into Ireland up to 1979, when deals with the EEC began to end in line with EEC accession negotiations with new members in the Mediterranean. The benefits of the new EEC Ireland helped to create a widening gap in income between commercial farmers and small farmers. In Meath the wealth that accrued to farmers from EEC programs and subsidies helped to convert most farms of 100 acres or more into successful businesses. The profits made in agriculture made all farmers, regardless of acreage, aware of their role as European citizens and farmers. From the early 1970s Meath large farmers had become immersed in international agricultural marketing, prices, governmental policy and consumer tastes. They received a stream of information about Europe from the IFA and other farming bodies, through the wireless, at their auction marts, from the local and national print media and, not least, from their fellow farmers, who had even started taking their holidays on the continent.

115

Not only were the majority of Meath big farmers driving newer and bigger cars, educating their children for the professions, and demonstrating consumer tastes unheard of years before, but they were also becoming businessmen in an international arena. For their own good Meath farmers kept themselves informed about European markets. In the late 1970s Meath beef went to Germany, Meath cereals and lamb went to France, and Meath calves were being shipped to Italy. Overall, Meath farmers' knowledge of international trade was comprehensive and impressive to me. For example, at Meath IFA meetings I heard discussions of Italian dairying as detailed as any discussion of Irish farming. The new international 'Euro-farmer' of Ireland was to be found in Meath in numbers unlike most other Irish counties. Wanting to control the factors of his business as much as possible, the Meath big farmer sought the knowledge and capital to act on situations rather than to react to them. I was often surprised and almost daily impressed with the confidence and expertise of the large farmers of Meath, who had learned and experienced a great deal after Ireland joined the EEC.

In Meath the boom years of EEC membership changed more than the economics and politics of large farmers' lives. The glut of home construction and the expansion of Dublin turned the southeastern part of the county into a suburb of the capital (in 2011 this suburbanization has spread to all of the county; Navan, the central town, is today very much a suburb of Dublin). The demand for agricultural and residential property forced up the price for land until it was almost out of reach for farmers, but only almost. Banks competed with each other to lend money, for so much money was being made in Meath farming, construction, mining, and furniture manufacturing. In fact, banks made it so easy to borrow that most large farmers modernized their farms, bought new land and changed their cars, clothes, home conveniences and leisure activities, all within the decade of the 1970s, in the first era of EEC Europeanization in Ireland.

The years of recession that began in 1979 and lasted to the Celtic Tiger years of the 1990s also put pressure on the new Euro-farmers of Meath. High inflation rates, changes in the national tax system, the overpricing of land, the end of Ireland's transitional status within the EEC and the curtailment of credit led to a period of economic constraint if not decline in the lives of the Meath farmers. Most large farmers, however, came to realize that designations like 'boom and bust' and 'good and bad' years obscured the realities of their new status within both Ireland and Europe, one in which their social, political, and economic circumstances had changed irrevocably.

The economics of their businesses remained a bond among most large farmers, however, a bond that was strengthened within the EEC. At that time farmers experienced remarkable degrees of capitalization. One result of this was that many younger Meath farmers, better educated and perhaps more willing to depart from traditional farm practices, turned to dairying as their principal farm enterprise. This led to a growing social differentiation between the commercial farmers who had adapted to a high technology, high cost, high output and high income agriculture, and those who had not (Commins 1986: 55). Although the differentiation between commercial and subsistence agriculture was traditionally based on farm size, by the end of the 1970s this gap had been widened by the differences in output, expenses and incomes. The increasing demands placed on farm businesses required that farmers have

117

more commercial and social intercourse with fellow rural and urban businessmen. This also seemed to take many of these commercial farmers away from the activities and organizations that seemed to hold farmers together in Ireland. Furthermore, in one other result, in this period the IFA was seen to be increasingly dominated by large farmers and beef and cereal production, while the ICMSA supposedly had more small farmers and dairymen.

In Meath, in reaction to their new sense of business and their new economic influence, large farmers (Protestant and Catholic, the self-made and inheritors of wealth) met often with other large farmers for a variety of professional reasons. They met at cattle auctions or with meat factories' representatives. They organized themselves into farmers' cooperatives. They stood for office as local, regional and national leaders of the IFA, making Meath one of that organization's most supportive counties. They served as agricultural contractors for their friends and neighbors, who needed seasonal labor and specialized machinery. They also formed sizable and influential minorities in political parties locally.

Throughout most of the 1970s increased wealth yielded changes that seemed to affect all large farmers of the county. Farmers' social and leisure lives changed as rapidly as their businesses. Because earlier ethnography described farmer poverty and marginality, it was especially startling to me in 1976 when first I visited Meath to observe the degree to which strong farmers enjoyed the delights of conspicuous consumption. At that time the above mentioned home appliances and electronics, such as dishwasher and color TV, were becoming commonplace, when just a few years before, farmers recollected, there were still some sizable farms without indoor plumbing. By 1979, when the first major stage of my field research was drawing to a close, the leisure concerns of a growing Meath rural middle class seemed to reflect many needs, values and joys found among the middle classes across the globe. In the years I was initially there, and certainly in the years that followed, young large farmers, many of whom had gone to agricultural college or university, had changed from people newly interested in the four locally received TV channels to those who formed private cinema clubs that could show uncensored films, to those who nightly double-parked their cars in town in order to run into the video shop to get tapes for themselves and their children. Today of course they have cable, blu-ray, internet, etc, and it is almost as common to see a New York Yankees baseball cap in Navan as it once was to see certain English football supporters' gear.

Perhaps the changed social lives of 1970s Meath commercial farmers demonstrated best the changes that had affected their roles in the social classes of Ireland. Large farmers' wealth, education, professional obligations, and widened expectations had made them the backbone of the rural Meath middle class. Nowhere was this more evident than in the restaurants, pubs, and sports clubs of the county. The dance halls and formal dinner dances of the past had given way to the informality of the 1980s in which many large farmers, men and women, used their golf and tennis club memberships as the bases for social circles of meals, drinking sessions, charity events and sporting contests, hardly affected by either the seasons or even such traditional farming concerns as hay making. Meath had four golf clubs and one nationally ranked tennis club. In the summer farmers were as likely to be taking their evening meals at the country club as they were to be at home. They frequented the local hotels or nationally known restaurants for dinner parties as often as any of their fellow members of the Meath middle class. Local pubs underwent remarkable modernizing facelifts, to approximate the living room decor of mirrors, plush couches, and stained wood so popular in the trendy pubs of Dublin. The number of pubs socially acceptable to the growing middle class of Meath also grew, to keep pace with the rise in the spending of time and money in order to relax and enjoy. The days when the strong farmers of Meath socialized almost exclusively at the parish hall, the Gaelic or rugby clubs, or at the local crossroads pub seemed to be gone, and from the perspective of 2011, are perhaps gone forever.

Changes in the social lives of Meath large farmers reflected too some basic transformations in their social organization. Most young farmers, who either had inherited or who were principal heirs to the land, married when they felt it was certain that they would have control over the farm. This usually meant that they would take over the home place when the farmer was old, ill, ready for retirement, pressured into it by family opinion, delighted by a son's choice of mate, desirous of an Old Age Pension, or afraid that his chosen heir was fed up and leaving. Seldom would a son who wanted the farm be able to attract and marry a woman when she knew that it would be years before the farm was theirs. In some instances, when the young woman was both liked by her suitor's family and recognized to be an attractive prospect, that is, when she had a job that was well paying and prestigious locally and therefore very much in demand, a couple's 'doing a line' (courting publicly) would bring very strong pressure to bear on the father.

The two most attractive jobs locally for women were teacher and nurse because they were respected positions, they paid well, and were always in demand in the local labor market. They were also publicly appreciated as 'women's' jobs that allowed the wife to be at home often, to take care of their domestic duties. Today, this world has changed for women, but not perhaps as clearly and as overwhelmingly as it might have, or has happened for women of similar class position elsewhere in Europe. But in the late 1970s, the changes to come through the feminization of Irish society had come slowly and in small but important ways.

A farmer had many choices regarding his successor if he did not himself want to relinquish the farm. He could draw up a new will to which the son was party, build a new house on his land to establish the new couple, make the son farm manager with at least nominal say over the business, begin to transfer bank accounts over to the son, or give the son complete control over a portion of the land, with written agreement to hand over more in the future. Whatever the farmer did, it had to be open and public. He would have been shaming his son and severely limiting his chances for a desirable marriage partner if he kept the younger man on the farm in no capacity other than as the dutiful and hopeful son.

Although the use of such terms as 'boy' to refer to farmers' sons who did not have their own farm was not common in my experience in Meath (as it had been in Arensberg and Kimball's Clare), such a person's status decreased steadily each year. Simply put, a man of thirty, let alone forty, was not considered a 'social adult' by the farming community if he had reached that age, wanted a farm, and did not have it. The older he got the poorer his chance of getting married. And although marriage was not necessary for the running of a successful farm and household, it was necessary if one hoped to claim some prestige within social circles. A wife and children were considered part of a successful farmer's life cycle. To attract a wife, however, a young farmer had first to deal with the 'boss.' And a farmer knew that he must compromise in order to keep his primary heir interested in working the land.

While government and EEC programs intended to stimulate early retirement had largely failed in Meath, they had served to make farmers more aware of the national concern with making agriculture 'younger' and more efficient. Farmers could not help wanting to hold on to the position of preeminence that had taken them up to thirty years to achieve, while they waited for their fathers to relinquish the farm. In Meath, the farmers did not wait to transfer ownership until there was a marriage agreement between their sons and girlfriends as had been reported for Clare and other areas. Most transfers occurred before both the death of the older man and the marriage of the younger, and these transfers sometimes happened gradually, fitting a national pattern in which, on farms of 100 acres and more, fully one-third of male farmers did not become farm managers (a prelude to ownership) before they were 35 years or older (Commins and Kelleher 1973:24).

Overall, large farmers' children seemed to have a good chance to go into the professions (for employment locally, in the cities, and sometimes for emigration), business, service industries and farming. Their fathers' wealth, if any, gave them an education, initial capital, and the ability to improve their geographic and social mobility. But at least one son (or a daughter if there were no sons) stayed in farming on the home place, and it was in that capacity that large farmers had maintained their influence in Meath society. There were mounting social and economic pressures on farm children to leave farming, however, due to the time and labor demands, the up and down of agricultural markets, the lure of professions for the well-educated, and an overall societal conception of farming as traditional and not modern or progressive.

The farm enterprise that had been the most profitable over the previous generations had been beef production, the 'ranching' for which Meath farmers were so famous. After 1973, however, many of the largest Meath farmers had adopted dairying as their principal farm enterprise. In the 1970s EEC grants and guaranteed prices, easy credit terms, and a stable market enticed the most ambitious and daring farmers to transform their businesses. Although EEC curbs on milk production in the 1980s subsequently limited their profits, Meath dairy farmers were at the end of the twentieth century among the most successful of those enterprising farmers of the nation whose farms had been newly mechanized and commercialized. And it was these farmers, leaders in the political parties and the IFA, who had been most affected by the Europeanization of Irish farming and society.

Thus changes in agricultural production, in farm output and incomes, and in statuses and social expectations were reframing local perceptions of 'large farmer' life in Meath at the beginning of the 1980s. The 'big men' of Meath were clearly seen, by themselves and other observers, to be members of Ireland's middle class. Some of them were new to such class positioning, while others, such as those with wealth made elsewhere, or the descendants of ranchers or other strong Protestant farmers, perhaps had longer familiarity with middle class roles and expectations. The term 'rancher' had evolved in Ireland as one for a resident or absent landlord who owned a vast estate, and was usually engaged in some form of pastoralism. Arensberg and Kimball used the term as a synonym for the large farmer. In my experience the term was no longer widely used in Leinster, in part I suspect because of the forces which I reviewed in this chapter. When it was used in my company I concluded that it was a mildly pejorative term utilized by small farmers and townspeople to imply that a farmer was not a worker, and was not of the soil. This was most definitely not an applicable term for the vast majority of large farmers in Meath in the 1970s.

Whatever the origin, large farmer influence was defined by a combination of their wealth, capital and income, by their social and political networks, their education, their conspicuous consumption, and their values and expectations. Large farmers were employers whose businesses not only provided direct farm employment but also indirectly supported the many agricultural service industries in the region, such as agricultural contracting, auto and farm machinery, meat factories, trucking and construction. Meath strong farmers also participated in social and political networking that drew them closer to an urban middle class, in a country that even as early as the 1980s was shrinking in terms of local notions of both geographical distance and community boundaries, a process of urbanization that was accelerated in the 1990s. When once Navan was seen to be just an hour from Dublin, today one may take the motorway and be there in half the time. But some wags might suggest that all you have to do to go to Dublin is to visit the Navan shopping centre or some of the town's outlying housing estates.

It seems that one no longer needs to travel to interact with Dubliners, for they, and Dublin culture, have come to Meath. But such things were only starting in the late 1970s, when the diversification of the cultures of the shrinking number of Meath large farmers was a harbinger of the redefinition of rural and urban class relations in Ireland which, I suspected then and have seen the evidence of it since, had a great deal to do with the EEC and the reformulations of Irish society and politics. Thus not only did their changing roles in the control of much of the means of production make Meath large farmers into members of an expanding national middle class, but the changed conditions of work and political influence which they faced also redefined their roles and expectations in local and national politics. To fully appreciate how much things were changing in Meath political culture in the 1970s, however, it is necessary to consider how these farmers had fared as a political elite in the decades before.

Chapter 4

Ethnography and the Past Politics of
Local Government in Meath

Before the years of my doctoral research, anthropological accounts of Irish politics had principally viewed local politicians as political patrons and brokers who were mediators between local political actors and individuals and groups external to local communities. With few exceptions, these studies lacked a historical perspective, a charge often made against the ethnography of Ireland in general at the time. While some ethnographers certainly reviewed some salient moments in national political history in order to provide some temporal context to their community studies, most anthropological accounts of local politics presented their institutions and organization in ways which did not involve very deep investigation into the roots of local behavior, values and attitudes. This shallow historical depth to Irish political ethnography was surprising to me at the time due to the complex, often exciting history of local party politics throughout Ireland, a nation which was then and perhaps still is renowned for its attention to all things political. At the time, the political anthropology of Ireland mirrored political anthropology elsewhere in Europe; before the 1980s ethnographers seldom investigated party politics at the local, regional, and national levels.

The literature of Irish political studies suggests that Irish political party cleavages date from the ideological split that led to the Civil War of 1922-23. My ethnographic research in County Meath revealed a more complex picture, in which many

127

individuals and families in the 1970s remembered the events of the 1930s as the key ones in the determination of their party loyalties and identifications. Crucial to their families' initial choices of party affiliation was the patronage that was made available to them from their local and national politicians. The early years of the Irish Free State were heady times for many politicians and for their political programs and activities, when political networks based on patronage and clientage flourished.

After the 1934 local government elections, however, both the government and political parties began to limit county councillor control of scarce goods and vital services, thereby diminishing the power of local government. The moves to centralize political influence in the hands of a national government eventually lead to the County Management Act, 1940. This act, in turn, saw councillors' roles as patrons quickly change to those of brokers. This chapter explores some of the changes in local political patronage which resulted from the processes of party and government centralization in those years of drastic political change in the new state. It also examines some of the origins of 'traditional' political roles in county Meath in order to focus attention on how anthropology may contribute to the scholarly study of contemporary political parties and ideologies in Ireland.

As an initial step towards these goals, it is important to also consider the local political studies which have been done throughout Europe by ethnographers who, in the generation after the Second World War, were instrumental in placing patronage studies in the mainstream of political anthropology. In fact, the anthropological analysis of local politics in Europe was stimulated by the groundbreaking case studies as those of Kenny (1961), Pitt Rivers (1961), and Silverman (1965), which in turn were part of a new anthropological interest in local communities' relations with institutions and people at more complex sociopolitical levels (see, for example, Barth 1965; Bailey 1969; Worsley 1968; Wolf 1966). A new wave of ethnographers analyzed the political economy of European communities and regions through the investigation of political and cultural patronage and brokerage (Campbell 1964; Boissevain 1965, 1966; Blok 1974; Schneider and Schneider 1976; Hansen 1977). But in ethnographers' efforts to identify non-corporate groups, secret societies, culture brokers, and merchant capitalists, in order to show that community studies cannot and should not be arbitrarily left at solely the local level, they tended to overlook many of the social and political institutions to which these patrons and brokers belonged.

Ethnographers became increasingly imaginative in the ways that they analyzed patrons and brokers. Network analysis (Barnes 1968; Boissevain 1974) became an important tool in the identification of webs of social and political relations which bound community members both to themselves and to outsiders (and network analysis continues to be an extremely valuable tool in the hands of politically minded ethnographers, although it has gone out of favor, along with the concepts of culture and community, among many more post-modernist anthropologists; we will return to a consideration of anthropology today in the concluding chapter). In the 1970s and 1980s in European ethnography the analysis of social networks provided clues to the sources of patrons' power and authority, which were often external to localities and just as often missed by ethnographers in their more narrowly focused community studies. But the success of these revisionist patron-client studies in delineating the many non-institutional and non-corporate ties that villagers and rural people had to the outside world often obscured or just ignored the institutional aspects that were integral to patron and broker personal networks. In fact, the institutions that these people belonged to became an ethnographic backdrop, a political *mise-en-scène* to the more important and increasingly stylized and idealized personality cults of patrons and clients.

With few exceptions (see, for example, Berger 1972; Cole and Wolf 1974; Kertzer 1980), local political studies in Europe at the beginning of the 1980s had largely emphasized the analysis of the informal politics of brokerage in all its forms, furthering the view of patrons and clients as ideal types. As a result, the ethnographic literature of Europe tended to present patrons and their networks as the major, if not dominant, political forms at all local levels. Political scientists and, I daresay, politicians of the time would have marveled at the provinciality of this position. Political parties were then, and continue to be, the source of many of the political symbols, wealth, communication networks, political ideology and labor which underpin all aspects of government and politics, and are the sources of much that gets politicians elected and in power. At the very least, in a Western Europe which has become increasingly international through the organs of the European Union, political parties are national and regional institutions that are both the cause and the effect of local political processes, and they serve as agents of national integration which outlive most of the local players in the political game. Their presence as well as their historical role in local communities should be a principal concern of political and historical anthropologists wherever they study.

In this chapter I explore some of the ways that people in contemporary rural Ireland reinterpreted their political pasts in order to correspond to contemporary party practices and ideologies. Although the origins of party affiliations were remembered in many contradictory ways by Meath people, individuals and families doggedly held to the almost universal belief that their party loyalty was traditional and unswerving. The dialogical relationships between the creation and re-creation of national histories and identities, and the same processes at local levels, have too long escaped critical ethnographic investigation (see, as exceptions, Herzfeld 1987; Layne 1989). The interpretation of the meaning of political culture, for actor and observer alike, should be the concern of ethnographers, who, after all, often play a role in recording and interpreting those meanings (Handler 1988). In twentieth-century Meath the changing definitions of patronage and brokerage, because of political parties and local and national governments, have been key to citizens' reconstruction of their histories and political symbols. They also illustrate the ways that historical analysis by ethnographers, in what might be termed historical ethnography or ethnographic history, can illuminate contemporary sociopolitical processes.

Irish political culture

No conclusion is clearer or more universal in the literature on Irish party politics than that regarding the origin of the two-party split in the early twentieth century. Those for and those against the treaty with Britain which ended the War of Independence became the core groups in the formation of today's two major parties, Fine Gael and Fianna Fáil. The basic ideological split over the partition of Ireland which took place after independence then fostered the Civil War (1922-23), when the two treaty factions took arms against each other. And it is these events that many historians and political scientists point to as the bedrock of twentieth-century Irish political party cleavages (Whyte 1974; Carty 1976; Gallagher 1985).[1]

From 1923 on, according to the literature, national and local politics in Ireland took on a stable and predictable character, influenced by such factors as the British political tradition, nationalism, peasant society, Irish Catholicism, authoritarianism, conservatism, anti-intellectualism, loyalty, personalism and localism (Chubb 1974, 1982). With few exceptions, however, these aspects of Irish political culture were investigated only at the national levels of political discourse (Higgins 1982). Although there have been a few ethnographic case studies in local politics, they have focused on the roles of national politicians as patrons, and have examined in the main the importance of local political machines in national political life. In fact, the two most celebrated case studies of local politics in Ireland, namely those by Mart Bax (1976) in County Cork and Paul Sacks (1976) in County Donegal, described local politics but largely ignored the importance of local government in rural society. Local politicians' input into county councils was reviewed by these scholars not as part of an analysis of governmental decision making and administration but as a testament to the many ways in which local politicians retain their standing in the community. Analyses of the structure and function of local government within local and national politics are still major lacunae in the scholarship on politics in Ireland.

This book is offered as a contribution to the analysis of local politicians' roles within the local government system, which are necessary complements to their roles within a local party system. The politics of local government and local party help to create and maintain local and national political elites. As I have argued throughout this book, the elite status of large farmers in Meath in this century has been due in large part to their participation in local government.

Overall, ethnographic studies of politics in Irish localities have supported the view that has become crucial for both party members and party analysts alike: Irish citizens have traditionally supported the two major parties because of individual and family traditions that date from the Civil War. My ethnographic research in county Meath, however, suggested a much more complex political culture and history. As they occurred in Meath, the Economic War (1932-1938), the 1934 local government elections, and the beginnings of the processes of centralization of political parties and national government all indicated to me in the late 1970s and after that the above conclusions regarding national party allegiance and local political behavior were incomplete. Local government in Meath, especially the county council, went through the greatest changes in the twentieth century precisely because party loyalties had not been determined before the 1930s, and the power available at the local government level presented a threat to the establishment of both party and government hegemony at the national level.

The case of rural county Meath in the 1930s demonstrated that economic factors, principally within agriculture, had a tremendous effect on the creation of individual and family party allegiances, and that the wherewithal of local political patronage was taken away from local politicians precisely because the national party leadership wanted both to curtail its use and to be its source. Thus the role of politicians as brokers that has become so familiar in the literature became set for local and national representatives after the party leadership removed much of their power in local government, particularly after legislation in 1940.

In effect, from 1925 to 1942, county councillors in Meath were members of highly decentralized political parties, and real and effective patrons because they controlled the distribution of scarce resources within the political arena. The County Management Act (1940) made the majority of local councillors into brokers by removing their control of resources just when the conditions of the Economic War had begun to cement both personal political followings and party allegiances. After 1940 the national party and state leadership became the real patrons of Irish political life. Meath councillors had to accept the less powerful status of political brokers due to the co-option of power by their parties and the state.

This transition from political patronage to brokerage in the role of local Irish politicians was clearly remembered by Meath people during my research, but it was also a memory that often contradicted the more commonly told tale of origins of most individual and family party allegiances. However, ethnographic historical research in local Irish politics is more than the recording of social memory. The distinctions in contemporary political culture that the ethnographer makes, between the 'real' and 'ideal' and the 'possible' and 'probable', inform the analysis of past

134

political events. This is especially true when there is no written history or there are few data with which a researcher may prove or disprove what people remember about their ancestors' behavior.

The historical dimension to Irish ethnography can provide valuable diachronic case studies for the analysis of comparative Irish and European politics. In Meath the events of the 1930s suggested at least one way that political patrons, long the interest of ethnographers worldwide, can lose power and control of material resources to the political parties and governments that they had helped to establish. Their new role of brokers - people who present themselves as decision makers and power holders but who increasingly rely on imaginary patronage and the exchange of information - may provide clues to the problems for local populations which result from the processes of state centralization wherever they are studied by ethnographers. The analysis of changes in political leadership in Meath generations ago serves as a useful starting point in the comparative ethnography and history of Irish political parties.

Patrons and brokers in local Irish politics

So many scholars have discussed the relations of patronage, brokerage, and clientelism (Gibbon and Higgins 1974; Higgins 1982; Komito 1984) that it is beneficial to define some terms here. A client is someone who receives material or nonmaterial aid from those who either control scarce resources or those who are the link to others who control such resources. The client's perception that aid is received - aid which may at times be all or largely imaginary - is crucial to every definition of clientelism in Ireland, whether that definition is that of the local citizen or of the scholar. Aid is also always associated with the efforts of a patron. As long as the client believes that one or more patrons played some effective role in the provision of the needed or desired goods and services the social relations at the heart of the patron-client dyad can be sustained. Sometimes, though, these relations may balance precariously on the edge of a client's suspension of disbelief. Sometimes, perhaps often, the political client may suspect that the patron is ineffective, ineffectual or simply lying in order to maintain an image and to take credit for actions and results that are out of his control. In most cases it does not take too much effort to play the role of client, in case—just in case—the patron will provide that valuable service, if not now perhaps at a later date.

The role of the client should also be clarified in terms of the support given the patron or broker when a debt is called due. In modern Meath this debt has most often been paid when the client casts a vote in an election. In some instances, however, the client also provides a service when called upon. Here it is not inappropriate to conjure up the images at the beginning of the first Godfather film, when Don Corleone, after chastising one of his clients for possible disrespect, informed him that his request would be honored, but that in return he might one day be called upon for a reciprocal service. In that film the Godfather made clear that such a day might never come, but in Meath the continuing support of a political client, who after all might be best seen as a political supporter, was always required, and always monitored. In Meath, as in other such political relationships found elsewhere, some clients volunteer a service in the name of friendship, family, locality and shared identity. For example, one of the Meath politicians whose career I tracked over my field research dutifully received fresh eggs from a client's farm every Sunday morning! As the politician explained to me, that supporter's family had been served well by the politician's father, and now both the support and the patronage had been bequeathed to the next generation.

Overall, however, in this patronage system in local politics, it is expected that the more a client receives from a patron, the more service might be expected from the client. As a result, political clients are often busy at election time at tasks ranging from canvassing to making sandwiches for party workers to putting up posters on crossroad telephone poles. Thus, the political patron is assumed to be able to provide material resources which are seen to be strategically more important to the client than anything the client could supply the patron in return. And a broker often mediates between the patron and client in a role seen by the partners as necessary for a satisfactory outcome. Because of this vital role as intermediary, the broker takes on aspects of both patron and client.

In Meath in the 1970s, the relationships among these roles had much to do with tradition, rural-urban dichotomies, and the development of Irish political culture (see, for example, Chubb 1974, 1982), but they were also the expression of a common desire to manipulate and control scarce resources to one's own and one's family's benefit. This basic point is too often absent from the literature of Irish politics, but in Meath it was always at the forefront of citizens' explanations of their own political history. In terms of the creation of political loyalties and affiliations, the material aspects of Meath political life, the economic issues which have influenced each generation of

Meath citizens, were discussed by Meath people as being as important as any ideological or political development in this century (rivaling, for example, Ireland's partition in 1921 and the Economic War in the 1930s). And regardless of one's role in any interaction in this brokerage culture, a person participated in the political process in order to improve those conditions which were perceived to be capable and worthy of change.

Many leaders in Meath politics and farming today emphasize the ideological origins of their political parties and their local party leaders' roles in the Irish War of Independence and the Civil War. In their own narratives of both the organs of the state and the roots of their party allegiances, ideology seems to trump all other possible causes. However, in my field research Meath people tended to ignore economic factors in the formation of family party allegiance until and unless specific national economic issues were raised, such as the Economic War and the 'emergency' of World War II. Most Meath party members leaned towards presenting a rather ideal view of their modern parties by minimizing the extent of patronage in past and current party affairs. This muting of certain memories and stories concealed party and politician indiscretions and errors that proved embarrassing to later generations, and in so doing suggested a relatively unbroken descent from nationalist forebears and heroes of the independence movement. This was an attempt to supply an ideological basis to parties in a political system famous for its lack of distinctive ideologies, where with a few exceptions over the century Irish political parties have tended to group themselves at the center-right.

Although at the time of my ethnographic research the roles of Meath politicians had changed over the last two generations, people in the main still supported politician and party on the premise that local politicians 'got the job done' as patrons for their constituents. The rhetoric of party politics upheld this view and distracted voters from the realities of brokerage by appealing to traditional supporters and by ignoring the events of the 1930s and 1940s, all of which would point to the relative powerlessness of today's politicians by highlighting just how much more in terms of jobs, services, and influence were provided by past politicians. Voters of the 1980s still expected their representatives to get the job done, but my research allowed me to clarify the changing dimensions of patronage and clientage in Meath, where the provision of scarce goods and services was no longer the sole domain of local politicians. Their days of getting the job done had ended in the early 1940s.

Meath politics before 1932

In the decade after independence and before the Economic War, the Irish government was dominated nationally by the Cumann na nGaedheal party. All the services that past county councils had provided were continued under the new Free State system, and some were added. After the Local Government Act (1925) the Meath County Council was in complete control of local health, sanitation, sewage, water, waste disposal, road construction and maintenance, defense, fire and safety, social welfare and public assistance. It also advised the national government on such matters as education, agriculture and telephones. But the most important powers that the new Meath county councils had were the striking of the rate each year, which determined the amount of tax that property holders had to pay to maintain services, and the hiring of the majority of county council employees. Alas, the corrupting influence of the latter power became clear quickly, and was the subject of the first move in the long struggle between the center and peripheries of power and administration in Ireland when the national government established in 1926 the Local Appointments Commission. This body was charged with selecting and appointing well-qualified nonpolitical persons for the principal offices in local authorities. The Combined Purchasing Act (1925) also gave Dublin some control over the spending of local authority funds.

From the beginning of the Irish Free State the government party did its best to support those who took its side in the Civil War. Compensation acts provided pensions for the wounded and disabled who had fought in the War of Independence and with the National Army in the Civil War (Kelly 1936: 91-93)· Opposition veterans were all but entirely excluded. Once Fianna Fáil formally entered politics in 1926, however, it quickly gained great support from small farmers, shopkeepers, and rural and urban workers across the country, including in Meath. The economic policies of the Free State had favored wealthier farmers, professionals and businessmen. A 1925 law made employment in the civil and local government service dependent on the signing of a declaration of allegiance to the Free State Constitution. It has been contended that in at least one county council government grants were awarded to local councils on the condition that they give jobs such as roadwork to supporters of the Free State (Bax

1976: 20). Thus, the practice of the ruling party's rewarding its supporters was quickly established in the state's early years, making it in effect national and local policy.

In this new era of local government the Meath County Council administered the county through a series of committees, made up of councillors and co-opted members of the community and advised by local government officers. Each committee, charged with dealing with county electoral area health, housing or road maintenance, had its own recommendations regarding which workers should be hired, the amount of funds needed, who was to be awarded council contracts, the types of service the council needed to provide, and the county's service schedules. Although the county council through its chairman had to approve all such orders, the majority party heavily influenced council decisions. All necessary services were provided in Meath in ways that were meant to guarantee that the electorate did not become disgruntled over a lack of desired services. The parties realized that the only way to gain and keep electoral support in Meath was to take care of their own.

In the 1970s and 1980s older Meath residents remembered the first two decades after independence as a time when politicians made the decisions necessary for the provision of almost all local services, a period in which elected representatives gave instructions to local government employees and seldom received bureaucratic resistance. Most of the memories concerned the provision of 'county' jobs or 'jobs on the Council,' or the allocation of council public housing. Although the accuracy of such memories must be considered in this and in any research into the ways people

141

Table 1. Meath county council members, by occupation, 1920–45

Occupation group	1920	% total elected	1925	% total elected	1928	% total elected	1934	% total elected	1942	% total elected	1945	% total elected
Farmers	17	45	21	55	20	55	25	71	17	57	19	58
Laborers	7	18	10	26	8	22	1	3	6	20	4	12
Professionals	2	5	0	0	0	0	2	6	2	7	3	9
Merchants	1	3	5	13	2	6	5	14	4	13	4	12
Company directors	2	5	1	3	1	3	1	3	1	3	2	6
Other	9	24	1	3	5	14	1	3	0	0	1	3
Total	38	100	38	100	36	100	35	100	30	100	33	100

142

remember activities that often have a poor paper trail, nonetheless it seemed clear to me from corroborating evidence in the council and local newspaper archives that Meath people in the early years of the state voted for the local representatives who could best champion their interests against and among other similar champions who acted for their own CEAs.[2]

These champions in the past constituted a local political elite in Meath who dominated local government and politics in the years before the county manager system was established. This local elite was largely composed of farmers and agricultural workers (see Tables 1 and 2, based on data collected from county council records and local newspapers). From just 45 percent of the council in 1920 (in a group with many agricultural workers, shop employees, and clerks), the farmers' share of council seats rose steadily, to a peak in 1934 of 71 percent (twenty five) of the councillors elected or appointed from that election year to 1942 (the year of the largest and most powerful council in county history). However, it should also be noted that this preponderance of farmers in the council did not signal their allegiance to any particular party, for farmer representatives were evenly distributed between the two major parties.

This balance and this influential position of farmers continued for some time. Before the 1970s their numbers never fell below 55 percent of the total council. It was not only the number of farmers on the council that was significant, however, but their role in the county economy. From 1925 to 1942, most of the non-farmer council members depended on agriculture for their livelihood. Perhaps more important, the parties themselves were in large part farmers' parties (except for Labour, which in Meath was primarily an agricultural workers' group), and they

143

reflected not only Meath agricultural interests but also national party politics. Laborers and merchants were represented on these early councils, but their political importance declined upon the rise of the Farmers and Ratepayers Party, which represented medium to large farmers and would eventually form, along with the declining government party Cumann na nGaedheal, the new Fine Gael Party, just before the 1934 elections.

During this period the Meath county council began

Table 2. Farmers by party, Meath County Council, 1925–45

Party	1925	1928	1934	1942	1945
Fianna Fail	0	4	12	7	8
Fine Gael	0	0	13	2	1
Independent	2	3	0	2	5
Labour	1	0	0	0	2
Farmers and Ratepayers (Farmers, Independent Farmers)	14	13	0	6	0
Cumann na nGaedheal	3	0	0	0	0
Cumann na Talmhan	0	0	0	0	2
Other (Old IRA, Republican, etc.)	1	0	0	0	1
Total	21	20	25	17	19

some practices which gave it a character for which it is still remembered today. The county council favored pro-treaty people for low-level county jobs such as clerks, road workers and lorry drivers, thereby winning it a reputation for cronyism and favoritism. It did its best to minimize the taxes that the ratepayers would have to pay for services, in its effort to reward political supporters with land and capital, and in order to soften the economic blows that all people in the new state were experiencing. And the members of the council argued often and well the important national political issues of the day, such as the state versus the Irish Republican Army (a proscribed secret army), the treaty, and trade and agricultural policy.

As a result of these trends in council affairs, in the years before 1934 council committees that were set up to provide basic services had as one priority the rewarding of party workers and supporters. Members of the new Fianna Fáil party were not included in such deliberations and rewards. The council also provided a forum for political party discussions, which would in turn be monitored by the party leaders in the Dáil, the principal legislative house in Parliament. This early politicization of the council became even more pronounced as the 1930s wore on, in what was perhaps the most decisive decade in Meath's local government history.

What then of farmers' roles in politics at that time? In almost all the interviews I conducted among Meath farmers, regardless of their family's political traditions or wealth, the first answer I received when I asked about the origins of their party allegiances was that it depended on the side taken by the family in the Civil War.[3] However, when I pushed people to describe the events that immediately preceded their families' choosing sides, they consistently drew their evidence from the years of the Economic War, a decade after the initial split. Most people had little to say about their families in the Civil War (not, I believe, because the events were still too sensitive but because most of their ancestors had not been directly involved) but were quick to discuss the opposition leaders' deviousness, their electoral and administrative practices, and their unfair patronage and use of force in the 1930s.

It is also worth noting, given the nature of ethnographic research into historical events and memories, how historical data is presented as fact, despite inaccuracies regarding chronology, personnel, and events. There seemingly was no gap in the logic offered by my informants in the 1970s and later when they presented data based on the 1930s as evidence of decisions they asserted were made in the 1920s. It was almost as if their families had become pro- or anti-treaty because they knew that in the following ten years the 'other fellows' would act the way they eventually did. The losses to Fine Gael families in the Economic War which were argued by one side were countered by the other side with condemnations of the riches of the pro-British graziers and the strong-arm tactics of the 'fascist' Blueshirts (an organization which helped form Fine Gael and which admired and mirrored some continental political movements of the right).

It was clear that Meath people of the 1970s cared less about the reasons for their ancestors' original political choices than about the fact that, in their view, the behavior of the other side during the Civil War and the Economic War clearly validated those choices, whenever they were made. As related to me during my research, farmers in Meath viewed their families' party affiliations as clear and necessary responses to an attack on the material conditions of their lives. For the farmers of Meath - especially the large farmers of Meath, who had served as the principal political elite in the county for so long - it was the events of early Fianna Fáil and Fine Gael party formation that helped cement their political loyalty up to the present. And, as has

146

happened often in subsequent years, it was a series of economic problems that first so politicized them.

The Economic War and Meath

The Economic War between Britain and Ireland began in 1932 when the Fianna Fáil government refused to pay money due Britain in the form of land annuities. Britain retaliated by putting duties on Irish agricultural imports. Meath's agricultural economy was devastated. Meath, the county most famous for the size of its farms, numbers of fattened beef, and wealth of its farmers, depended in the 1930s on an internal cattle trade in which it served as the final stage in the fattening and sale of beef which originated in the West of Ireland. In Meath, cattle were killed for local consumption, for consumption in Dublin, or were exported to Britain. The majority of her sixty-one thousand people (1936) made their living from agriculture, in a county dominated by farms of over two hundred acres. In 1926 almost 40 percent of the county's crops and pasture were produced on these large farms, the highest percentage in the state, and at the same time Meath had the lowest number of milking cows (three) per hundred acres in the state (Central Statistics Office 1928).

The social groups who dominated Meath society were the various large farmers, who were a mix of gentry holdouts, former tenants, agricultural entrepreneurs, and owners of bloodstock farms. Their dominance of the Meath economy was due to their relationships with each other and their networks outside the county in government, commerce, banking, and the church.

147

The big farmers of Meath, who had supported the Farmers Party and Cumann na nGaedheal over the years, were especially hard hit by the Economic War. The war itself followed an agricultural depression that had Meath farmers expecting help, not disaster. In the nation as a whole, agricultural income had fallen 12.8 percent between 1929 and 1931, and the price of one- to two-year-old store cattle fell by 17.2 percent between 1931 and 1932, sliding to 58.8 percent below the 1931 level in 1935 (Orridge 1981: 7). In an effort to save their businesses, many farmers refused to pay either their annuities or their rates (real estate taxes) to the Fianna Fáil government. Nationally, in 1930-31, 14.1 percent of rates were not paid. Within two years, nonpayment rose to 36 percent. The refusal to pay occurred primarily in prosperous counties like Meath among large farmers, both Catholic and Protestant, among Protestant small farmers, and among some Catholic and Protestant commercial interests in Leinster (Orridge 1981: 9-11).

As we have seen, the nature, timing, and recipients of Meath county services were the sole responsibility of the committees controlled by the members of the county council (MCCs) who were delegated by the council as a whole to sit on them. The party that controlled the council controlled a large share of the patronage the council could command. Before the Economic War large farmers, members first of Cumann na nGaedheal and later of the Farmers Party, dominated the council. Most Meath political power rested with them, and most of that power was in the hands of the farmers of the majority council party.

The central government attempted to curb local government functions and control civil service hiring, but its relative failure to do so before the 1930s is a testament to the decentralization of Cumann na nGaedheal and the absence of an organized opposition party. Thus, the strength of both local government in Meath and the interest groups elected to it were linked to the development of political parties in the county. Before 1934 in Meath the parties of the nation took a backseat to the local election of people who would best represent the constituents of their CEAs. The parties themselves began to command more attention at the 1934 local elections. These elections were of national significance because they were the first major test of the popularity of the Fianna Fáil government. In Meath, they were also significant because a victory for the party in the county election would ensure control of goods and services. This last belief was a new development in Meath because, for the first time, local patronage was viewed as the domain of the political *party* that controlled the council, rather than just the people elected to the council. This belief seemed to be largely due to the rise of Fianna Fáil as a strong centralized opposition party in the 1930s.

Before the parties became the chief instrument of power in Meath, local representatives who sought to champion their constituents' interests needed the cooperation of representatives from the other CEAs, who themselves wished their communities to benefit from such schemes as road construction and rural electrification. The task of satisfying clients' individual needs was time-consuming but the best way to gain voter support. If an MCC got the job done, then that representative could expect a person's, and often a family's, vote in the future. Services provided included individual health benefits, getting a man a job as laborer 'on the roads,' and getting a council house for a newly married couple. A lot depended on the committees to which the MCC was appointed, along with the relationships and working relations which the MCC had built with fellow party representatives and with those in the other parties.

As the 1930s progressed, Meath councillors stopped debating the great national issues of the day simply because neither their constituents nor their parties wanted or expected them to continue. Meath people remember the first decade of the new local government as one in which they supported their local MCC because he represented not only their CEA but their way of life. Large farmers quickly became the representatives with the most influence. Many small farmers, mindful of the differences in wealth, culture, and nationalist ideology between themselves and their larger neighbors, could not afford the time and money to run for office, nor did they have the networks necessary to run a successful campaign and to ensure a productive working relationship with other MCCs even if elected. Thus large farmers who served as MCCs ostensibly looked after the interests of all farmers, but many Meath farmers at the end of the century contended that these original farmer MCCs looked after the interests of large farmers first. However, this rather decentralized party system changed with the successes of Fianna Fáil.

The Economic War followed hard on the heels of Fianna Fáil's taking control of the Dáil. Its new opposition party, Fine Gael, provided a platform which brought together many former political enemies and friends. The national seriousness of these events was mirrored in Meath. When British markets were removed, the major markets for Meath animals became the home one of Meath itself and those in

Dublin. And in the county council of 1928-32, which had only five Fianna Fáil representatives, MCCs were relatively powerless to aid their county's farmers. Because of strict Fianna Fáil government control of international marketing, most Meath politicians could neither rely on favors due them for past services nor look to their party for help, because their party was not in power. Fianna Fáil had formed the national government, and the country was feeling the political aftershocks of this significant turn of events. In Meath, the need for affiliation with *national* parties that could form national governments and national economic policy became apparent to the Meath MCCs.

In order to sell cattle in Meath in the early 1930s, a farmer had to provide export licenses or permits. But these could be obtained only through the Department of Agriculture, a ministry in Dublin serving the government controlled by Fianna Fáil. In Meath such licenses were available from the local Committee of Agriculture, a committee of the county council but one controlled by a combination of Fianna Fáil MCCs and local Fianna Fáil supporters.[4] As supporters of both parties remember in Meath, the principal way to get a license back then was *not* to go to your MCC or the Committee of Agriculture directly, but to go to the new Fianna Fáil Cumann (club) in your community. These clubs supplied sales licenses through their patrons on the committee and in Dublin. If you did not 'turn' Fianna Fáil in this period by joining the local club, and if you did not have a considerable number of local butchers and merchants in your network of social or business contacts, then your animals were almost worthless.[5] As one farmer related, 'My family was all for law and order, and the government and treaty parties, but he [his father] had a difficult decision to make in the hard times of the Economic War.' Another believed that the Economic War was Fianna Fáil's way of taking its revenge on the large farmers who supported the treaty.

Thus, it was in this period that most large farmers turned towards Fine Gael. They did this for many reasons. Some large farmers were motivated ideologically, based on differences in perspective on the Civil War and Treaty divisions in the nationalist movement. Some suffered from being outside the patronage of Fianna Fáil and their political leaders and supporters. And yet others decided that if they were ever to be able to counter the dictates of a centralized party and government such as those of Fianna Fáil then they would have to do so in a similarly structured and organized political party. Thus, as Meath moved into the 1940s, Fianna Fáil had become the party of small and medium farmers.

Although past political events and nationalist ideologies played key roles in party divisions, in Meath the ability to sell animals, pay taxes, and keep a farm was just as important in aligning voters then as in the period of my field research. Even those large farmers of the 1930s who were willing to forget past political differences found it difficult to gain Fianna Fáil patronage, because, simply put, a terrible market for beef left the party's patronage severely limited. Thus in the 1930s political allegiance in Meath began to have a great deal to do with fattened-beef sales. As can be seen in Table 3, beef cattle numbers dropped sharply in the early 1930s. Three-year-olds decreased by 15.4 percent between 1931 and 1932, and by another 8.1 percent and 10.9 percent in the next two years. Two-year-olds dropped 13.1 percent in number at the height of the Economic War. As a result, many Meath beef farmers began keeping calves and yearlings. They hoped to survive the current economic troubles and have replacement stock for the revival. But they were to have a long wait. By the end of the decade, long after the end of the trade Economic War, three-year-old Meath-fattened beef had dropped by 35.9 percent, from sixty-four thousand to forty-one thousand head. Only the one-year-olds increased, by 29.1 percent, between 1931 and 1939.

The early 1930s was a crucible for many due to the swings in fortune in both the economy and polity. Many poor farmers, urban workers, and small businessmen in towns and villages joined Fianna Fáil because of the patronage it promised as well as the republican ideals it espoused. Many of these supporters were irate citizens who had been denied county council and Cumann na nGaedheal patronage. They felt that it was then their turn to receive some material rewards.

Government legislation supported this position, and fostered the view that government was a way to reward party faithful and in reverse to settle old accounts with opponents. An ambitious legislation program set about doing this. Whereas in the past they had only been awarded to Free State veterans, army pensions were now supplied to Republican veterans (1932). In addition, compensation was paid to all those people whose property was damaged when they aided the Republican side in the Civil War (1933). Service pensions were also awarded to old Republicans and their families (1934) (Kelly 1936: 91).

Table 3. Meath cattle, 1930s

1 June	3 years old and older	% change	2–3 years old	% change	1–2 years old	% change	Total (including bulls, cows, heifers in calf)	% change
1931	64,633 (−9,939)		73,594 (−3,434)		39,664 (+1,833)		225,952 (−8,336)	
1932	54,694 (−4,455)	−15.4	70,160 (−1,116)	−4.7	41,497 (−2,179)	+4.6	217,616 (−4,015)	−3.7
1933	50,239 (−5,479)	−8.1	69,044 (−9,019)	−1.6	39,318 (+960)	−5.2	213,601 (−11,225)	−1.8
1934	44,760 (−3,218)	−10.9	60,025 (+7,376)	−13.1	40,278 (+10,909)	+2.4	202,376 (+23,570)	−5.2
1939	41,542	−7.2	67,401	+12.3	51,187	+27.1	225,946	+11.6

Source: Central Statistics Office, Dublin.

154

their families (1934) (Kelly 1936: 91). Fine Gael, the new opposition party, was formed around a nucleus of large farmers who had been demoralized by the weaknesses of the old Farmers Party and were unhappy with their powerlessness in such organizations as the Blueshirts and Cumann na nGaedheal (Manning 1971). To both major parties, a demonstration of electoral strength was needed as a clear sign of the new political alignments. The 1934 local elections were to be a test of their political future.

Fianna Fáil was the first to recognize the importance of controlling locally elected bodies. The benefits in providing services to local constituents notwithstanding, such control would cement the local to the national party structure and present a picture of almost unilateral government and party solidarity at every level of government and administration. Fianna Fáil was especially interested in taking political control of municipal local government, because they knew that municipal bodies, through non-cooperation, could block the government's programs.

To break its opponents' hold on municipal and local government, and to win the first local elections after its victory in the Dáil, Fianna Fáil had to change the local franchise, which at the time was only given to ratepayers, i.e., those who paid property taxes (Kelly 1936: 93). To achieve this, the Fianna Fáil government injected money into local government through the Local Government (Extension of Franchise) Bill (1933), which gave the vote to every citizen twenty-one years of age. This new bill was a calculated move by Fianna Fáil to extend the vote to those groups who had become its national voting support. The Seanad (the second house of Parliament) delayed the bill, however, so that in the 1934 elections only the ratepayers voted. Fianna Fáil expected a loss. In Meath, a county hard hit by Fianna Fáil policy and one in which most standing MCCs campaigned vigorously against the national government, their defeat was expected.

The 1934 Local Government election

Besides extending party and governmental power into rural constituencies, the 1934 elections were significant in other ways. A victory for the government party would vindicate its economic policy, and the local elections were the first after the start of both the Economic War and a Fianna Fáil Dáil majority. The local elections were also a test of strength for the new party, Fine Gael. Local party organizations, hastily constructed and placed in every CEA, were being tested for the first time. And the elections also served as the first electoral contest in the history of the state in which economic issues were as important as political or ideological ones.

In Meath these local elections were clearly fought over economic issues. All the major parties saw them as a contest for control of the politics that were crucial in local government. As such, the elections were the first major party-politicized contest in Meath County Council history. They were, in the end, a battle for competing patrons, who wanted to meet the needs of their supporters and to attract new ones. Thus, in early 1934 Fianna Fáil increased the agricultural grant to county councils, a move aimed to please both farmers, whose rates would drop, and local councillors, who would not have to strike a high rate to tax their constituents. In Meath this increase aided small farmers (giving relief to

156

the first £20 valuation, which in Meath was roughly the first twenty acres of one's land) by giving a total of £11,000 to the county, making it fifth in receipts among the nation's counties and the biggest recipient in Leinster *(Meath Chronicle,* 24 February 1934).

Perhaps not surprisingly, the debates in the Meath county council that followed these governmental moves to curry favor focused on the issue of rates. Council chair John Quinn contended that the rate relief was nothing in the face of an economy which made rate payment a problem in itself: 'We see unfortunate people having their cattle seized and driven away by the bailiffs because they were unable to pay the rates.' James Kelly, Fianna Fáil Member of Parliament (TD) and MCC, countered by asking if Quinn was condoning the nonpayment of rates, a question answered with cries from the floor of 'No, no!' Kelly went on to question the money being made by big farmers who had invested in tobacco, wheat, oats and potatoes, and who surely were not suffering as much as they claimed. The Fianna Fáil TD then attacked the major supporters of the opposition by asking them, 'Why don't the ranches go into tillage, instead of employing one or two men?' This reference to large farms as 'ranches' criticized them as beef fattening enterprises which were not labor intensive.

Labour Senator and MCC Michael Duffy also attacked the economic strength of many in Meath when he wondered at the wealth of the 'market manipulators,' the 'banks,' and many of his Meath neighbors, for 'in the country they could see hundreds of expensive motor cars at Blue Shirt meetings' *(Meath Chronicle,* 3 March 1934). Many MCCs were also quick to point out the role of past governments in the provision of services in Meath. Lamenting the situation in which the outgoing government had left the countryside after ten years of power, one Fianna Fáil MCC concluded that 'it was strange that in these years of prosperity they had not built a cottage for the rural worker. In Meath alone, under Fianna Fáil, 700 cottages had been built in two years' *(Meath Chronicle*, 9 June 1934). It is important to note though that such patronage came from Dublin. These local politicians were using the actions of national parties and governments for whatever rhetorical and other gain they could. The new government followed patterns established by its predecessors and offered substantial material benefits to locals who aligned themselves to Fianna Fáil.

The Blueshirt organization feared the economic power of the government. In an article entitled 'A Carrot for Meath,' in the Blueshirt official newspaper, *United Ireland* (7 July 1934), the Blueshirts denounced the government for the false rumors it had spread in Meath regarding a beet processing plant that it would open which would employ seven hundred men. The Blueshirts claimed that Fianna Fáil promised that 'farmers would more than make up their losses on cattle by their profits on beet.' And although no factory was built, the Blueshirts were aware of the power that the government wielded through its ability to provide such valuable economic services. Without access to scarce resources vital to patronage, the Blueshirts and the new Fine Gael party could only ask farmers to use the 1934 elections to fight Fianna Fáil on the land annuities, a policy which had divorced them from British markets, destroyed their beef industry, and put the titles to their land in jeopardy. It was clear to Fine Gael that this would be the first local election fought along party lines

(*United Ireland*, 26 May 1934). As a Fine Gael TD announced at a Meath rally, 'Any person with a vote, particularly the farmers, who did not use it at the elections next month, was not fit to be called a citizen' (*Meath Chronicle*, 19 May 1934). This belief in democracy was espoused, perhaps surprisingly, by the Meath Blueshirts, who contended that they represented a true cross section of county life:

> They had people from the cottage and people from the Castle; they had the farmer, the professional man and the business man, all marching under the Blueshirt banner . . . the spearpoint of Fine Gael (*Meath Chronicle*, 19 May 1934)

Fianna Fáil campaigners believed that, unlike Fine Gael, they themselves 'were not putting forward Captains and Colonels and Generals. . . . They were putting forward plain people; many of whom had fought in the IRA' (*Meath Chronicle*, 19 May 1934).

Although Fine Gael had announced a local government scheme in early June which promised rate relief for rural and urban ratepayers, a national reconstruction scheme and new social welfare programs, their campaign also decried the economic and political policies of Fianna Fáil. They feared a 'Party dictatorship' (*Meath Chronicle*, 10 June 1934). But these maneuvers on the part of the Fine Gael and Labour parties in the end did not succeed.

The 1934 election in Meath returned twenty Fianna Fáil MCCs out of a total of thirty-five (Fine Gael won fifteen seats, Labour none). Of the thirty-five seats, twenty-five, or 71 percent, were held by farmers (twelve FF, thirteen FG); it was the largest farming representation in county history. Across the nation, fifteen of the twenty-three councils that were contested were won by Fianna Fáil. In Meath, James Kelly felt that his party's victory was a vote of confidence in his party's actions at all levels of government, and that the new politicization of local government was right and proper. Kelly 'at all times believed that politics should enter the County Council chamber' *(Meath Chronicle,* 7 July 1934). He promised Fianna Fáil's political opponents that they would suffer no 'victimisation' and 'intolerance', but neglected to add that Meath's Fianna Fáil would now control local government both as the agent of its national executive and as a dispenser of patronage.

The 1934 election marked an end in large part to non-party political localism in Meath, in which constituents voted for the person, regardless of party, who would best serve their local interests. From 1934 on the parties saw to it that local electors believed that the parties were the best means of serving local interests, so that they should vote for the individual who was best suited to satisfy voters' needs. Now in one sense this was commonsensical, but the point made then by Fianna Fáil, and one copied by all political parties in Ireland since, is that the party will meet voters' needs, instead of local leaders whose personalism or business contacts will get the job done. Said differently, political parties were taking up the mantle of picking the right people, with the right contacts and networks, who were able to get elected and who would serve local constituents' needs. The party could no longer tolerate its self-construction from below.

In Meath the choice for farmers who needed to support one or the other party was largely influenced by the conditions of the Economic War. Although 1932-1942 were years in which the political center continued to take power away from the political periphery, it was also a time when the party politician in the county council became the 'patron' so famous in fact and fancy in Irish political culture. From the 1930s on Meath farmers began to believe that the best way to influence both local and national politics in order to improve their material conditions was to participate in party-organized politics, a belief that began to change only in the late 1970s.

A new breed of politician stepped into the political arena of the 1930s and 1940s. This new politician relied on personalism, familism, localism, and the networks provided by both occupation or profession, and the resources and imagery of political party, to get the job done to the satisfaction of local electors. One of the most successful in this new breed of politician was Pat Fitzsimons, Sr., who founded a Fianna Fáil organization in Navan which is still instrumental in party affairs in the county. This organization controlled most of the county councils up to the 1970s and provided a political legacy that was passed on to two sons, during the course of my fieldwork, and to a grandson today.[6]

Pat Fitzsimons, often called 'the Godfather' in later years due to the popularity of the Hollywood film, allegedly ran the committee system of the county council to his party's advantage for ten years after the 1934 election and was the party leader in the council for a generation. Everyone in Meath in the 1970s it seems, and regardless of their political

161

loyalties, was aware of the power Fitzsimons and his party had wielded in the past. All services, jobs, favors, and political commitments asked of Fianna Fáil representatives, it is said, crossed his desk. Many former Fine Gael and Labour MCCs remember with regret and a sense of amusement, some with sheer hate, their lack of control over the resources they needed for their constituents and for the success of their political careers. Not surprisingly, some Fianna Fáil MCCs, who envied Navan Fianna Fáil's control of the county party organization, did not remember old Pat fondly either. And although it was all but physically impossible for Fitzsimons and his local Navan Fianna Fáil club to have controlled as much of county affairs as both their friends and their enemies have charged, it is clear that Fianna Fáil controlled the majority of the vital county committees of 1934-42 and was influential in many council relations with both local businesses and the national government. As evidence, for example, of his political reach, it was often recounted to me that the national bus line's only stop in Navan, until the 1980s and re-zoning in the town, was at the doorstep of Fitzsimons's pub and shop.

To get things done in the Navan area in the 1930s, it was clear that most Fianna Fáil people had to go to Fitzsimons's pub to get a chance to talk with him; it was a pub that until the 1990s people visited to speak to Jim, the son who was a TD and later a Member of the European Parliament (MEP). Many a pint has been taken there while the drinker (sometimes an inquiring anthropologist) waited to ask a favor. The 1930s then was the time of the Fianna Fáil-dominated county council but also of a Navan-dominated Fianna Fáil, and a Navan organization run by a network spun around one

162

family. If Meath ever had a political machine on the model presented by Bax (1976) and Sacks (1976) for Cork and Donegal, then it was Fitzsimons's Navan Fianna Fáil.

This period of transformation in the power of county councilors was destined to be short-lived however. After 1934 the Fianna Fáil leadership did not intend to give more power to local government. Eamon de Valera, Taoiseach (prime minister) and leader of Fianna Fáil, believed in the centralization of power in the party executive and through it the party leader. De Valera, however, did not have the desired control of the country's political system and electorate. The 1937 election saw a Fianna Fáil victory in the voters' acceptance of the new constitution, but it also saw Fianna Fáil suffer a number of setbacks. Perhaps for the first time, Fianna Fáil realized that it had to pay more than lip service regarding nationalism in order to keep the votes it needed to remain in power. The Economic War had proved that even the smallest farmers needed material incentives in addition to nationalist rhetoric. The 1937 election showed the effects of that war. 'In short, for the first time since the foundation of the Irish State, a substantial body of electors followed their local and personal preferences in economic and social matters, doubtless from the conviction that the Treaty-Republic issue was moribund' (Hogan 1945: 30-31).

For this and other reasons, de Valera's Fianna Fáil concluded that it could not allow a local government system to provide power bases in the counties, which given current legislation and local government administration could not be controlled from Dublin. Local political control of political goods and services had to end. Thus, ironically, it was a Fianna Fáil government that made county management a nationwide institution in 1942. In Meath, Fianna Fáil had been the party best served by local political control, yet it was the one to change the conditions that were necessary to maintain a high level of local political patronage.

The County Management Act put an end to both party control of local services and the committee system. In 1942 all counties were appointed managers by the Local Appointments Commission. Each manager was entrusted with all 'reserved functions' of the county council, that is, with all administration and decision making not specifically given to the elected members. In Meath the sources of local patronage quickly dried up as the centralized and increasingly powerful local government service resisted political interference and began to administer the county with the help of the elected representatives. The control of scarce resources passed to Dublin, forcing local politicians into the role they have become so famous for in modern Ireland, that of brokers of information. Centralized parties and governments became the sources of material rewards in the political game, so the game in Meath had to change.

No party, individual, or occupation ever again enjoyed the power that had been held by those people who were in Meath local government before the 1940s. Pat Fitzsimons continued to be the leading politician of Navan and Meath until the early 1970s, but his battles with fellow party men for political prestige became as heated as any he had waged for his constituents' benefits in the past. All of this came to a head symbolically in the 1970s, when the Meath County Council suffered the loss of its last great power, that of raising and spending its own revenue.[7] The centralization of party leadership, civil service administration, and government decision making had changed Irish political patrons into people who could only hope to convince people of their power. Getting the job done had become a matter of 'telling them the job is done', of getting them to believe that the politicians could get the job done.

Ethnography and political studies

Few Irish local political studies have dealt with the role of local government and politics in the creation of both a national political elite and a national political process, either within or outside the party system. In fact, because local politics is such a neglected area of Irish social science, it seems that, beyond the oft-mentioned comments on constituency support for parliamentary representatives that emphasize a political culture steeped in localism, clientelism, and personalism, Irish political scientists have found little of importance in the role of local politics in national politics. Their assumption appears to be that the form of local politics is remarkably homogeneous nationwide (wherein it is taken for granted that local parties, interest groups, and electoral politics are structured alike by county or constituency and are but subsystems of the whole), but that the content of local politics differs (one or the other party dominates locally, and some independents can command local votes). In this vein, local politics is often inferred to be a by-product of local history, with its present configuration of little import to a political scientist who may very well assume that local politics functions alike in all constituencies. A survey of Irish political studies at the time of my field research, and this is a conclusion that has stayed with me since, suggested to me that local politics in the view of political scientists cannot itself be fruitfully studied as a political system.

This chapter has disputed such assumptions and inferences. The structure of local politics and its role in electoral politics, political recruitment, policy making, and the articulation of local interests at the national level were in the 1970s, and are still, matters for empirical research. Local politics has played a key role in national policy making and party formation since the creation of an independent Ireland, and it had taken on new significance in an Ireland that in the early1980s was for ten years a member of the European Community. National political discourse up to that time had suggested that parties formed and gained their electoral support because of nationalist issues that came to a head in the Civil War. My analysis of Meath political parties suggested something more. 'Traditional' political cleavages in Meath were at the very least due as much to the economic conditions of the 1930s as they were to Civil War divisions, and it was precisely because local politicians in the past had so much power within the local government system that electoral support quickly became linked to politician and party patronage.

From 1925 to 1942, at the high water mark of local councillor power in Meath, there were definite barriers to enlisting certain politicians as patrons. Past nationalist views and Civil War animosities combined with CEA residence, voters' occupations, and party policies to limit one's access to certain politicians and their political influence. Those people who became disaffected with Fianna Fáil quickly turned to the new Fine Gael party in order to build a network of patrons for a hoped-for future when they would have

166

majorities in the county council and/or the Dáil. But Fine Gael never had the opportunity to wield this power in Meath local government. Fianna Fáil, in an effort to prevent the decentralization of political power, established the county manager system, which has effectively made today's political brokers out of yesterday's patrons. The facade of power is all that remains to the Meath local politician who, along with his party, is eager to persuade people that it was the nationalist issue that was the origin of party allegiance. To remind people of the choices they made in the Economic War is to remind them of powers lost by the politicians

Irish political studies rely heavily on generalizations about political behavior based primarily on national voting patterns, party membership, and socioeconomic correlations. Field research in the social and economic roots of the political behavior of individuals, families, and larger social groups continues to be the greatest need in Irish political studies today. My study also shows that due scholarly attention to political economy demands that class and culture be considered in the ethnographic examination of local political history. This consideration might very well subvert scholarly findings on Irish party politics, such as the one offered by Carty (1976: 200):

> The long-standing differences that divide political parties in Ireland do not correspond to any social or economic cleavage in Irish society.... only in Ireland is the structure of the voter alignment underlying the *party system* unmarked by any social cleavage. The cleavage that divided Irishmen and structured the nation's party competition was political.

How important the events of the Economic War were in the alignment of voters within the Irish political parties outside Meath remains a matter for further research. The changes in political roles and the origins of party allegiance in Meath suggest that much work still needs to be done on Irish political behavior. The explanation or description of political cleavages through the use of political variables alone or in greatest part cannot do much to benefit a comparative and historical social science.

This chapter's case study offers an example of the relevance of ethnography and history to the analysis of the origin and development of political parties in Ireland. It also seeks to show how ethnography may contribute to an understanding of the past and present of political parties beyond Ireland. In the European context, for example, parties are integrative bodies closely linked to modern national development. As such, they rely on the imagery and symbolism of national history, and they are not above reinterpreting this history to suit their needs. Parties are also a means of centralization, whether at regional or national levels, and therefore have an important impact on all types of local political leadership, much of which anthropologists have discussed both historically and contemporaneously in terms of patron-client networks.

If political studies itself cannot escape the issues of personalism in political practice, where what is exchanged through political networks runs the gamut from information to jobs to votes -- and there is much to suggest that political studies anywhere in the world cannot escape the analysis of political networking and personalities (see for example Weingrod 1968; Bailey 1969; Schmidt et al. 1977; Eisenstadt and Lemarchand 1981) -- then political studies must treat such networks as problematic. The historical dimension is a crucial one in the Meath case, because it not only demonstrates the change of political patrons into information brokers who continue to act the part of dispensers of goods and services, but also illuminates the disparity between local people's memories of the events and their interpretations of the historical reality. The symbols they choose to remember and privilege from their past reinforce national political culture building and de-emphasize other aspects of their local political history in ways that anthropologists have observed elsewhere (see, for example, Herzfeld 1982, 1987; Layne 1989).

The lack of fit in the construction of national political culture, between on the one hand what is presented as national party origins and what is contended locally as the origins of local party political culture, and on the other hand the clear and concrete memories people have of their own and their families' lives in the 1920s and 1930s, does not pose a problem to Meath people themselves. It is not a contradiction in their lived memories or in their quotidian lives. It is indicative, however, of the important role political parties played in the creation of modern political culture in Meath, of the part they played in delimiting the bases of local political power outside the party, and of their interpretation and reconstruction of both national and local histories.

This Meath case study thus also shows the importance of ethnographic studies of local political history for a fuller understanding of national political process, but it does so at the expense of what has become an ideal type in political anthropology, the patron-client network. Patronage and brokerage studies are ways of understanding local and national political processes. Their discovery and analysis should not be the goal of ethnographic and historical research but a means to an end, the understanding of politics and culture. The study of the real and changing roles of political middlemen and their supporters must include the analysis of the dialogue between cultural historical memory and the realities of that historical change. In Meath, the ideal model of the local political patron reflects beliefs that have been at the core of contemporary Irish party politics for generations, suggesting that anthropologists have much more to investigate, and much more to offer, in the understanding of the structure and process of party politics in Ireland and elsewhere.

Notes

1. At the time of writing this chapter, in March 2011, the recent election in the Republic of Ireland offers evidence which must give pause to those who still see the major cleavages in party loyalty, affiliation and electoral support to be based on the Civil War of eighty years ago. The decline of the Celtic Tiger, the worldwide recession, the return of emigration as a panacea for social and economic ills, globalization, secularization, the peace initiatives in Northern Ireland, diasporan politics, corruption and abuse scandals and many more forces for change have converged to transform Irish political culture.

2. From the 1930s Meath has had five county electoral areas (CEAS) and twenty-nine members of the county council (MCCs).

3. The sources for this historical research were many: county and national newspapers; county council minutes and records; formal and informal

170

interviews (totaling over sixty hours) with fifteen former MCCs who had served in the period under investigation or just after, one member of Parliament (TD), and two senators, who also served on the Meath County Council in this time period; interviews with all elected and co-opted members of the Meath County Council from 1974 to the present; interviews with the descendants of MCCs from the period; a number of family diaries and record books shown and, in some cases, lent to me for copying; and finally, ten years of formal and informal interviews (and observations) of Meath farmers, discussions which often turned to their families' political history and heritage.

4. Although the majority of the committee was not Fianna Fáil, the connections that the Fianna Fáil members had with their party in Dublin, coupled with the department employees' reluctance to antagonize the government party, quickly made all committee members take note of Fianna Fáil influence.

5. One family from North Meath remembers the parish priest as its network man most responsible for buying and selling local cattle during the Economic War.

6. One son was a MEP and TD, the other was an urban district councillor and MCC in Navan, and the grandson currently serves on the Navan Urban District Council.

7. In his comprehensive review of Irish local government Roche (1982) points out the effect this loss of power had throughout Ireland.

Chapter 5

Political Leadership and Brokerage in Meath Local Government

The power and influence of large farmers and other elites, both rural and urban, which developed in Meath local government and politics in the years shortly after national independence, did not survive in the same forms into the 1970s. An increasing centralization of Irish political power within what amounted to a two-party system, similar to that which exists in the British parliament, meant that each national government was formed by a majority or minority with either Fianna Fáil or Fine Gael providing the prime minister, who in Ireland holds the title of An Taoiseach. This centralization of political power in Leinster House (the seat of Dáil Éireann, the Irish parliament) and in the national government also led to a shift in most power and influence to Dublin. This also resulted in a gradual erosion of political influence and power at local levels, to a point, as we have seen, where locally elected political representatives in county and urban councils had little power to get material benefits for constituents.

Nevertheless, many if not most politicians in Meath played a game of 'imaginary patronage', in ways similar to the case which Sacks presented for Donegal. Local politicians made entreaties to ministers of government or to national or local civil servants to get things for their constituents. Most of these requests went unheeded, and for various reasons. Sometimes the request was unreasonable, was uneconomic, was not under the domain of the government representative solicited, or was illegal. Sometimes the request was ignored because of the rocky personal relationship between civil servant or government minister and the politician, for example, who might be members of different parties, or electoral competitors. At other times the request was received positively and the constituent could get a satisfactory answer or other result. This too may be due to the personal relationship built up over the years between politician and government agent, also sometimes influenced by past political loyalties and relationships (civil servants in Ireland were duty bound to not be partisan in their dealings with all members of the public, but most politicians at the time in Meath were reasonably certain of the political party leanings and past actions of local government employees at all levels of government).

The politicians, once the representations to power-holders were made, in turn suggested to constituents such things as: 'they have done what they could', 'let us wait and see', 'if it did not pan out as we had hoped then somebody must be playing unfair with the politician', or, on some occasions, 'nothing seems to be possible in regard to this matter'. On other occasions, when the request or service was heeded by government or civil servants, some politicians suggested to constituents that it was the politician's intercession which was the cause of the positive result, despite the distinct possibility that the service was in fact received in due course as part of the everyday actions and regular duties of government agents. Thus, party politics played an important role in local government in the late 1970s, wherein the wheels of government and administration could still be greased by the unction of party and governmental politics. In this chapter we examine how some politicians, in positions of authority,

174

sometimes could make a difference in local politics and government in the 1970s and 1980s.

Irish political studies have emphasized national political culture and partisan politics, often concentrating on national elections and party organization. Studies of local politics have looked mainly at machine politics and the informal and personalistic aspects of political patronage and brokerage. Even when such local political studies focused on aspects of national political culture, they tended to analyze party and patron-client electoral mobilization (Garvin 1976; Carty 1981). Largely ignored in these analyses of local politics were many of the formal and informal roles that local politicians played within local government.

Although local government had figured in some political studies, such as in regard to the problems posed by the county manager for county councillors (Chubb 1982: 301-304) or the roles of local government officials in the 'imaginary patronage' of county councillors and TDs (Sacks 1976), more often than not local government was portrayed as a backdrop to the principal drama of local party politics. These local politics, in turn, served as dress rehearsals for elections, or microcosms of a national system of patronage and cronyism. This secondary status assigned to local government and politics was ironic, as the local government system had long also been recognized as providing powerful bases for national political leadership. It was in local government that politicians learned about governmental administration, created political networks, and added to their prestige and status within their parties and their communities.

Over the last sixty years, however, politicians elected to local government bodies have lost much of their elite status and their power and influence. Yet people still have sought political office, in the face of increasing centralization of government and political parties. When elected they were often treated with deference and respect in light of their political position, and they enjoyed advantages in their social, economic and political lives. The position of greatest significance in these ways was that of the elected leader of the county council. If there was any influence and power to be gained in serving in local government then it was clear to me and to my respondents during my field research that it was to be found as chairman of the county council.

The politics of the chair

Because a great deal of local politics revolved around the machinations of competing political brokers, it was surprising that the scholarly literature on local government and politics in Ireland had virtually ignored the position of the chairperson of the county council, a key figure in partisan local and constituency politics. His influence largely derived from his considerable political networks and to his powerful role as spokesperson for the elected members of the county council.[1] This role allowed him both to serve and to compete with his colleagues within his party and in the county council (competing especially with those who either served or hoped to served in the Oireachtas, in either the Dáil or the Seanad). This chapter reviews the role of the chairman of the Meath County Council in local politics and government in the late 1970s, the main reasons why people served in that office, and some changes which reflected the problems that had developed in Meath politics at the time.[2]

The chairman of the Meath county council was elected each year by majority vote of the twenty-nine member-body. The vote was strictly conducted along party lines, in what in Meath was considered to the most politicized event in county council meetings each year. This notion that the election to the chairman of the county council was extraordinarily politicized, a view expressed to me often by both councillors and county officials alike, was ironic, in that most of what was said and done at county council meetings was in my view both political and partisan. It was also indicative of what politicians and civil servants considered to be 'political', i.e., their public display of partisan loyalty in a contest that must be won by one side or the other. Politicians at council meetings went to great lengths to show that their actions were motivated by their sense of civic responsibility, their charge as public servants, and the needs of their constituents. Thus, publicly, they seldom wanted to be seen to be partisan, especially when the press was covering the event or developing a story. But the subtext of all council meetings was how to walk a successful line as an electoral area representative while simultaneously supporting party wishes and policies.

The chairman's first and foremost public duty was to chair all monthly council meetings (he was also an ex-officio member of council sub-committees) which he did from the dais at the end of the main county council meeting room at the council offices in Navan, seat of the county council of Meath. Arranged to either side of him were the county manager, county secretary, assistant county manager, county engineer, and assorted officials and staff officers responsible for the many services that local government provided to the nearly 100,000 residents of Meath. Along the southern wall, at right angles to

177

the dais, the Fianna Fáil members of the council faced their opponents in Fine Gael, who were arranged opposite along the north wall. In the center of the room were the members from the Labour Party and all non-party councillors. They sat at one table and to view some of the proceedings had to look over the heads of members of the press who were seated prominently at a small table just in front of the dais.

The chairman ran each of the formal council meetings by acknowledging all speakers, reminding them of standing orders, and instructing officials of the council to reply to queries or charges that come from the floor. Ideally this function of the chairman was apolitical and was based on council traditions, standing orders and precedents, as well as good manners and common sense. His central role in the public functioning of the council was one of his principal areas of influence and was used to varying degrees of advantage by the chairs (who were observed by me at all of the council monthly meetings from 1977 to 1979).

The chairman's primary responsibility at council meetings was to see that they were conducted in accordance with standing orders and the general standards set by decades of past meetings. The standing orders dictated the order of business, the time and days of the meetings, and the order in which items appeared on the agenda. The chairman's ruling at these meetings was final. His legal responsibilities also included the signing of the minutes of the meetings, after which the minutes served as a full and accurate record of what had transpired at the meeting. The chairman also had the right to cast the deciding vote in all matters where there was a drawn result, except in regard to the election of the chairman. The chairman's full statutory powers, seldom if ever used in Meath, included the power to adjourn council meetings, call special meetings of the council, appoint a deputy council manager if the manager and assistant manager were suddenly incapacitated, and demand that the manager furnish whatever information regarding county government business which was in his possession.

Although it was the command of the council meetings that was his most obvious public function, other functions of the chairman's role also served as the basis for his influence among his political colleagues, the staff of the county council, and Meath overall. It was the chairman's duty to witness the affixing of the seal of the council to all legal documents and he had the right, if not also the duty, to be present at the opening of all business tenders for the awarding of local contracts. His role as protector of the interests of the elected members of the county council, as a quality control over the council's decisions and their implementation, also gave him a role as protector and representative of the people of the entire county; a status no other elected politician in the county, including TDs and Senators, could realistically claim.

The chairman's right to obtain information from the county manager in relation to any aspect of the council's business, if the chairman made a written request for the information, was a potential source of friction between the county manager and the chairman. In fact, in Meath among the councils I observed from 1976 to 1980, the chairmen and the manager had remarkably good and close working relationships, due in part to the managers' strong and effective administration as well as the ability of each chairman to obtain necessary information without resorting to formal requests and demands. During the tenure of the county councils which sat in Meath

179

from 1974 to 1984 there was no 'Section 4', i.e., a council command to the Manager to act in a matter directly related to the legal functions of the council, if the funds are available. In other counties these directives; often in the area of housing planning permissions, seemed to be a regular order of monthly business.

All but a few members of the Council I interviewed, and all of the staff members of the County Council, perceived the Meath record to be a testament to the close and amiable relationship between the Council and the local government staff in general, and between the elected politicians and the manager in particular. The stability of this relationship had a great deal to do with the one man who had served as County Manager from 1976. However, in late 1980s this relationship was strained due to the manager's imposed restrictions on planning permission, especially in regard to the building of residences on the primary national roads and in the areas of Meath adjacent to County Dublin. In fact, in the 1980s the processes of the suburbanization of Meath had begun to change aspects of the political culture of Meath, a topic to which we return in the concluding chapter of this book.

Subsequent events notwithstanding, the close working partnership between the chairman and the manager during the last three terms of the council in the 1970s had resulted in an amiable and cooperative relationship between the manager and the elected members of the council overall. Because the manager consulted his council before discharging his duties, and because he had to discharge these duties in accordance with the council's policies and the law, it was imperative that he keep in regular communication with the chairman. Although the manager was free to contact any councillor directly, and often did so, when something significant was developing anywhere in the county the chairman was kept informed. Thus the chairman's access to vital information made him an enviable and formidable politician who, in turn, was attractive as a political ally to politicians and manager alike.

In the latter case this was especially important when the manager needed council approval of an important proposal or when he needed help in regard to any local issue in one of the county's five electoral areas (CEAs). For his part; the chairman often had first crack at the information regarding the approved, pending or declined provision of such council services as public housing, traffic safety, water supply, sewage schemes, and planning permission for residences and businesses. This first access to key information placed the chairman in a central position in the system of real and imaginary patronage that was at the core of modem Irish political life. His job was clearly seen by politician and constituent alike to be the holder if not the conduit of timely and significant information.

This situation in 1970s Meath local government was to a great extent only a generation old. As we saw in the last chapter, before the County Management Act 1940 the elected members were at the peak of their power and influence. During that time every bit of administration had to go before the council which often met for eight and nine hours and then was forced to apportion much of its business to its many sub-committees. Although many decisions were influenced by the advice of local government officials, council members did not have to follow their recommendations, and often did not. The chairman of the council often acted on his own authority without recourse to his political colleagues or council staff. His power was immense and largely unchecked, and his ability (and some might add, his right) to provide valuable services such as jobs and housing to his constituents was unquestioned. Many Meath residents remembered that time to me with mixed feelings. Although charges that corruption was rampant in the early days of the new Irish state still surfaced during my research, many people also seemed to miss the days when locals had more control over vital services, before the time when an appointed local government officer was in charge.

It was surprising to me at the time of my initial fieldwork that the man who held the chairmanship longest in the history of the Meath county council (nineteen years), Senator Patrick Fitzsimons, did not lament the passing of the old-committee system. A staunch Fianna Fáil supporter, he concluded that it was right to support the national initiative to make local government less corrupt and more efficient, especially as this initiative was launched by the leader and founder of his political party, Eamon de Valera. Fitzsimons also concluded that the county management system took much of the pressure off of councillors, and that the working relationship between chairman and manager that had developed in Meath between the 1940s and the 1970s enabled local government to provide a better overall service to constituents. It did this while simultaneously eroding the influence of the councillors and the chairman in the everyday and in many important affairs of the council.[3] This loss of power and influence continued into the 1980s in Meath, thus calling into question for me what Meath farmers, businessmen, and professionals hoped to achieve when serving as councillors and, if they were ambitious, clever, and lucky as well, as chairman of the council.

The reasons that Irish local and national politicians served in local government have been examined in some depth (Bax 1976; Sacks 1976; Chubb 1982), and these works have emphasized that patronage and clientage were the chief reasons for both entering politics and supporting politicians (Higgins 1982). A number of studies from the time of my fieldwork had begun to temper this view by investigating councillors' satisfaction or dissatisfaction with their jobs, and their own perceptions of their roles in politics, government and society (Zimmermann 1976, 1978; Carey 1986). Local politicians' were also compared to their counterparts in local government in Northern Ireland (Birrell 1983) and England (Collins 1980), to see what part national styles of administration and politics might play in similarities and differences in local politicians' actions.

These studies informed my own research, but in the end I was best guided by what I observed and by what councillors told me. County councillors in Meath clearly served for a great variety of reasons, some of which they would not admit to me until after months, and in some cases, years of interviews or familiarity. These reasons, which were as much ideological as they were about the economics and politics of their jobs, were often shared by members from diverse backgrounds and experience. In fact, most councillors gave very similar reasons to me to explain their willingness to serve as elected representatives, although their reasons as a group seemed to change as my study entered the 1980s.

One thing was clear to me about the members of the three county councils I observed in action: they expected the chairman to be their physical and symbolic representative. Testament to this was the remarkable fact that all of the forty-six councillors whom I interviewed on this subject gave good to excellent reviews to the current and past chairmen. They praised these chairs for their hard work, their political acumen, and the many ways in which they represented the council at public functions.

The aspect of the chairman's job that drew the greatest praise, however, was the chair's actions at monthly council meetings. When questioned about the chairmanship, councillors (whether they had served as chairman or not) turned to the many ways in which the chairman could acknowledge partisans at meetings, be fair or unfair to opponents, direct information to the press, support or confront members of staff on the dais, and limit or expand discussion on topics harmful or useful to individuals or groups present or absent. In fact, it was this attention to the behavior of the chairman which I encountered in early interviews with politicians that led me to focus on the chairman of the council as an institutional broker for his twenty-eight colleagues, and for his party members who were behind the scenes. The more I investigated the chairman's role in the workings of the council the clearer the personal goals of each councilor who held or aspired to the office became to me.

Among the politicians I interviewed in Meath, the most discussed aspects of the chairmanship were the political advantages the job offers to both the individual who holds the office and to his party colleagues. At a personal level the considerable prestige that comes with the post approximates that of TDs and Senators in Meath society. If the stuff of politics at a local level is to acquire the patronage of a local political leader, then who is bigger on the local scene than the county council chairman, who after all has direct access to the county manager? And the proof of the chairman's privileged position was in the weekly Meath newspaper, where there were multiple photos of the chairman attending a wide range of public functions across the county.

Further proof of the chairman's elite status was the frequency of his attendance at all major Meath public and civic events, such as a bridge opening, a school groundbreaking, and welcoming visiting politicians and dignitaries. Photos of these occasions, which figured prominently in the *Meath Chronicle*, almost always included the county council chairman. His photo was not all that mattered in the news stories of these events. His 'statesmanlike' status in Meath made him a principal respondent to questions about county politics and government from the press, who were often chagrined by the relative silence they received from county administrators in the council offices.

Indeed, it seemed to me that the more the chairman of the council had to say on public matters, especially if he was able to express himself with a colorful turn of phrase, then the more he appeared in the *Chronicle*, and the more often he appeared on the front cover! The *Meath Chronicle* was at the time the most widely read weekly newspaper in the county, and anyone who had a regular place within its pages, in photo and in print, had a decided edge in local politics. Thus the chairman's status was both a result of the publicity his office engendered but was also one of great potential for enhancing the image and political reach of the individual politician and his party. As county statesman the chairman was the only elected local politician who had as his right and responsibility to travel throughout Meath representing the council. All other members of the county council only represented their own electoral areas, of which there were five in Meath. And although Meath

TDs also represented the entire Meath constituency at parliament, and four of the five sitting TDs (in 1987) were also MCCs, their attendance at county public functions was often seen as a political maneuver by partisans and opponents alike.

However, in general the future electoral goals of the chairman were considered by the public to be secondary to his role as council leader and representative, a status that considerably enhanced his credibility as an elder politician relatively untainted by the exigencies of local partisan politics. This attitude on the part of the Meath electorate, clear to me whenever the chairman's name or job arose in discussions during my stay in Meath, was always mixed with comments about how clever ('cute') the man was as a politician, but often too the office itself seemed to confer enough prestige to at least make people curtail such comments. As a consequence the local political advantages to the office were immense.

The chairman's status as elected public representative was second only to sitting parliamentarians. The chairmanship had thus come to be seen by local politicians as a substantial base for a campaign for higher office. As publicity was a key political advantage in local politics, the increased publicity that the chairman received in the local media was significant. Moreover, the chairman had prior access to local council information which was vital to his fellow politicians. Because it was his job to know about major decisions or council achievements even before they were announced, the chairman was expected by his partisan and electoral area colleagues to use the information to best political advantage, for them and for their party.

In the brokers' world of imaginary influence, this usually meant sending a letter, making a phone call, or dropping by a constituent's home with the information that the service which had been requested was granted. The chairman, of course, could not physically inform all of the residents of Meath of the decisions made at the council, nor would he want to do this because of the political enemies he would make by not sharing the information and allowing other politicians to gain credit from this circulating imaginary patronage. However, the information at his disposal allowed him to either inform his own electoral area residents before any of his local colleagues, thus adding to his local political support and gaining the clients necessary for party electoral success or for his own future bid for national office. The information at his disposal also enhanced his role as an information broker, whereby he distributed valuable information regarding government services to party members, and sometimes even to party opponents.

At the very least, the public perception that the chairman was privy to more council matters than the other local representatives made him a prime political candidate and a patron/broker worth contacting. The chairman's travels around the county thus enabled him to meet many more potential political clients than he would otherwise have met if he had stayed in his electoral area bailiwick. These travels in fact served as substitute 'clinics', the name most commonly used for the regularly scheduled open-house meetings between elected representatives and their political constituents. The chairman of the council did not need to hold such clinics because his regular activities were seen and heard throughout the county. Overall, this role, which was a rotating one among the parties represented on the council, precluded much intra- and inter-party jealousy, precisely because it was seen to be a perk of the job and a job that would fall in turn to each party.

187

Although, for example, the chairman of the council in the mid-1980s used that office as a base from which to launch a successful campaign to be a TD, few chairmen of the council had been able to move up in politics in recent years. Most, however, had tried to gain nominations or the seats themselves. Of the nine chairmen whom I observed in that office in the late 1970s and early 1980s, all but one had actively campaigned for either the Dáil or Seanad, most of them more than once. Two of them had served in the Seanad, and one in the Dáil. This success rate of one in three was high, however, considering the strong familial and personal networks of many of the sitting TDs during that same period. In fact, the importance of having a seat on the council for national politicians, so well-documented elsewhere (cf. Bax 1976), was clear in Meath. Of the nine TDs who represented Meath from the 1977 general election to 1987, eight had also served as MCCs.

In Meath it was patently clear that the chairmanship of the council gave a candidate a decided edge in local politics, and it is widely held in Ireland that all local politics are national politics. At the very least, even unsuccessful parliamentary aspirants in Meath often ensured success in future local elections after serving as the chairman of the county council. Overall, then, the potential personal political advantages induced many MCCs to set their sights on the chairmanship.

The political advantages to the chairman's party were also many. The information he received and contacts he made at the council were expected to help his party colleagues almost as much as himself. The line between serving one's own political career and those of party members was a fine one, and Irish party politics are famous for their intra-party competition, especially in elections that are run on the single transferable vote system. A chairman relies on his fellow MCCs to act as information brokers too. He is also mindful that with a rotating party chairmanship he cannot afford to make an enemy of someone who may indeed be the next chairman. Thus party members sometimes shared their information across the chamber regarding the provision of services, and in the main did so in ways that were legal, expected, and very much reinforced by other politicians and civil servants. In varying degrees all MCCs relied on the chairman to act as their information broker.

The party also gained politically by having the chairman cast the deciding ballot in a drawn vote at the council, something that seldom occurred in Meath, unlike many other councils that often decided all major matters according to strict party discipline. The MCCs from the three councils whom I interviewed concluded that they were a relatively apolitical body because they often agreed with each other, regardless of party, especially on local electoral area matters. Although it was my view that while in the council meetings they were acting more in a non-partisan way than in an apolitical manner, outside of the council chamber councillors were both political and partisan.

One last political advantage to being chairman of the council should be noted. Because of his status, high profile and information networks, the chairman could play an important role in Seanad elections. Local authority councillors from across Ireland voted for candidates for the five interest panels for the Seanad, thus attracting many candidates to Meath who paid courtesy calls to the chairman, usually in search of advice about which MCCs to approach and how best to do this. In many cases these visitors were themselves MCCs from other counties, people who had met the chairman previously at such venues as conferences, party meetings and sporting events. In fact, most Meath chairs had served for a time as Meath's representative to the General Council of County Councils, a national body that meets in Dublin (and was begun with the help of the founding father of the Meath County Council, John Sweetman).

This role as representative to the General Council of County Councils was an attractive one for an MCC because it paid the expenses of a trip to Dublin and it offered an arena in which to meet influential councillors from around the nation, improving one's own chances for a possible Seanad run. When hosting visitors to Meath the chairman was often asked to put in a good word with local MCCs. In return the chairman built up a network which might someday help to put him in the Seanad.

Thus the chairman, like all MCCs, always wore at least two hats, that of public representative and that of party supporter and member. The reputation one made as a chairman of the county council was also an intra-party one, and it could aid others in their pursuit of the party-dominated elections to the Seanad, a process which one eminent scholar of Irish politics has called 'unnecessarily complicated and not particularly democratic' (Chubb 1982: 212).

Other advantages

The other advantages to being a leading figure in local government, i.e., those material advantages which were not directly political but were important influences in the life of a politician, were sometimes clear but just as often clouded in an

190

air of suspicion, jealousy and conjecture, a murkiness made thicker through the embellishments of political history, myth and prejudice. One conclusion that I reached when I conducted my field research was that none of the chairmen of the Meath council over the last political generation had used their office illegally and certainly none had made any noticeable financial fortune through the exercise of their duties. That some local politicians had been able to use information at their disposal or their status within the community to gain a business advantage was often charged but difficult to judge and more difficult to prove.

After all, it was often the more successful farmers, professionals and businessmen who had the time and the capital to serve as elected local politicians, which was an unpaid and part-time calling. However, if there were considerable social and economic advantages to being a MCC and perhaps even the chairman of the council, and I concluded that there were, these advantages were also part of intricate networks of obligations and pressures that might be seen, and frequently were seen by local politicians, as disincentives to taking on the job of public servant.

County councillors were not paid a salary or wage, and their voluntary service incurred many personal expenses. To compensate them for their time away from home and business and to pay their travel expenses when attending required meetings of the council they were paid £10.45 per meeting plus 53P/mi. travel costs (1986 rates), if they lived outside the community where the meeting was held, which in Meath was usually Navan. If a councillor resided in the location of a council meeting or other function then the expenses compensation was £15.40 per meeting. This was not a large sum when one considers that the regular monthly council meeting lasted from 2 p.m. to 5 or 5:30 pm. and that many councillors had a 30 to 45 minute drive-time to and from Navan. The cost of petrol alone was a sizable expense. Still, some Meath councillors were renowned for their clever use of existing transport facilities in order to make their expense money go farther. One long-standing member of the Meath council had been appointed for years to a number of the council's committees. His appointments reflected his years of service, political acumen, constituency work, sincerity, and his many contacts in the sports and farming worlds. But he was also justly famous for hitching rides with fellow councillors or neighbors to all council meetings (and, as some of his colleagues were quick to point out, never paying a penny for expenses), thereby putting his expense money right into pocket (app. £28 per monthly council meeting).

A number of councillors also occasionally attended more than one meeting on one day. If both meetings were in Navan, the expenses might be doubled regardless of whether the councillors returned home for dinner or not. Although these were rare occasions, an MCC could collect £30 to £60 for such double service. It was also tax free. All of this was quite legal, however, and not enough to provide a councillor with much more than it was intended: to pay for petrol, automobile depreciation, food, and time away from other, potentially more lucrative, activities.

Nonetheless, nationwide abuses of the local government system in Ireland had not escaped the attention of either the general public or the press in Meath. But as one leading Meath local government official concluded, in an interview with me in 1979, ninety-nine per cent of the allegations were either false or

192

a reflection of left-over Victorian ideas that demanded that public representatives should not be paid. In his words, the Irish citizenry 'want the council to operate in business-like fashion, but once the council did it was criticized for it.' He used the example of government ministers' cars: most constituents think it right and proper for government leaders to have all the prestigious trappings of office that any advanced Western democracy should have, but then the public turned around and criticized those same politicians for *driving* anywhere in the cars, especially when doing the very same work in their constituencies which made them minister material in the first place. As another official in Meath told me years ago, such reasoning was not confined to the Irish citizenry, but seems to seep into both the media and academia as well.[4]

The media were often critical of the system of public official expenses. John Kelly in the *Sunday Press* (2 March 1986) reported that Dublin Corporation councillors made as much as £160 a week in expenses. This was achieved by councillors who served on a number of standing committees. Kelly also pointed out the sharp rise in such expenses throughout the nation (in Sligo alone councillors' expenses increased by 176% in two years). He concluded that the rise was due to inflation and the increase in the number of council committees everywhere in the nation (ironically, these committees were often set up to deal with the added paperwork created by so many other new councillor committees). These criticisms stimulated an exchange in the *Sunday Press* when an anonymous civil servant indicated the many other ways politicians could make a profit out of their public service. Besides the creation of extra sub-committees, he charged that many MCCs called for 'deputations' being sent to the Minister in Dublin, which when sent were deemed to be council business, while other local politicians were quick to attend conferences, often for very slim or transparent reasons. Some councillors who were also TDs or Senators could claim double expenses by putting in requests to two different government ministries. At other times councillors might adjourn meetings early in order to meet again, at a later date and with added expenses paid, or, taking the opposite strategy, they might extend discussions, to a point where they might take advantage of overnight subsistence allowances to stay in Dublin or at a conference. For example, he noted that a councillor from Cork or Mayo could collect over £200 for a 24-hour trip to Dublin (Cynical Public Servant 1986).

The chairman of the Meath County Council at the time, Noel Dempsey, who also served as Secretary of the Local Authority Members Association, replied to this attack. His letter (Dempsey 1986) highlighted many of the gaps or weaknesses in the earlier articles and how exceptional Dublin was. In his view, committees were established in order to facilitate policy decision-making and were more efficient precisely because of their small membership. Moreover, he asserted that public representatives had the right and responsibility to be well-informed, and deputations to Dublin would not be needed if Irish government was more decentralized. He went on to charge that public transport was so inefficient that rural councillors had to use private means, and graft and corruption by 'double-jobbers' were not the rule.

Although some questions still remained after this exchange, it served to highlight the comments of the Meath official quoted above. Some people believed councillors could not be trusted to claim their just expenses, while others questioned why elected officials should receive any compensation at all. This became even more ironic when, as Dempsey pointed out, MCCs, unlike TDs or Senators, must pay all of their own postage and telephone bills. And the more successful one was as a politician the more bills one had. Was it dishonest if three councilors from the same electoral area drove to a meeting together and all received their expense money? If the Meath MCC mentioned above was 'cute' enough to arrange lifts for forty years, or hardy enough to bicycle to Navan whenever needed, was he not owed his expense entitlement? Perhaps a look at the ways that the chairman of the county council plays his role in this complicated arena will help illustrate the ambiguities inherent in a situation in which a councillor seldom gained either sympathy or sizable income.

The county council was considered by many people in Meath to be a group of representatives little interested in the big 'junkets' that have been a cause for concern throughout the local authorities of the nation. Although it would be expected that the chairman be given first opportunity to represent the county council at national and international meetings, the opportunity to do so could be only one, relatively minor, attraction of the job. In the long run the most money a chairman can make in a predictable and legal way was through attendance at regular council and committee meetings. However, as must be clear given the nature of his political duties and expectations, the chairman had the potential to make the most money in subsistence and expenses of all the councilors on the council. It was also expected by both his own majority party or fellow coalition members that he be put on most of the senior committees of the council, including the North-Eastern Health Board, Meath Local Health Committee,

Vocational Education Committee, the old County Committee of Agriculture, and the Library Advisory Committee. The chairman's opportunity to sit on these bodies depended on his occupation (for example, it was rare to see the same MCC sit on both the VEC and Committee of Agriculture), his interests, and the favors owed to other councillors in the party. Because the chairmanship was itself a reward for service and recognition of talent, Meath councillors found it inconsistent to not have the chairman appointed to most of the 'prime' committees, i.e. ones that dealt with the problems which were most important to their constituents (especially health-related matters) and which were covered by the press. Thus, the chairman of the council had the responsibility to attend often at the council chambers.

Although the regularity with which a chairman attended to his duties in Navan would be all but impossible to determine, as would how much he was paid in subsistence and expenses, I was able to estimate the number of times a chairman *should* attend meetings, depending on the committees he was on. This estimate was only a minimum figure, however, because the chairman was often called into Navan to witness or review council business. Five of the last nine chairmen estimated to me in interviews that they were at the County Council offices twice a week for eleven months of the year. A look at the committee duties alone of a long-serving chairman made clear to me the demands on his time. Patrick Fullam, from Drogheda, was chairman in 1977-1978. At that time he was a member of the North-Eastern Health Board, the Local Health Committee, the Committee of Agriculture, and the Library Committee. He also represented Meath at the General Council of County Councils. Because each of the Meath committees meets once a month (except in August) Fullam had to attend 55 times in Navan, including the monthly county council meeting. Although he may also have had to attend other committees, and most certainly was required to travel from his home in east Meath in order to deal with council paperwork, his frequent attendance at Navan meetings was similar to the activities of other chairs over the course of the three Meath county councils I witnessed during my field research in the 1970s and 1980s. If the chairman met with committees fifty-five times in Navan, and had a journey of fifteen miles, his expenses and stipend would total approximately £1485 per year (based on an allowance of £10.45 subsistence and 53p per mile).[5] This sum would not include attendance at Dublin-based committee meetings or any electoral area meetings, which were also liens on the official's time and money. Here I use the number of fifty-five Navan meetings because chairmen in the past have certainly been required to attend that number.

One thing was clear to me in all of this discussion of Meath politicians and the economics of their roles as elected representatives. Travel expenses were certainly covered for local representatives, but the sums they received must be weighed against their postage, phone and petrol expenditures. In the end the two figures could never be balanced with each other, or with the time politicians were away from family and business. Noel Dempsey, TD and Chairman of the Meath County Council in 1986-87, estimated his phone, postage, travel and miscellaneous expenses for three months, from September to November, 1986, at £2174. He was reimbursed £541 by the Meath council for the same period (personal communication).

Despite this pressure on them, and perhaps partly due to the ways that reimbursements and other perks might be enhanced through careful manipulation of travel and schedule, the number of committees on which Meath MCCs might sit seemed to grow over the time I observed council activities. This was due to changes in local government and to other forces external to the county. In 1987, for example, there were no less than twenty-one statutory, non-statutory and national committees in Meath on which councillors served, ranging from one representative on such bodies as the Eastern Regional Tourism Organisation and the Irish Public Bodies Mutual Insurances, to fifteen on the Local Health Committee. In 1986 these committees met at least 120 times, a number which did not include the regular monthly meetings of the council (eleven per year) or the new electoral area meetings (four per year), the latter at which much of the basic constituency work was then done due to the absence of the press and therefore without the need to stand up and be quoted on all major issues.

Thus, in 1987, councillors, and especially the chairman, had the opportunity to serve their electorate in many ways and in many political and governmental forums. In doing so, it was possible to more than cover one's initial role-related expenses, but even sums of over £1500 tax-free could not make a wealthy man of a councillor who had to spend so much of his own time and money in public service.

Another possible economic advantage of service as councillor and chairman was the benefits that might accrue to one's business. Certainly the greater one's status as a politician the likelier it was that he would attract more political clients who, in turn, might also bring their custom. The 'gombeen' aspects of local politics have been covered in depth elsewhere

198

(cf. M. D. Higgins as quoted in O'Leary 1981) and they have certainly been well represented in Meath's political past. I was often reminded of cases where the chairman of the council who was a publican kept clients waiting in the bar before seeing them. When doing research with publican councillors in the town or country village I often observed customers ordering a pint while waiting to speak to their representative. But in my experience in Meath any charges of usury or of custom in exchange for favors were rare, and often referred to the years before the County Manager system. Obviously, Meath politicians acted as patrons and brokers in order to get votes, but how far that spilled over into unethical or illegal behavior was difficult if not impossible to determine. Rumors about businessmen-politicians acquiring valuable information before the public were aware of it, and thus giving an important advantage to the politician in his business, persisted.

I observed all nine of the chairmen of the council who collectively served in that role over a decade and none had, to my knowledge, added substantially to their land or business holdings, or had markedly improved their standard of living. In fact, some had clearly neglected their businesses or occupations and had to hire more staff (for example, by adding an extra chemist to the chairman's pharmacy) or had to rely increasingly on family (for example, in agricultural contracting) to keep their businesses functioning. Others were only able to serve because they were retired or had employers who gave them the time off. Clearly, chairmen of the county council did not serve for the money or the wealth.

Changes in the role of the Chairman

The chairmen of the Meath county council over the period I observed them seemed to serve their communities out of a sense of duty and in the spirit of good citizenship. However, political service also functioned as a leisure-time activity among politicians. Most councillors were members of the middle class who eschewed such other pastimes as sports, theatre, travel and other leisure activities. Most of their perceptions about their own roles as MCCs and chairman of the council included many of the perceptions voiced by councillors in other parts of the country. They were, alternatively and sometimes simultaneously, ombudsman, information broker, patron and local policy-maker. These political leaders, like their colleagues in the three councils whom I interviewed, were distressed at the changes that had taken place in local government in general and in their roles in particular.

The chairman had lost status and power commensurate with the council's losses at the hands of state centralization and the removal of a local authority's right to raise most of its own funds. This latter attack on local government power dated from Fianna Fáil's 1978 decision to take domestic rates (property taxes) liability off of the taxpayer and transfer it to the central government. At the same time, to prevent local authorities charging the central government for too high a rate of tax to pay for local services, the government set a limit on how much of an increase in local rates could be requested by local government bodies. The result in Meath was twofold. First, councillors resented their almost complete dependence on Dublin for the funds to provide local services as well as their obvious loss of prestige. Second, from 1979 councillors had increased their demands for spending by the central

200

government precisely because many local government costs were not passed on directly to their constituents, but remained the domain of local authorities to provide and budget.

The chairman, also a leading party man, was caught between the councillors and the government, a situation that was especially awkward when the government party was his own. In regard to local services and policies, the chairman had to do what was feasible according to the county manager, what was fundable according to the state, and what was necessary for his constituents according to his peers. Clearly the powerful days of the era before the County Management Act 1940 were long gone, but the changes that had occurred to the chairman's influence since the 1970s were just as important as those of 1940. The chairman was increasingly a mediator for his fellow politicians. He was someone who was perceived to make decisions and to get things done, but, in fact, he passed on requests or information about decisions made by others.

The Meath chairman was in a position where he had to listen to the county manager and the Minister for the Environment about matters over which he and his colleagues would like to be seen as having some control. Such things as planning permission, health benefits, and development plans depended on much of the information that councillors supplied to local government officers, but depended much less on anything else the politicians could do. Thus the chairman, as symbol of the council, suffered in reputation because councillors were perceived by constituents as 'messenger-boys'.

To counteract this loss of real political influence and power, in the years I observed the council, chairmen had increasingly adopted an attitude of wanting to be seen to be

201

doing a good job, and did much to gain the publicity needed to create that image. Because they could no longer act as patrons who could supply goods and services directly to their clients, and because their role as information broker had been curtailed by the loss of most of their power as a council, the councillors had turned to the image of the patron as the yardstick by which they were judged to be efficacious. Just as in the day to day constituency work, which is itself about the sending of information up the line and its retrieval from actual decision makers, which also falsely suggested that the councillor was in some way responsible for the positive outcome (he would rarely take the blame for a negative result), councillors depended on their image in the press for their reputation and electoral support. Perhaps most important, however, the chairman of the county council played a pivotal role in the relationship between press and politician, and he played that role at the monthly council meeting.

Representatives from the three local newspapers sat in the middle of every county council meeting. The meetings began precisely at 2 p.m., the first Monday of every month except August. From the beginning of the meeting the chairman controlled the pace at which the council went through the agenda (although the agenda was set by the county manager and his staff). The speed and ordering of the agenda were of principal importance to the councilors because they needed and wanted to comment, debate and introduce related or new business. There were seldom matters for discussion that all the members could not predict before the meeting, but it was only the chairman who could facilitate or obstruct a councillor's participation in such discussion and debate, and of course the opportunity to be quoted in the media.

202

The chairman set the pace of discussion and the nature of the political debate and rhetoric in many ways. He could simply allow a discussion to continue so that all councillors were able to participate, or he could allow councillors to extend a discussion in order to stretch the meeting, preventing the council from addressing a later agenda item before the press left precisely at 5 p.m. In this manner the chairman acted in league with his party colleagues with whom he conferred before the meeting in order to find out the issues they wanted to raise and the ones they wanted to curtail or to avoid altogether. For example, in Meath at the time Fianna Fáil actually had a formal meeting of its councillors before 2 p.m. The issues that would enhance the position of opposition parties were obvious choices for curtailment or avoidance.

The chairman also had the power to acknowledge councillors in the order that he saw them raise their hand. This was a valuable tool because of its subjectivity. Who could judge accurately whom the chairman saw raise a hand first? In some cases the chairman had agreed privately beforehand to acknowledge party colleagues, electoral area colleagues, or others first or early, giving them an opportunity to state a position on a matter after which other councilors would find themselves in the less attractive role of just agreeing or supporting. All the councillors were aware that the local journalists did not copy down everything that was said, but, rather, concentrated on the cleverly worded comment, criticism and question, or the first few comments when the councillors generally agreed about a topic.

The order in which councillors were acknowledged by the chairman thus allowed the first to their feet to make the statements that in all likelihood would be quoted in the subsequent issues of the papers. This was almost a certainty given the familiarity and repetitiveness of the phrases used in this traditional and stylized political forum. The political value of having your name listed as someone who seconds a motion was negligible when compared with the dramatic phrase that would be highlighted on the front page of the *Meath Chronicle*, maybe even in a headline. The chairman made both friends and enemies through the seemingly reactive position of calling on councillors with the press in attendance. In fact, the presence of the press made the meeting more of an exercise in rhetoric and posturing than it did an actual exchange of ideas or analysis of issues. Not surprisingly, the chairman was often quoted because of the summary statements he made after long-winded or heated arrays of speakers. One thing was patently clear in regard to the press and the councillors - after 5 p.m. few councillors made the dramatic pronouncements that were so popular with journalists, and the agenda was dealt with rapidly and efficiently, although many councillors' pet projects were tabled until the following month's meeting when the press would again serve as witnesses and chroniclers .

Because of his key position the chairman was often approached for comment by the press before and after meetings. This gave the chairman an extra electoral advantage because it all but ensured his continued publicity in the papers. Most local news stories did not identify when and where local politicians made their pronouncements, and they sometimes included quotes from politicians from the day after the event in question. This was often a product of the journalist's faulty notes or his subsequent realization that he did not appreciate the significance of the events when the journalist attended the earlier meeting. The chairman thus became a prime informant for the press. The more descriptive and illustrative he was in his perspective on the issues and on the meeting then the greater his chances that his words, his name, and his photo would appear in the next issue of the paper.

As we saw above, publicity had become an integral element in the councillors' job, and the role of chairman brought with it the opportunity, more than any other councillor except those who were also TDs, to gain more publicity and to build better public relations. And although a good reputation was always necessary for re-election in Meath politics, all the councillors I interviewed agreed that their media image had become as important as, and some felt more important, than their constituency work, at least when it came to political reputation and image. The chairman's job thus had great publicity potential, which reinforced its worth politically. The chairman's valuable political role became apparent when the county council members began to rotate the chairman's job each year.

Before 1975, no elected chairman of the council had served just one year (although two had done split terms). From 1975 on, however, each of the majority parties had agreed to share the job of chairman among its members. Changing the chairman each year began under a coalition majority, i.e., a union of Fine Gael and Labour parties with independents on the Meath Council which reflected coalitions at the national level. Each year from 1976 to 1984 the nomination of a new chairman by the coalition members was a way of keeping their majority in the council. If Labour and non-party members were not offered the chairmanship for a year, they could pull out of the coalition and give the party majority to Fianna Fáil. Thus the chairman became part of a political compromise. The people chosen to be chairman were selected because of their years of service, their political skills, their personal characteristics, and their own perceived need to gain the publicity necessary to add to their chances at the next local elections (in 1979 and 1985). But when Fianna Fáil gained the council majority in 1985 they, surprisingly, continued the practice of changing chairmen each year.

The reasons for this were many. The party members acknowledged the value of the chairman's job in gaining publicity (important for at least one councillor running for his first Dáil seat) and in honoring past service (the 1985 chairman had been a Senator without ever being the chairman of the council, despite years of service). Sharing the post among five councillors (the next local election was scheduled for 1990) also reflected the lack of central leadership in the county's party, after a generation where Navan party members dominated. As one Navan councillor told me, in Meath at the time 'there was no big strong man, and rotating the chairman will keep it that way'. By sharing the wealth, so to speak, intra-party competitions ensured that no one councillor would pull ahead of others in terms of national prominence. By selecting chairmen from each of the electoral areas the party also hoped to bolster its support in future general and local elections.

The personal and partisan political values of being chairman of the county council surpassed all others in local government, but the politics of local government had changed so profoundly over the preceding generation that being chairman in the 1970s and 1980s entailed many changing rights, duties and responsibilities. Local politics depended more on image and public relations than on supplying goods and services to constituents. Politicians had become commodity

206

middle-men, with information being their principal commodity. The majority of a chairman's activities reflected this new emphasis on being seen to be doing a job which in fact politicians no longer could do. The power to provide for voters' needs was in the hands of county officials and the central government. And with the loss of control of local finances, which began in 1978, councillors perceived themselves to be hamstrung.

The chairman, of course, continued to serve a valuable statutory role by chairing meetings and witnessing council proceedings, but his political role had become one of information broker for his fellow councillors, and perhaps a bigger information broker than he could ever have been if he were not the chairman. The chairman clung to the mantle of 'county statesman' but, in fact, his election was increasingly just one of the party spoils distributed among partisans as rewards and incentives. Although the job still carried considerable prestige and influence, it was slowly being reduced to one which was principally used to get more publicity and prestige for its holder and his party members. The days of using the chairmanship to decidedly improve one's own or one's supporters' economic well-being were over. The only way a politician could utilize the job to help himself and his friends was through the manipulation of information and the proper manipulation of others with information.

The revolving chairmanship signaled both the relative powerlessness of the post as well as the demise of machine politics, long an aspect of Fianna Fáil in Meath. Power had become centered in the bureaucracy, the parliamentary party leadership, and the administration and government, locally and nationally. This changed domain of local government and politics highlighted to me the need to better understand the relationships between and among public servants and politicians at all levels of administration and government. In the case of Meath, the chairman owed his influence as much to the press as to the county officials, but he continued to act as if it devolved from his office and the activities of the elected members. This contradiction did not bode well for representative local government wherein councillors could both make and implement their decisions. In Meath at the time the 'statesman' of the county had become as imaginary a role as most others in local politics. It was, however, good press. So too were other matters related to the changing political culture of national and local politics and government, among them the changing roles of farmers in politics.

Notes

1. In this chapter I use male pronouns in reference to the chairman of the county council because up to the early 1980s there had never been a female chairman of the county council, but there has been since.

2. Meath County Council is the primary unit of Local Government in County Meath. The Council was established in 1899 following the enactment of the 1898 Local Government (Ireland) Act. Local Government was given constitutional recognition in 1999. There are twenty-nine members on the Council. Members are directly elected by the system of proportional representation by means of the single transferable vote. Meath County Council is one of the County's major employers, currently employing over 700 staff.

3. This section of the chapter owes much to an extended interview I conducted over a few days with Senator Patrick Fitzsimons in October 1979.

4. During the interviews I conducted with public servants, i.e., non-elected local authority employees and civil servants in Meath and elsewhere in Ireland, my respondents were candid and forthright in their analyses of Irish local and national politics but all asked that their comments be shared with others in a discreet way because of the nature of their jobs. None wished to be quoted because of the possible impact on them. The two Meath officials I quote here were, in my experience, reflecting views held by the overwhelming majority of local government officials and elected members that I interviewed and observed.

5. The expense figures I am using are based on 1986 rates and the mileage I have chosen is arbitrary and is not intended to indicate any particular councillor.

Chapter 6

Farmers, Tax and the Transformation of Irish Politics

One of the reasons why farmers in Ireland have traditionally supported the country's two major political parties was to influence governments who made national farm policy. However, Ireland's entry into the European Economic Community in 1973 shifted the locus of much of agricultural policy-making to the continent and greatly changed the ability of Irish politicians to control the provision of certain goods and services to their constituents. The large farmers of County Meath were quick to see that their economic livelihoods demanded a redefinition of their political roles. The national tax dispute of 1979 established a pattern in Irish politics in which Irish commercial farmers eschewed many of their former political roles and joined ranks within the increasingly powerful national farmers' organization, the Irish Farmers' Association, in order to affect national and international agricultural and tax policy decisions. This chapter offers an assessment of this Irish case as an example of an international phenomenon. On the one hand, it describes some of the forces at work that have eroded the material bases of a decreasing population of family farmers. On the other hand it chronicles some farmers' efforts to influence policy determination by a government that had once accorded farmers more favored status.

Within the Irish context, and in regard to local political change in Meath, this chapter also examines the effects that Ireland's membership in the EEC had on the relationship between farmers and politicians in eastern Ireland. It shows how there was a major weakening of clientelist party politics within the agricultural community of County Meath, due in part to the changes in the business of commercial family farming which followed Irish accession to the EEC. The new relationship between farmers and politicians became apparent at both the local and national levels when in February 1979 the Irish government proposed modifications in the national tax laws in order to include more farmers in the tax net. The resulting confrontation between the farmers and the government transformed the nature of agricultural politics in Ireland as a whole, but also illuminated how local politics and government had been transformed, into new relationships of policy making and political power which undermined the more traditional bases of local politics and government in Meath.

Accession and Europeanization

Ireland's accession to the Common Market on 1 January 1973 marked a turning point in Irish history. Membership in the EEC opened a network of political, economic, social and cultural ties that have altered Irish society in ways that were both predicted and welcomed and in ways that were unexpected. The international arena within which Ireland became so firmly placed helped to change much that mattered in the daily lives of farmers. Membership in the EEC raised the standard of living, made Irish industry the most productive in its history to that date, shifted the bulk of Irish exports to the continent, rearranged national political loyalties, affiliations and networks, and diminished many British cultural influences while seeing growth in things European. These latter processes, regarding changes in attitudes, loyalties, networks and other forms of culture, are part of what has been called Europeanization,

212

where Ireland and Europe have slowly but surely changed each other in what can be seen as a feedback situation. They have done this for centuries, but with perhaps greater intensity and effect since 1973 and EEC membership (for some perspectives on this important relationship, see McCall and Wilson 2010).

The initial EEC years also had negative effects on Ireland and its people, due to increased prices, a rise in unemployment, high inflation rates and the increasing demand to understand and adapt to political and economic affairs outside of the country and beyond Ireland and Britain. The citizens perhaps most influenced by such changes were farmers, who responded to processes of Europeanization in ways that radically altered their roles in Irish society and polity, making the 1970s a landmark decade in the agropolitical history of the Irish state.

Within the Irish agricultural community the people whose wealth increased most markedly since 1973 were the large farmers. As discussed in previous chapters, the county in Ireland most associated with large farms was Meath. In this century Meath has been the county with the greatest number of cattle, the most fertile land, the largest farms and the richest farmers. In the 1970s Meath, in an area of 577,000 acres, had 5,000 farmers (out of a population of 100,000) and the highest ratio of land devoted to agriculture in the Republic of Ireland (95% of its land was devoted to tillage and grass) (Central Statistics Office 1982). In Meath, famous for both its large landholdings and the people who own them, a large farm was reckoned to be 200 acres or more. Fully one sixth of full-time farmers in Meath in the late 1970s had farm holdings of that size. To the small farmers of Ireland, holdings of this size often represented both a fortune and an unattainable goal.

Meath's reputation as a beef-producing county was due to its role as the terminus of Ireland's internal cattle trade, a role it had played since the eighteenth century (Freeman 1972). Traditionally calves born in the west of Ireland were sold to farms in the midlands as store cattle, which in turn were sold at two years of age to farms in the east where they were fattened for national consumption or export (Gillmor 1977). Meath's farmers had long been suppliers of this fattened beef to both Dublin and Britain, and in recent years had sold cattle and beef products throughout the EEC. Although Meath farms were known nationwide as beef farms, after 1973 many of the largest had turned to dairying and most farms grew combinations of cereal, root and clover crops

Meath large farms were mostly owner-occupied and had been commercial enterprises throughout the century. From 1973 on, however, many small farms in Meath had also become going commercial concerns due primarily to the benefits offered by the EEC Common Agricultural Policy. Strong farmers particularly profited in the first five years of the EEC because of higher prices, guaranteed markets, and available grants and credit, but they had already been established members of the rural middle class for quite some time. These large farmers functioned as an elite in a number of ways: they owned and rented the best agricultural land, they controlled the cattle trade, they served as merchants and cattle agents (often setting up family members in village businesses, such as shops and pubs), they established agricultural co-operatives and livestock marts, they helped form and lead farmers' organizations, and they controlled the elected council in local government for most of this century. This elite status began to decline, however, when Meath became part of the EEC. To understand this, a brief reminder of large farmers' role in local politics in Meath is on order.

Farmers in local politics

Most formal political influence and power wielded by Meath large farmers has been within the two major Irish political parties, Fianna Fáil and Fine Gael, and within the local government system, principally in the county council. Party organizations and government at the county levels had given local representatives both national prominence and local power. The large farmers of Meath had consistently used their base in local politics as a springboard from which to both launch their own political careers and to make demands of national policy-makers in Dublin, especially in regard to agricultural and social policy. These farmers held power in the local political system through the manipulation of many informal and non-institutional means, including their mobilization of kin and business networks for the electoral support of party and politician, their financial backing for neighbors and party patrons, their leadership in fraternal, occupational and religious organizations (such as the Irish Creamery Milk Suppliers Association and the Knights of St. Columbanus), and their control of the scarce resources of land, cattle and milk in local markets.

In the past, in order to maintain this influence, Meath farmers often served in local government. This meant that they had to serve as patrons to clients and to act as the key mediators between their constituents and local and national civil servants and policy-makers. In essence, in order to keep their preeminent position in local politics and society, they had to

215

gain and keep political party and electoral support. They did this through the supplying of jobs, acquiring government grants, arranging cattle sales, and getting telephones and stop signs installed.

As we saw above, Meath farmers elected to the local government were at their most powerful in the 1930s when government services were provided through the organs of local government and when civil servants often took orders from the county councillors. Since the 1940s, however, all executive functions had been slowly taken away from the elected members, and councillors had increasingly been constrained in their efforts to influence either national or local government policy. For two generations councillors had seen a steady loss of power to both the parliamentary parties and to the state bureaucracy. By the 1970s Meath councillors claimed they performed services that they did not. Their role had become one of a broker only, one who channeled information up and down and who could no longer be a patron in control of governmental goods and services.

The rapid exodus of farmers out of local government in the 1970s was testament to their perception of its increasing powerlessness. In the 1930s 75% of the county council was farmers, and from the 1940s to the 1970s their percentage never fell below 55. In the three councils elected from 1974 to 1985, however, farmers went from 38% to 17% of the twenty-nine elected members (the lowest figure in history). The loss of financial power, greater state control of local government, the elimination of local patronage, the rise of workers and professionals in local politics, and the steady decline in Meath's farm population all combined to lower farmer participation in local government. And while over the years the majority of farmers elected to local office had been strong farmers principally because they possessed what their 'smaller' neighbors did not, namely the wealth, networks, and freedom to leave their businesses for many hours at a time, this freedom of movement and access was no longer enough to warrant the effort to be a politician. Other changes in Irish life had also given big farmers the wherewithal to achieve political ends by other means. The introduction of the EEC made the 1970s a time of great change both in the business of farming and in the politics of farming.

Accession to the EEC greatly improved the agricultural economy. Between 1970 and 1978, the volume of gross agricultural output increased by 35%. The decade ending in 1979 saw the per capita money incomes of Irish farmers increase by over 400%, which in real terms meant that farmers more than doubled their income. In the first five years of membership alone agricultural prices tripled, while per capita payments to Ireland from the Community farm funds were higher than for any other member country. In fact, CAP policies up to 1978 increased the Irish GNP by as much as 15% over what it would had been, during a period when the volume of Irish GNP increased by 38% (between 1970 and 1978). In 1979 EEC expenditure on agriculture in Ireland was the equivalent of £415 million, while state expenditure on agriculture was only £158 million. In 1976 alone, at the start of my research, there was an increase of 400% in EEC expenditure in Ireland, with a corresponding 25% increase in state expenditure (Department of Agriculture-Ireland 1978; Sheehy 1978, 1980, 1984; Cox and Kearney 1983; Duchêne et al. 1985).

In Meath the effects were transformative. Guaranteed prices, incentives for increased production, the expansion of state and private credit, and the proximity to a rapidly growing Dublin market established most Meath farms, regardless of size, as viable money-making concerns. Overall, Meath society boomed with the advent of foreign manufacturing and service industries seeking access to the EEC market. Housing became an issue in rural and urban Meath due to the influx of money, the expansion of suburban Dublin across the county border, and the coming of international mining with the opening, in Navan, of the largest lead and zinc mine in Europe. The availability of funds inflated the price of land, further adding to the wealth of established commercial farmers. An acre of prime farm land that had sold previously for less than £1,000 in 1975 was worth £3,000 (approximately $6,000) in 1978. Many farmers quickly used their new capital base to borrow funds for business expansion, in order to change their farm enterprise, mechanization, or type of agricultural production. Farmers also used their new wealth to change or expand their types and rate of consumption. Overall, Meath farmers experienced an unprecedented rise in their standard of living. Money seemed to be everywhere in rural Meath, and much of that money flowed to and from the farmers.

Because most of their capital was invested, however, the energy crisis in 1979 hit these farmers hard. By the end of the year, banks began cutting back on credit because of changes in the CAP and the declines in agricultural prices and European market demand. Irish agricultural production fell by 3.5% between 1978 and 1981. The price of land also fell, bottoming out at the mid-1970s prices. In 1983 the EEC added to farmers' problems by announcing their intention to curb agricultural production in order to drain the European milk 'lake' and to cut down the butter 'mountain.' This was especially distressing to those Meath farmers who had taken advantage of the available credit to transform their beef farms into intensive dairying farms (Duchêne et al. 1985).

This great and rapid change in the fortunes of Irish farmers notwithstanding, agriculture remained the healthiest sector of a depressed Irish economy, due still to the CAP. In the 1980s, however, even the CAP was under threat because of European-wide dairy overproduction, the member nations' disputes over payments to the EEC, the wrangling among member states over revenue collection for the CAP and the Regional and Social Funds, and the problems associated with integration of the newest EEC members, Spain and Portugal. These threats were largely out of Ireland's control due to the nature of policy-making at the Community level. This was a process which Ireland had been notoriously poor at influencing (Shanahan 1981; Bums and Salmon 1977), but one which they would learn to affect in the decades that followed. At the time, however, Irish agricultural policy was principally decided by the diplomats and governments of the twelve member states of the EEC, a group in which Irish diplomats had to negotiate to best represent the interests of their nation and farmers.

Thus, beginning in 1979, Meath's firmly established commercial family farmers faced economic pressures that threatened the high profits and standard of living to which they had become accustomed over the previous five years. Large farmers, who for three generations as leaders and members of their respective political parties had organized local politics as a way to influence national rural policy, found their influence in county politics waning. This was doubly serious because it had become clear that *national* politics could no longer control the policies so vital to agriculture. They had to both adapt to a change in their political status in Meath and to the changes faced by their occupation in the national and international political arenas. This changed situation was clarified for government, farmers and many other groups in Irish society alike in February 1979.

The government strikes back

The sharp rise in the income and standard of living of farmers, and the perceived dip in same among workers in urban settings, soon became a national political issue. The party in power, Fianna Fáil, estimated that in 1979 Irish farmers would pay a total of £52 million in income and real estate tax, or 5.5% of farm income. This represented an increase from 1978 of 1 % of farm income, while government subsidies for agriculture had increased significantly in the same period. In fact, combined aid to Irish agriculture from both national and EEC sources was estimated at a minimum of £545 million. The government concluded that it could no longer treat agriculture as an underdeveloped sector of the Irish economy and that farmers should pay a more equitable share of the state's expenses. The government was determined to see this happen. The government was also under considerable pressure from the wage earners of the country, as expressed through unions, the media, and political party channels, who felt it was they who were subsidizing agriculture. In 1978 alone, employees in Ireland paid about £526 million in income tax, representing 16% of their earnings (Government Information Service 1979).

As a result of these quick and radical changes in the balance of economic sectors in Ireland, on 7 February 1979 the Irish government's Budget Proposal for that year called for a widening of the income tax net to include 6,000 more full-time farmers. While this was a move considered inevitable by many farmers throughout the country, just as many farmers were unpleasantly surprised by the second, unprecedented, proposal of the government. Ostensibly to pay for the costs of education, research and advisory services, the government announced a 2% levy on the sale of all cattle, milk, pigs, sheep, sugar beets, and cereals, to be paid at the point of sale. The government estimated that this levy, which would go into effect on 1 May 1979 for cattle and milk and 1 August 1979 for the remaining products, would raise approximately £16 million in the financial year.

The farmers of Meath were outraged, and immediately opposed this levy on many grounds. They argued that the government was acting unconstitutionally by establishing a tax quota for a particular community, and then establishing programs to raise a desired amount from that community. They also rightfully saw this levy as a very high tax on net income. Although the levy was only 2% of the purchase price of agricultural goods, this could mean a high percentage of income after expenses. Beef farming, the mainstay of Meath agriculture, would be hardest hit. Although a fattened bullock might sell for £500 the profit on that animal could be as low as £30, which would leave only £20 after the £10 levy was subtracted. This amounted to over 30% tax on profits. Meath farmers concluded too that this new tax was being rushed into effect and that the government had not done their homework, particularly in regard to the economic and social needs and

221

consequences of such a program in rural areas. In the government's moves to implement this scheme, for example, it was unclear who was to collect this levy at the point of sale.

The farmers' reaction to the government's move was not based on economics alone. Many farmers felt that, in some respects, they were being betrayed by a government which the farmers had returned to power in 1977 by the largest majority in the history of the state. This sentiment was conveyed to me by the vast majority of farmers I interviewed in Meath at the time on these issues, and public media reports reinforced my conclusion that this was a widespread reaction among farmers across the country, but particularly in those areas of Ireland where both old and new commercial farming had been successful. The farmers of east Leinster, whose landholdings were the largest in the country, had been instrumental in the national swing in large farmers' votes away from their traditional party, the opposition Fine Gael. They were thus astounded by the change in Fianna Fáil policy. In essence, the government that farmers had helped to put into power was seen to be attacking farmers. To add insult to injury, the major reason for farmers' support of the Fianna Fáil government was to voice their disapproval of the tax system introduced under the previous government, a coalition of the Fine Gael and Labour Parties, who first taxed farm income (Farrell and Manning 1978). Furthermore, farmers felt that the government's new taxes were the result of political pressure from tax-paying wage earners. Farmers believed they were being used as scapegoats in order to placate politicians' urban constituents, who had recognized that the EEC had brought higher prices for consumer goods and thus lower spending

222

power for workers, all the while farmers seemed to get wealthier.

The budget was announced in February but the levy was not planned to go into effect until May or August. Farmers throughout Ireland mobilized their political resources to get the government to reconsider its position. Meath farmers were quick to react to the government's announcement, but did so in ways which began to break with local political tradition. Large farmers did not attack the government *because* they were traditionally Fine Gael supporters, *nor* did smaller landholders in Meath support the Fianna Fáil party that had been their sponsor since the 1920s. It seemed that all Meath farmers, or at the least all who belonged to the IFA, opposed the government. Perhaps for the first time in Meath political life, the farming supporters of each major party considered that their welfare as farmers was not synonymous with that of the welfare of their political parties. The interests of farmers as a profession, an occupation, a class and/or an interest group were clearly trumping ideological and historical considerations.

New appreciation of their changed political and economic conditions did not mean that farmers needed to jettison old, tried and true means of acting politically. Thus pressure was applied on the government by farmers in Meath and across Ireland through the informal channels of political clientage. But within the time frame that these events were being played out, nothing of significance could be accomplished by farmers by the early summer. In Meath it was also clear that the large farmers had not completely abandoned their traditional party loyalty, but were willing to hold it in abeyance in favor of other strategies. For example, it was widely held in Meath in 1979 that the strong support by Meath farmers for Fianna Fáil in the last general election was a protest against tax, not against the principles of any one party. The main thrust of farmer opposition, then, developed within the Irish Farmers' Association, the non-partisan occupational society organized for the improvement of Irish agriculture through research, communication and services. Since the early 1970s, as more and more farming bodies were incorporated into the parent IFA, it had become the primary agricultural lobby and pressure group in the nation. It represented the majority of Irish farmers, drawn from each region and involved in every aspect of agricultural production, and acted for farmers' interests both within Ireland and in the EEC.

Up to 1979, however, the IFA had never successfully confronted an Irish government over policy decisions. In regard to the 2% levy the IFA's goals were clear. It had to establish a united farming front whose interests would supersede former political alliances in order to stop the levy. The IFA knew that all the political parties were sensitive to the swing in voting patterns at the last national election. Large scale social disapproval of Fianna Fáil's tax policies was sure to make the government anxious, especially in light of the forthcoming June 1979 elections to the European Parliament, the first that was based on a popular election in each member state. The IFA wanted to capitalize on these fears.

The farmers of Meath as a body felt especially threatened by these events of 1979. The high profits they had been making since 1973 had been largely reinvested into their businesses. Farm improvements such as mechanization, new buildings, silage pits, milking parlors and land drainage had resulted in considerable farmer debt. The new tax system would cut into the profit necessary to keep these farms functioning.

224

Furthermore, Meath farmers were concerned that if the government initiative was allowed to go ahead uncontested and unchanged, then the government might feel free to put even more pressure on farming income in the future. Unlike previous periods of farmer opposition to the government, however, and despite Civil War and other loyalties which had so influenced voter cleavages for the last fifty years, Meath farmers quickly allied themselves with the national leadership of the IFA in order to back that organization's opposition to the new tax scheme.

The levy

From 7 February 1979 on, the major topic of conversation for friend and foe of the Meath farmer was 'the 2%.' From the craftsmen of Navan's furniture industry to the North Meath farm laborer to the East Meath stud farm owner, all of Meath wondered both at the audacity of the government and whether the farmers were powerful and organized enough to let the government get away with it. To some Meath people, most notably in the towns, it was about time the farmers paid their fair share of the costs of the state. The farmers, regardless of past political persuasion, began to see this as the first battle in a new struggle, that between the new European farmer in Ireland, keen to protect his livelihood and way of life, and the old Irish politician. This was a dispute between Euro-farmers and the traditional politics of locality and nation in Ireland. Farmers perceived that the IFA had the organizational infrastructure needed to lead the fight.

Following directives immediately put into effect by national headquarters, the county executives of the IFA met as soon as possible in order for branch members to disseminate the organization's official position to Ireland's villages and rural townlands. Although each county executive, composed of an elected administrative body, a national IFA appointee and the representatives of the many county branches, would receive little information not covered in the press, they would receive the important message that the IFA was going to champion their cause. If farmers wanted to change the new policy they had best join together within the ranks of a united Association.

From the outset of this dispute the IFA leadership in Dublin had called on the farmers of the country to use whatever means necessary to put personal pressure on their politicians, but above all to no longer abide by past political understandings. The IFA line was for farmers to trust those most interested in protecting the rights of all farmers throughout the country, namely the IFA. To find out how that was to be done, they were urged to attend their county executives' meetings. To show he meant business, Paddy Lane, president of the IFA, 'warned the Government that farmers would soon have an opportunity to show that they no longer had blind allegiance to a Government that reneged on their election promises to farmers' *(Irish Times,* 10 February 1979). The unveiled threat, which referred to the elections upcoming in June, was one of many that the IFA was to make in the days that followed.

On 12 February 1979 the Meath IFA county executive met at the Beechmount Hotel in Navan in what was one of the best attended meetings ever held in county history (the largest IFA gathering by far of those I witnessed in over two years of research up to then). Almost 200 farmers packed the small meeting room, both to hear what the Association had to say and to voice their own grievances. The tone of the meeting was set by the county chairman who announced that the 2% levy was introduced by the government 'to appease the Trade Unions.' The calls for action were many: unanimous support for the IFA leadership in Dublin, contesting the unconstitutional levy in the courts, voting the present government out of office, starting with the June Local and European Elections, refusing to pay any levy, and directing the County Council Committee on Agriculture to protest the government's move. They also considered strikes, marches, pickets and overall economic harassment. These suggested avenues for action were all made in the presence of a number of farming county councillors and some farmers known throughout the county to be interested in either elected office or IFA positions of authority. Most notable was a past Fianna Fáil candidate for the Dáil who was then the chair of the Committee of Agriculture of the County Council and whose present and future political career depended on the good will of the farming community. The councillor attempted to point out his party's line that the levy was earmarked for the payment of advisory services. But the militancy of the meeting precluded any such party plank explanations.

It was clear that these Meath IFA men and women would not even consider the government's position. A local small farmer, known since the 1960s for his support of farmers' rights, countered the comments of the councillor by saying that farmers should not have to pay for services they did not control. The implications were clear: farmers no longer could allow politicians the luxury to control services and policies. Farmer control had to be more direct and predictable. By the end of that important Meath meeting (which, testament to the seriousness of the moment, lasted beyond the 11:00 p.m.

closing hour for the hotel's pub, depriving the members of their traditional post-meeting pint of stout), a number of courses of action were decided upon: all branches were to hold meetings and contact their county parliamentarians, a delegation from the county executive would themselves approach these county representatives to Dublin, a special meeting of the executive would be held on 21 February, and the county executive agreed to support in any way they could the directives of the national leadership.

The great turnout at the meeting was unprecedented. Individual phone calls and personal visits from IFA leaders had mobilized branch members who, from IFA newspaper reports, clearly knew the issues that the IFA wished to discuss. The Meath meeting was held not so much as a fact-gathering exercise but to demonstrate to all interested parties that the county's farmers were united in their opposition, and that the IFA was the means whereby that opposition would be articulated and sustained. The legitimacy of this position was reinforced when local politicians, by attending that first meeting, seemingly disavowed the actions of the government and aligned themselves with the farmers.

Meath farmers looked to the IFA administration in Dublin for a guide to their next moves. From the beginning of the growing dispute the Association claimed that the government was not only going back on its promises to the farmers who voted them into office in 1977, but was attempting to undo years of Irish and EEC policy. As Lane announced on 9 February: 'the massive support given by farmers to the present Government almost two years ago was given on the basis of getting a fair deal and an opportunity to develop their farms in order to compete with their fellow farmers in Europe' *(Irish*

Times, 10 February 1979). He requested that all branches and county executives meet to discuss the government's 'unjust measures.' At the same time a dairymen's association promised legal action.

By 11 February the IFA and the Irish Creamery Milk Suppliers Association (the IFA's chief national competitor and an organization up to then reluctant to become allied with the more powerful IFA) had agreed to cooperate completely to coordinate all resistance. The government was seen to be accomplishing what years of discussion could not. Farmer unity within a combined national effort of farmers as an interest group had all but sprung up overnight in result to the government's tax plan. When the IFA announced it also intended to send a questionnaire to each TD to discover his/her views on this issue before the next election, many rural TDs became alarmed. The farmers themselves were also considering direct action, following the lead of twenty farmers from the West of Ireland who went to the Dublin offices of the Agricultural Minister on 9 February to get some answers.

If the government was surprised by the universality and vehemence of farmer protest, it was very unhappy to see the direct political effects which resulted. Within a week of the budget announcement, the papers were carrying stories on the popular support for a farmer running for the European Parliament. T. J. Maher, a famous leader in the Irish Creamery Co-Operative Movement, was being touted as a farmer who would independently serve the interests of farmers in Europe. The Fianna Fáil government knew that, if he ran, one of the 15 national seats being contested would definitely be in jeopardy. The IFA was also against such independent political moves, as well as the desire of pig producers to negotiate with the government independently, because it believed that farmers' overall position was weakened. At the same time, the Association sought to make the issue an international one.

On 16 February it was reported that the IFA had requested the EEC Commission to give an opinion on the legality of the 2%. If the Commission deemed it to be a contravention of the Treaty of Rome, the IFA would challenge it in the European Court. Their position was a simple one: the 2% did not allow Irish farmers to receive the full EEC guaranteed price for produce covered by the CAP *(Irish Times,* 16 February 1979). The IFA was demonstrating, perhaps for the first time, its belief in its new role as a representative of the new Irish Euro-farmers, especially when the Irish government threatened farmers' EEC-based rights. Through its actions at home and in Europe the IFA was also tacitly identifying the new power bases for Irish agriculture.

Although initially surprised by the reactions, the government had not been idle since 7 February. However, much of what it attempted met with little success. Its directives to the Fianna Fáil party organization to support the government line did not meet with local approval in the countryside. Although the *Irish Press*, the national daily newspaper that was closely aligned with the Fianna Fáil party and perspective, supported the government in principle, it had little to say about the methods selected by the government. The *Irish Times* and *Irish Independent* ran stories which went from middle-of-the-road accounts of the need for farmers to pay more tax to outright attacks on the new budget. When on 13 February a Fianna Fáil TD from Cork announced he was going to question the 2% levy at the sacrosanct meeting of the parliamentary party the next day, the country quickly grasped that at least some Fianna Fáil TDs were in open rebellion. Many TDs felt it was up to them to represent the interests of farmers in their constituency and were loath to let the IFA encroach on this role. Many politicians quickly came to the conclusion that their support for the rash tax program would in the end jeopardize their electoral political futures.

Both the IFA and ICMSA could not stop Maher from running for the European Parliament or his championing the pig producers' separate delegation to Dublin. They took a different course of action by charging that the government sought to split farmer opposition by dealing with separate sectors of the farming community. When the pig producers attempted to enter government offices they were blocked by farmers from Clare and Meath. In fact, the members of the Meath IFA were among the most vocal and organized of all farmers in opposition, a role they maintained throughout the dispute.

By the third week of February there were numerous calls from within Fianna Fáil to either change the new farm tax policy or rethink the entire tax system for the country. The government was in a dilemma. Compromise on the tax issue ran the risk of angering either farmers or wage earners, but if the government did nothing it courted political defeat. They faced a difficult decision, which on 21 February was announced by the Taoiseach. The 2% levy was removed from the proposed budget, which by law would have to be approved by the Dáil. Instead, the levy would be put into effect through Ministerial order, which needed no parliamentary vote and could last for a year. It was clear that Jack Lynch, the Taoiseach, had decided to use the weight of his office, government and party majority to force the issue. As the IFA deputy president said in reaction to this move: 'We will not pay. At this stage the gloves were off. The time has come for action' *(Irish Times,* 22 February 1979).

The farmers of Meath reacted just as swiftly. At their second IFA county executive meeting of the month they decided to send a large contingent of farmers to support the announced meeting in Portlaoise, outside of Dublin, between farming leaders and the government, and to send an equally large number to protest at the Fianna Fáil annual convention, the Ard Fheis, which was taking place that weekend, 23-25 February, in Dublin. Lynch's directive, which was announced on the eve of his party's meeting, sought to quiet party dissension. It made Meath farmers angrier and more determined than ever to stop the government initiative. Furthermore, the farmers of the whole country reacted in similar ways. Spontaneous demonstrations, road blockades, sugar beet delivery delays, milk strikes, withholding of dairy products, and a shortage of fresh meat were immediate nationwide occurrences, and were the handiwork of farmers of all sorts of farm holdings and enterprises. This was a response of farmers unlike that of the farm dispute of the 1960s in which the IFA unsuccessfully confronted the Fianna Fáil government of the time. In that dispute the IFA failed to equally mobilize small and large farmers, and farmers drawn from across the country. This was largely due to the Association's reputation of being a large farmer body; small farmers had in the main joined other farm interest groups.

In 1979, however, the IFA and ICMSA had mobilized the nation's farmers in opposition to a Fianna Fáil government which had been voted in with the greatest margin of victory in Irish history. The country's farmers felt that they had been

232

largely responsible for that victory and were just as sure they could use their influence to make that same government reverse its policy. In short, the IFA (and, to a lesser extent, the ICMSA) provided the organization and national prominence to effectively bypass the old means of affecting national policy. The position of the farmers of the IFA was that they were no longer *asking* the government, they were *telling* the government. The country wondered what Lynch, who had decided on the new strategy, would say at the Ard Fheis, in reaction to farmer protests

In the end it was not Lynch who voiced the reaction at the convention. On Saturday, the Minister for Finance announced that the levy would not be applied to the sale of sheep and pigs or to cattle slaughtered under disease eradication programs: It would also not apply to sugar beet production in the west of the country, or the first 5,000 gallons of milk delivered to creameries or milk plants. This effectively freed 35,000 milk suppliers from the levy and partially relieved 43,000 other farmers *(Irish Times,* 26 February 1979).

The government's strategy was clear. By removing the levy from these activities it was again subsidizing small farmers throughout the country. By doing so it still hoped to split the united farming front that had quite literally erupted two weeks earlier. Furthermore, these small farmers had consistently been Fianna Fáil supporters since the party was founded in the 1920s. The Fianna Fáil leadership obviously decided that they could not afford to alienate the faithful in the face of the important June elections. Yet the government also clearly decided that it would not remove the levy altogether, for the precedent had to be upheld that the government had the right to establish measures to tax the 'special' category of

233

'farmer.' Besides, the prestige of the Taoiseach and government was on the line. When they first announced the levy, however, they had not predicted the degree of farmer unity or the strength and role of the IFA in that unity.

The farmers of Meath yet again were incensed by these concessions. As Monday's *Irish Times* reported, the announcements did not impress a hundred or so Meath farmers who picketed the conference all day Saturday (26 February 1979). As one Meath farmer said 'the levy exemption on milk supplies under 5,000 gallons was only the yield of seven good cows.' Simply put, the modifications affected Meath minimally. Few Meath farmers were involved in pig and sheep production, and their sugar beet was still liable under the 2% levy. While milk suppliers had their first 5,000 gallons free of levy, a large dairy farm could supply at least 100,000 gallons a year. Beef farms, the mainstay of Meath at the time, were untouched by the new program. Therefore, the Meath IFA resolved to double their efforts to support the Association at that Monday's mass farmer demonstration in Portlaoise, in County Laois, south of Meath.

For most Meath farmers there was really little choice. For the best of the young farmers of the county, who because of education, ambition, business acumen and overall social sophistication were seen to be 'progressive' or development farmers, the IFA had become the principal means to influence governmental policy. The high level of economic and political analysis that was demonstrated by the leaders of the Meath county executive showed clearly that the farming community leadership that in the past had served the county council was now in the IFA. It was clear to the sons of the old Meath farm elite that their best chance at political power was through their

234

interest groups and not through elected politics. As one young farmer (with a holding of 200 acres and a family political legacy that included both major parties and TD/Ministers in each) told me at the height of the tax dispute, he had a choice to make now that his farm and family were established. He could go into the county council and hope for a TD spot, or he could go into the IFA county leadership and perhaps use that as a springboard for national prominence. He did not run for party political office after that, and a few years later he rose to be a key elected leader in the national IFA.

It was these young farmers who joined the older generation, 5,000 strong altogether, in Portlaoise that Monday. Their cheers greeted Lane and Anthony Leddy (ICMSA leader) who told them that no government ploy would divide the farmers. Seeing these farm association leaders appear on the same podium and agree on these issues had to give both the farming community and the government cause for belief and cause for anxiety, respectively. Lane announced to those assembled at the meeting that the goal of the farm association was a 'single taxation system, such as every other sector of the community had. And . . . farming organizations wanted to be consulted and involved in the drawing up of that system' *(Irish Times,* 27 February 1979). They were in effect informing the government that if it wanted the support of farmers for its tax policies it had to negotiate with the farming associations. The old system of party brokerage could no longer be relied upon to mobilize and rely on farmer support. The implication of February 1979 was that the IFA spoke for the farmer because the new Irish Euro-farmer could no longer rely solely on his government to protect his interests, and when that government

235

itself was perceived to threaten such interests it too could be thwarted by a united farm lobby.

The political effects

On 28 February 1979 the government, in consultation with farming leaders, agreed to drop the levy, announcing instead that the government would seek from farmers an income tax yield 'in line with other sectors of the community' *(Irish Times,* 29 February 1979). Negotiations between government and farm groups were to take place up to 1 May at which time a mutually agreeable tax system for farmers would be announced. The victory was clearly the IFA's while the loss was just the first which the government would suffer in what was to become a long year for them.

This last announcement did not get the government out of its dilemma. By 1 March the unions of the country began voicing their disapproval of the deal made with the farmers. Old animosities quickly rose to the surface. The president of the Irish Congress of Trade Unions threatened action by the union movement and demanded 'rights similar to those now apparently won by farmers to negotiate economic policy with the Government' *(Irish Times,* 1 March 1979). Fianna Fáil TDs, especially from the cities, continued to dissent. The Labour Party was outraged. As one Labour TD put it, his party could not agree with the government's 'cowardly surrender' to the farmer. Within days there were impromptu work stoppages throughout the country and a series of protest marches was planned in many of the nation's towns and cities. On 5 March Lynch, obviously reeling, delivered a speech in which he asserted that the 'government did not surrender' to the farmers, and that the farmers would be forced to pay the same amount of tax already demanded of them. The people of Ireland did not agree with this assessment.

The urban center outside Dublin quickest to organize itself against the government's newest moves was Navan, the central town of Meath, a county known for its role in the IFA protest. Under the leadership of an independent county councillor a march was planned for 9 March. This march, the first of the nation's organized protests in response to the government's climb down with the farmers, had more than 1,000 people march both in support of a new national agreement between labor and government and in protest against the government and the farmers. The size of the Navan demonstration was impressive. Although many marchers were from out of town, most of the 1,000 were Navan residents and they formed a sizable part of the 5,000 strong urban district population. The significance for Navan and Meath politicians was especially clear. If an independent local politician could gather this much support in one urban district, and farmers were already alienated from party politics in rural areas, then they obviously had cause to worry about the effects of recent events and emotions on their candidates and parties in the June local and European elections.

The successful Navan march began a series of nationwide protests which culminated in the 20 March national union protest which saw 150,000 working taxpayers take to the streets of Dublin. Their goal was a 'total overhaul of the taxation system' *(Irish Times, 20 March 1979)*. While the demonstration, which was joined by marches of 40,000 in Cork, 8,000 in Galway, and 2,000 in Dundalk, was not particularly anti-farmer, the main message was antigovernment and pro-labor. The 22 March call by the Irish Congress of Trade Unions (ICTU) was for new tax and pay policies by 30 April, the day before the new farmer income tax deal was to be announced.

The events of March again caught the government unprepared. By trying to placate farmers it had sparked the largest demonstration in the history of the state (one national newspaper likened it to both the 1913 Lockout and the 1932 Eucharistic Congress). By attempting to maintain its hold on farming votes it had jeopardized its support among urban workers. Perhaps most important, however, the government had been seen publicly to be unpopular. After its unique successes of 1977, it had slipped to arguably the most unpopular government in Irish history up to that time. This was shown in the local and European elections in June, when Fianna Fáil suffered surprising defeats at the hands of both farmer-candidates in Fine Gael and independents.

In the months that followed these events the IFA continued its campaign to make the government rescind the levy and establish farm accounts as the only acceptable method of taxation. Surprisingly, the IFA still presented a united front, for even the farmers who were relieved from the levy supported the IFA and their fellow farmers in the East who bore its brunt. Selective government patronage did not split the new IFA. Farmers seemed to be united by the realization that as a body they could effectively pressure the government along a selected course of action. Farmers' votes were also influential in the national by-elections in November in which Fianna Fáil was widely defeated. By the turn of the year the leadership within Fianna Fáil had split, due in part to the government's alienation of both farmers and workers.

238

In Meath the results of the 1979 tax dispute were significant in a number of ways. It was clear that most farmers no longer participated directly in local government, and that this was especially true among young development and wealthy farmers who in the past had been the new core of the local political elite. Those farmers who stayed in both the county councils and party organizations did so with less enthusiasm, at least in their roles as farmers representing farmers. Farmers used their votes, as well as their newfound roles within farm lobbies and interest groups, in Ireland and in the EEC, as their primary political tools to affect agricultural policy. In fact, in the late 1970s farmers became widely known as the most volatile of voters throughout the nation. In 1979 it was rare to find farmers who were not willing to at least consider going against tradition in order to vote their perceived economic interests. This volatility helped to foster support for the IFA and other interest representations. In Meath this support began to siphon off the most educated, ambitious and well-known young farmers from formal political interests. The progressive development farmers of Meath in the 1980s were the farmers of the IFA. These young men and women recognized that interest group activity was their best tactic in winning their local, national and international goals.

The development of the IFA as the key farmers' organization has as much to do with the organization's own planning and development as it does with the impact of the EEC on Irish life. The IFA leadership campaigned vigorously in favor of Ireland's joining the Common Market in hopes of gaining the tangible rewards for Irish farmers that they did indeed enjoy in later years. It was also clear to the IFA that EEC membership would threaten political party control of

239

agricultural policy-making. They had learned a valuable lesson through their often unsuccessful confrontations with the Irish government in the 1960s. Thus, over the intervening twenty years the IFA had established a good grass-roots organization, with Meath as one of its strongest counties. This organization had sought to develop a strong and able leadership from within. Its emphasis on agricultural efficiency and education, coupled with its often timely support of parties and candidates, helped to establish the IFA as the chief non-partisan and non-government research body in the nation. By the mid-1970s its highly educated national farm specialists and its politically-savvy grass-roots farm leaders had established the IFA as an effective lobby for a newly international farmers' interest group, a group often at odds with its national policy makers.

Thus, the reorganization of the tax system and the implementation of successive budgets had proved sizable hurdles for Irish governments. Four successive governments were voted out of office after 1979, and at each election farmers demonstrated their willingness to vote the IFA line to achieve their interest group's goals. In fact, within the national political arena, in which many interest groups voted according to their economic needs, the group which was most damaging to government and party confidence was the farmers. Not only were farmers reluctant to continue traditional voting patterns, they had so enhanced the power of the IFA that its influence began to rival many organs of government. This power rested, in part, on the new internationalism of the farming body.

Irish farmers had joined their counterparts in the other nations of the EEC in the European farmers' interest lobby, COPA, an umbrella organization which brought together all of the major farmers' organizations from the then Community of

Twelve (Averyt 1977). The IFA maintained offices on the continent in order to affect all policy issues relevant to Irish agriculture. In Brussels and Strasbourg the IFA acted independently and in concert with other national farmers' groups to influence all decisions made at every level of the EEC, including those of the Commission, the Council and the Parliament. Their roles within national politics became stronger as a result, especially in those national policy domains directly related to European Community policy-making. Farmers' collective political voices had become louder in other nations as well because of increasing farmer interest in policy formation and their new international ties to other farming groups (Feld 1966, 1974; Buksti 1979; Andrilik 1981). The importance of these farming lobbies in all the nations of the EEC highlighted the differences inherent in national and international policy-making, when the needs of a national farming lobby can be at odds with its own national government but quite in line with the needs of transnational farmers and other governments (Newby 1980b). The farmers of Meath, who did so well initially within the Common Market, but whose occupations were later threatened by various national and international forces, had gone to the forefront of the new Europe-oriented IFA. In the 1970s, and since, these farmers clearly qualified as Euro-farmers.

Thus, 1979 saw an Irish government wholly unprepared for farmer reaction to its new tax programs. It did not predict the extent, degree and form of opposition. Perhaps for the first time farmers of every county, income level and farm enterprise had united for a common goal. In Meath the farmers of both major parties in large part bypassed their accepted political role in order to make their needs known through their national lobby, the IFA. Since then the IFA has effectively articulated the needs of the new Irish Euro-farmer. Meath commercial farmers can no longer depend solely on national government subsidization. EEC relations, by changing the role of Meath farmers in the national and international economies, had resulted in a redefinition and realignment of the role of Meath farmers within the national Irish political system.

In closing this chapter, it should also be remembered that the protests and elections of 1979 led to a great factionalism in political party structures as well, both in Meath and in the nation as a whole. This was particularly true of Fianna Fáil, whose success in elections had long depended on central party control of a tightly-knit grass-roots organization. Over the 1970s, however, Fianna Fáil had suffered a series of disturbing changes (Garvin 1981). Instrumental voting had helped farmers create an image of themselves as businessmen and agriculturalists with special needs and special powers. Recognition of the strong position of farmers in a united IFA had also increased wage-earners' dissension and electoral volatility. To all national interest groups the primary problem of the nation had become the government's management of the economy (Blackwell 1982). Perhaps among the Irish citizenry the real political crisis of the 1980s was one of confidence in government and politics. Trust and confidence were also factors important to an ethnographer conducting field research on politics in the midst of these other crises.

Chapter 7

Codology and the Ethnography of Politics

The ethnographic study of elites has been a concern of anthropology and sociology since the 1960s. For decades anthropologists and other ethnographers have examined the social and cultural dimensions to the political and economic control held and reproduced by relatively small groups of people who are strategically placed in social hierarchies (see, for example, Friedrich 1969; Schneider et al. 1972; Schneider and Schneider 1976; Murray and Hong 1988). In recent years, however, anthropological analysis has turned to the study of political knowledge, practice and culture, rather than the study of the political economy of elites' power, institutions and roles in society. And a great deal of political anthropology today has much more to do with the politics of ethnographic fieldwork, where the protagonist is the ethnographer rather than the members of the society being studied, and where the people who once were the subjects of research are now seen to be relatively uninteresting in the rush to examine the role of ethnographers in crafting ethnography.

Due partly to major changes to the ways anthropologists do ethnography, it is often difficult to tease out in current anthropological accounts where the politics of those being studied are different from those of the researcher. There are many sources for this change in research emphasis, but key among them are the increased importance of ethnographic reflexivity (Herzfeld 1987; Roth 1989), interpretive anthropology (Fischer 1977), and critical approaches to the process of doing and writing ethnography (Boon 1982; Clifford and Marcus 1986; Marcus and Fischer 1986). Not surprisingly then, in contemporary elite studies in anthropology the subjects of the study are often not approached as elites, even though it is often obvious that they are groups with authority and power who are recognized as such in society and who act in ways that acknowledge their higher statuses. However, some important but indirect studies of elites have been conducted, wherein the dilemmas of doing fieldwork among elites have figured prominently in a wide range of ethnographic case studies (see, for example, Gilmore 1991; Aldridge 1993; Hertz and Imber 1993).

One of the key problems facing ethnographers who attempt to study those who have power and influence, and it is a problem common to the ethnographic study of all groups of people, is the capacity of researchers to maintain neutrality and objectivity, even though they have definite sympathies and empathy for select groups of people in the host community. Long gone are the days when the ethnographer was but a fly on the wall. Ethnographers now debate whether it is even possible, or desirable, to avoid becoming advocates for the people among whom they live and study (Paine 1985; Hastrup and Elsass 1990). However, of critical importance for research among elites, ethnographers must devise strategies to establish rapport with people whose social, economic, and political statuses place them at levels equal to, or in many cases higher than, that of the researchers.

The dilemmas created by developing feelings of sympathy or advocacy for the views and roles of one's hosts become heightened when the ethnographer must deal in the gamesmanship of status in order to be accepted by the elite. Simply put, it is hard to sustain the illusion of neutrality when one is expected, at the least by one's hosts, to take sides, and when much of the research experience puts the ethnographer squarely inside one segment of the community. Furthermore, in order to gain access to elite circles, ethnographers must often develop social and cultural tactics that privilege one's own status markers, which are frequently based on the ethnographer's home culture, community, and/or social class. These markers often involve the use of a particular dialect or language, the wearing of certain clothes, the evocation of education and social status, and evidence of the social networks to which the ethnographer already belongs, and to which, it is hoped, some of the elite may desire access. As Hunter suggests:

> In the actual fact of studying elites the ethnographer cannot ignore the elite's power and must not ignore his or her own power in the relationship. Academically based researchers, especially, are wittingly or unwittingly likely to be drawing on their own human capital (advanced degrees, for example) and their institution's power and prestige in these relationships. Ethnographers must be self-reflexively sensitive to the fact that power relationships enter into the very process of studying power itself (1993: 37).

Although many ethnographers may balk at the notion that they have power, or are perceived to have influence, authority or power by elites whom they wish to study, most should agree that research among elites entails the creation of social status strategies which make the ethnographer attractive, welcome, understandable or agreeable to the elite who are the focus of the researcher's study. In short, the negotiation of status by ethnographers, to be accepted by members of an elite, to expand one's knowledge of the elite, and to gain access to their social networks, is an unavoidable aspect of elite studies. In the Irish political context, at least for me in County Meath in the late 1970s, this effort entailed the manipulation of information, for knowledge, whether real or imaginary, is at the heart of status distinctions among local Irish politicians.

As has been examined in the previous chapters, in County Meath, where I conducted years of field research, local politics was an arena wherein imaginary patronage had been central to the activities of politicians and public servants alike for decades. Despite the generally held notion that politicians had little power, and relied a great deal on their own manipulation of image and imaginary efficacious political networks, there was also a widespread perception that a vital and dominant political machine still persisted in Meath as late as the 1980s. Belief in the vitality of a political machine in this large and wealthy Irish county had lingered despite a great deal of local and national evidence to the contrary.

During the course of my fieldwork it became clear to me that one sign of the diminishing influence of local politicians in eastern Ireland was their attempt to incorporate me into their political networks. This acceptance and attempted exploitation suited me. It was my goal, after all, to be accepted by the elite so that I could do an in-depth study of them. But as that research deepened in focus, and as my visit seemed to transform into sustained residence, I became prey to some of the forces I was there to study: I was subject to recruitment into the networks of politicians and politically-minded people in local society, in ways which not only demonstrated to me the seductions of political networking, and some of the reasons that

246

political elites had such a hold on the realities and fancies of local political life, but also showed me how there was an air of desperation in such maneuvers, and perhaps evidence of political decline. Simply put, the way some politicians attempted to redefine my political role locally indicated to me that information had become their principal, if not only, political capital, and that the machine control of local politics had become little more than a facade.

Their perceptions of me as both outsider and insider led me to reconsider the role of an ethnographer who finds, in the midst of fieldwork, that he or she is seen as part of the political field one is there to study, and, in turn, to reflect on the nature of objectivity and subjectivity in the processes of ethnographic construction and reconstruction. This sort of analysis is offered here in the spirit of the changes in worldwide anthropology that were begun in the 1980s with the advent of more interpretive and reflexive ethnography. It also is offered to partially fill what is becoming a scandalous long-standing gap in the political anthropology of European societies, namely the dearth of ethnographic perspectives on political parties as institutions and as aspects of wider political fields.

Since independence from the UK, local political leaders and parties in Meath had reinforced misconceptions and myths regarding their own power and ability to supply material resources to voters. Rural voters had been especially susceptible to these efforts, and in response had often exaggerated the power and importance of 'their men' in office. One local party organization had been characterized by Meath people as a political machine, marked by its high degree of electoral control and political patronage. But Irish machines are not held together solely by the provision of real and imaginary rewards on the one hand and the return service of votes on the other. The values and ties of kinship, religion, class, and common political and nationalist ideologies had created a political culture which had formed local political factions, parties and machine cadres.

The successes of Meath's only political machine since state independence in the 1920s depended on the leadership provided by local politicians, who through various combinations of family ties, charisma, common nationalist ideologies, money-lending, and sociability had been able to gather a good number of clients around them. Such clientage had been translated into relatively stable and secure voter support at all local and national elections up to 1973. However, the asymmetrical relation between party boss and dependent voters which developed over that time had increasingly become an ephemeral or imaginary one itself, because since the 1930s Irish national politics had experienced a slow but steady centralization of state and party power. In this situation there were fewer opportunities for local big men to create their own semi-independent machines. And the state bureaucracy had succeeded in removing almost all of the potential areas of graft and corruption. In fact, local Meath politics in the 1970s were in the main the politics of administrative implementation and redistribution. If the imagery and imaginary of power kept many clients supporting politicians, then the actuality of local power made politicians into clients when they dealt with the officers and public servants of local government.

248

The Meath machine

Meath local politicians have many, often conflicting, views of what they do and why they serve. One thing is certain; they did not characterize their local political system in the rather rigid terms of patronage, brokerage, and clientage which political analysts, including me, use. After all, local politicians do not simply manipulate the symbols and history of local politics nor do they just exploit their ties to other members of their communities. They are themselves as much a part of the many fabrics of their communities' lives as are their supporters and enemies. Not surprisingly, politicians and party cadres often characterize themselves in such terms as 'hero' and 'villain', 'leader' and 'follower', 'cute' (clever) and 'thick' (stupid), and, simply, 'good' and 'bad'.

In the 1970s it was clear that local politics were undergoing great, perhaps transformative, changes, yet all contended that regardless of what happened in the future locally elected politicians would continue to play a major role in the maintenance of a high quality of life for local people. Their seriousness of purpose and their commitments to their communities and parties were most evident at election times. And it was in the run-up to the Local and European Elections of 1979 that I saw the remnants of a Meath political machine in action.

Since my arrival two years before I had learned a great deal about the Fianna Fáil (the state's dominant party since 1932) Meath machine. I quickly ascertained through interviews with Fianna Fáil county councillors and party workers that if such a machine still existed, then it survived where it arose, in the center of the county, in the urban and rural areas of Navan town. As the county-wide Fianna Fáil organization geared up

249

for both elections by looking for suitable candidates and profitable alliances among neighboring local political clubs, it also became clear to me that the peripheral areas of the county felt that the force to be reckoned with was the leadership of the Meath party, who were in the main in Navan. They based this appraisal on the power these leaders had from a number of sources. Some leaders were on the national party executive, and these privileged few were also the first ones to receive instructions from Dublin, thus enabling them to gain local political advantage both through prior notice as well as allowing them first interpretation of national party directives for the locals. This same Navan leadership had helped engineer a very strong Fianna Fáil election victory in 1977, including having a local Navan man elected TD. These Navan leaders were the successors to the traditional Navan Fianna Fáil political machine, and although these men were not elected themselves, their TD from Navan was the son of the man who fashioned the machine in the 1920s and 1930s.

Party chapters around the county described to me years of Navan domination of both general and local elections, in which the core leadership divided the county into electioneering zones designed to elect the candidates who suited them. This resulted in a great deal of intra-party jealousy and factionalism. Yet while many party cadres, as well as their opposition in other parties, were lamenting the strength of the Navan dominated Fianna Fáil machine, many were quick to point out the weaknesses in that machine.

These criticisms hinged on views of the one family which had been at the core of the machine since its origin, that of Patrick Fitzsimons, Sr. 'Old Pat' (so-called to distinguish him from his son 'Paddy') was then in his seventies and although still chairman of the Navan Urban District Council (the chair of the UDC is the closest thing to a town's 'Lord Mayor') he had decided not to contest the 1973 county council elections, thereby symbolically 'giving his seat' to his son James, who, in turn, was elected TD in 1977. His impending retirement from public life was seen by many as a possible political opportunity, i.e., 'the Boss' (this, a title common in rural areas, connoting power, loyalty, affection, respect and power, was also the nickname of a later Irish Premier, Charles Haughey) was losing control. Still others pointed to the many people Pat had groomed to run Navan's Fianna Fáil, both in party cadre posts and in elected office. After all, his son had already attained a TD post to which Pat had aspired but did not attain.

Pat had been a representative in Seanad Éireann (the Senate), the second house of parliament, but that was often viewed locally as a party accolade to a loyal Fianna Fáil leader, who was an original party founder and a supporter of Eamon de Valera. It was also widely rumored in the late 1970s that Old Pat was grooming Patrick Jr. for the posts, long-held by his 'da', of Chairman of the UDC, Chairman of the County Council, and Senator. Perhaps proof of the enduring influence of the Navan machine was that 'Young Paddy' had achieved the two chairmanships by 1990. Regardless of the conflicting critical views of Navan's Fianna Fáil leadership in the 1970s, all the people I questioned (and, I must stress, virtually all of the hundreds of Meath people with whom I discussed this subject) agreed that the senior Fitzsimons had created and run the largest and most powerful political machine the county had ever known.

In 1978 many Meath people called Pat Fitzsimons 'the Godfather,' but never, to my knowledge, to his face. The American film and novel had an impact in the county which, perhaps surprisingly, translated into a sentimental and affectionate view of the Godfather as power broker. It was in this way that the term was used in reference to Senator Fitzsimons. Nonetheless in many instances the smiles quickly disappeared when discussing the power of Fianna Fáil in Meath in the 1930s and Pat Fitzsimons' role then. Even his staunchest supporters reluctantly admitted that the leader had to make a lot of hard decisions for the good of the party and the county. The 1930s were a decade in which the Chairman of the County Council wielded a great deal of power in local society. This was especially true when the Chairman also led the most powerful local party, as Pat Fitzsimons did. This was all before the County Management Act of 1940 began to take power from the elected MCCs and their chairman. From 1934 to 1942, the height of Fianna Fáil power in local government throughout the nation, Pat Fitzsimons is reputed to have supplied county council jobs, arranged loans, assigned local government housing, and acquired government benefits for his clients.

Although much of this reputation remains problematic, because the data is mainly in people's memories and not recorded, the historical perceptions of power are persuasive, suggestive, and of a political validity all their own. It was almost unanimously reported to me, by Fianna Fáil friends and foes alike, that most requests for material goods and services that were made to Fianna Fáil representatives from throughout the county had to be either approved by him or, at the very least, he had to be informed of them. The only exceptions seemed to relate to a small rival Fianna Fáil faction in Navan, also led by a charismatic founder of the party, which never achieved local control. Nevertheless its leader became a TD and a Government Minister, and he provided services to his clients which were largely out of Senator Fitzsimons' purview.

Most of Fitzsimons' political influence derived from his control of the county council's committees, which were established to deal with every aspect of local government that by the 1970s was being run by public servants. In their heyday the elected councillors staffed the committees which decided upon, and then implemented, local policies regarding transportation, taxes, farming, sanitation, housing, and health care. This included hiring and firing, the schedule for the provision of services, and the contracting of private concerns to help the government. In this situation the possibilities for patronage were many, and the probabilities of political brokerage were high. In the late 1970s it was not hard to recognize Pat Fitzsimons' central role in the development of local politics, symbolized by the strategic placing of his two pubs, one at either end of Navan's main street. As one wag recalled 'He had us all coming and going.'

Senator Fitzsimons' power began to wane in the decades after the 1940s, however, reflecting processes going on throughout the land. The County Manager has become the real patron of local politics and government because he, the top county civil servant appointed by the Government, controlled most essential goods and services in the county. National political parties had also chipped away at local politicians' bases for patronage through the centralization of decision making in Dublin. Local political parties were as a result increasingly powerless to supply the 'pork barrel' rewards that were the mainstay of their earlier days. The irony of the parties' position became clear when both major parties campaigned heavily for admission to the EEC, an organization that would take even more of their control of valuable goods and services away.

In Meath in the 1970s local politicians saw themselves as being assailed from all sides. The legal basis for raising local taxes had just been removed by the national government. Their parties could no longer guarantee needed services. Their government was a weak partner in Brussels. And local politicians were beginning to be perceived as nothing more than messenger boys by the constituents who had looked up to them in the past. Many politicians openly expressed to me their frustration at being in a thankless job. Elected representatives, and the party cadres who elected them, were in a crisis of identification and political strategy. In the past they had perceived their role to include many vital services of government including legislating. Then, in the 1970s, they seemed powerless to achieve most of what their predecessors had done. 'What were they to do?' was an almost unanimous complaint of the twenty-nine sitting county councillors whom I interviewed in 1978 and 1979.

Desperate strategies

By the late 1970s Navan's machine had lost the institutional edge in local government which it had enjoyed a generation before. As Fianna Fáil's machine lost its credibility voters began to openly deride local politicians in community business meetings, at church gates and in the press. They also voted for opposition parties in great numbers in the 1973 elections, marking a period of voter volatility which has continued to today, forcing politicians to compete for votes at each election which in the past had been assured through traditional family loyalty. In response politicians sought ways to maintain their influence and prestige, to give them ways to gain voter support, election by election. Not surprisingly, for conservative parties in the conservative business of Irish political life, they responded as any good political brokers might: they attempted to expand their networks of people who could supply information and support. They essentially attempted to shore up the holes in their political front by doing more of the same, by doubling their efforts to get key information, and by expanding the membership of their networks and the machine.

This was extremely hard for them to do. As one councillor said to me in regard to the forces at work that were impeding efforts to succeed as politicians: 'they all had the wind in their faces.' Both local and national developments were against efforts to strengthen networks. It was now impossible to guarantee the goods and services which clients demanded. Perhaps more important, it was harder to convince clients that their traditional patrons had any role at all to play in the provision of local services. In a nutshell, fewer people were imagining the patronage. The reasons for this in 1977 to 1979 were many:

(1) Many aspects of national policy making were no longer the sole domain of Irish parties in Irish government. Ireland's entry into the EEC in 1973 had put such key areas as farm policy largely in the hands of European policy makers.

(2) Although EEC membership had provided a stimulus to foreign investment, by enhancing Irish tax-free incentives to foreign corporations, many local factories had recently closed. Jobs were lost, and foreign competition had virtually destroyed

255

the local Navan furniture industry. Politicians were seemingly powerless to stop the economic slide.

(3) Traditional constituent supporters had either declined in numbers or had transformed themselves into growing independent interest groups and international lobbies, such as the Irish Farmers' Association, who were becoming political forces in their own right. At the same time many Navan voters began to support independent candidates who had forsaken party affiliations in order, as they saw it, to be free to dedicate themselves to local concerns.

(4) Meath was increasingly becoming urbanized and suburbanized as Dublin city's population moved across the county borders. Dublin city centre was thirty miles from Navan, but Meath's border with Dublin city was 18 miles away, and during the 1970s Dubliners had bought and built so many homes in the region between Navan and the capital that many towns and villages had become social satellites of the city. Although this new population voted in the Meath constituency, they brought new political expectations to local politics, not the least of which was the rejection of rural pork barrel politics. Navan itself had gone from a population of 5,000 to 12,000 in just ten years. Many of its new residents brought with them party affiliations but not loyalties to local personalities.

(5) Finally, Meath and the rest of the nation were in the oil crisis recession of the late 1970s, which fostered unemployment, emigration, and the predictable backlash against 'old-style' politics that had failed to protect the local economy. It was clear to some politicians that the old ways of adapting to changes in politics would probably not do them much good in the face of such monumental changes. But many

politicians knew no other way, and many newer ones were disinclined to change old styles because the rewards were few.

The desperation that existed beneath the surface for many local politicians then, which continued well into the next decade, crystallized for me when I realized that many politicians and cadre members were attempting to change my role as an outside observer by making me part of their political networks. For some this was done unconsciously. It was a by-product of their attempts to help me, to make me welcome, and to fit me into a political climate and ethos which were important aspects of their lives. Others, however, attempted to co-opt me in order to use my information, my access to opponents' opinions and strategies, and my analytical skills. The more I became part of local political culture, and the more politicians figured prominently in my professional and social lives (at times perhaps almost indistinguishable for an ethnographer in the field), the more difficult it was to resist these efforts. In my attempt to return the confidences and hospitality of my hosts I often walked a narrow line between reciprocity and unprofessionalism. Suffice to say, as I became integrated into the local Navan political scene, a good number of local big men devised a variety of uses for me, in terms of asking for return favors as they cooperated with me in my research.

Let me be clear too about one matter. At no time were I and my services vital or necessary to their political success, but this was also largely true of many other tasks they embarked upon themselves in their daily political lives. Their efforts in creating and maintaining a network of political clients were often small and seemingly ephemeral in nature. But the art of politics in this regard is one which seeks gradual and cumulative effects. Large and small services and favors are meant to coalesce into a long and broad service that adhere a voter and a voter's family to a politician if not also to a political party. In the creation and maintenance of political support political ideologies also figured prominently, especially through their historical ties to the Civil War era in Ireland in the 1920s. But in Meath I also came to appreciate that patronage and clientelism also had ideological referents, wherein those with whom you share political community and society were seen to be more likely to help when a service was needed or demanded.

However, there was also more than a mild note of desperation that crept into the process while I was doing this initial field research in Meath. As I grew to appreciate my own role in a number of changing socio-political circumstances, I began to view a great many politicians' efforts to go beyond more traditional bounds to recruit networks as indicative of people who simply did not know how to proceed otherwise, and who were clutching at political straws. If the information I could provide was valuable to or desired by a local politician of the late 1970s, and many said or suggested to me that it was, then it was clear to me that there was a crisis in political control and information management in local politics.

Ethnographer as political extra

At no time in Meath politics did I ever play a significant role. But the more I learned about local politics, which was a function of my own skills as an ethnographer as well as the length of time I was there, the greater was the potential of my becoming an actor rather than an observer on the local political stage. In the end, I played a walk-on bit part, little more than an extra in the political melodrama whose production I was witnessing. Of course, using stage or screen metaphors to describe local politics would be humorous to Meath politicians, but their use is not entirely inappropriate. Most Meath politicians were public thespians to the core, and many expected me to act a similar role.

In early 1978, after a few months residence in Navan, I began to gain what was to become almost total access to any political deliberations I wished to observe. This became especially true of Fianna Fáil, principally because their party organization and 'chain of command' were so much more efficient and recognizable than the other major parties, who were equally forthcoming in their welcomes and cooperation but who quite simply were fewer on the ground and considerably less organized than Fianna Fáil. This is not to say that my initial ministrations were not met with resistance, if not opposition. But after weeks of camaraderie, network-building, and appeals to pride and politicians' sense of the scientific or educational value of my work, by me and early politician supporters of mine, I steadily became part of the political scene. When years later I returned to Navan for some summer field research, I visited a county council meeting in November, 1990, where many of the councillors joked that the stylish remodeling of their chambers had necessitated the removal of 'my desk.' This was a reference to the desk in the back of the hall at which I sat for over two years observing their deliberations, the only outsider admitted except for the press, and certainly the only witness to their much more politically heated meetings when the press left sharply at 5 p.m. (as they did at every such event after three hours of stone-faced note

259

taking). The near complete cooperation I experienced by mid-1978 was never without its doubters or outright enemies. Throughout the election campaigns of 1979 I was often accused, sometimes to my face, of being a spy for 'the other lot' (usually meaning the 'other' party, although the charge of CIA operative also arose in a few discussions!).

Some Fianna Fáil politicians became so anxious about my attending their secret conference regarding their strategy in claiming the chairmanship of the county council after their 1979 election victory, that I was asked to remain in the pub (a Fitzsimons pub, of course) while they held their meeting upstairs. They, and I, knew they would complete their plans before the pub closed, so I waited. When they returned one of their leaders slipped me a paper with the minutes of the meeting, whispering that he understood that I would like to follow this particular process 'from thought to action' and that it would be interesting for me to see their local strategies and factions as they materialized at the next county council meeting. Another MCC put it differently when he told me that some MCCs 'always make a mountain out of a shite [shit] hill,' and that many were afraid I might betray their plans to the opposition.

Such occurrences excepted, however, I was almost religiously invited to as many formal and informal party and Navan machine meetings as could be conceived by either myself or my hosts. Why? The obvious congeniality, sincerity, and clarity of purpose of ethnographers notwithstanding, the reasons why our hosts and informants cooperate with anthropologists are rarely addressed in our literature. They should be, if for no other reason than they help us to understand some values, perceptions, and forces at work in these communities. In Navan and in the wider Meath there seemed to have been a few reasons why politicians and their supporters were so helpful. Some I will not or cannot reduce beyond hospitality, graciousness, the belief that my studies gave them some long-due public attention, and/or that university research was valuable and worthy of support. Some, however, had more material or self-serving reasons. As outlined above they were looking for a number of ways of shoring up deteriorating political support. Many of these politicians clearly did not understand why politics had become so difficult and unpredictable. On the simplest level they wanted me to share my analysis with them. But over those years of research I also concluded that there were more complex reasons for their cooperation.

Some politicians and their agents, while helping me with information and introductions, attempted to enlist me in their networks, which I have already suggested were shrinking and increasingly powerless. Their projected roles for me were never consistently or uniformly requested, but most overlapped the both implied and explicit requests made by other colleagues. I have grouped these expectations of me into three categories: information broker, public representative and political advisor.

Adding me as a client, or attempting to use me to get to my 'clients,' was a strategy adopted often by politicians who could not stop themselves from using tried and true ways of maintaining their political edge. I saw their efforts regarding me to be benignly unconscious, and sometimes foolish and/or desperate. Nonetheless, because of my lengthy analysis of farmers in business and politics, politicians at times wanted access to my networks among farmers. They often questioned

261

me, slyly and indirectly, regarding the political support of farmers they knew I was close to or had interviewed. Among such questions were: 'Who was he/were they voting for?' 'What do they think of (a recent government action)?' 'I don't suppose he's gone a bit Blue (from Fianna Fáil questioners, referring to the color of the shirts of an old movement associated with Fine Gael, the main opposition party)?'

These sorts of inquiries sometimes also referred to the IFA. As that organization gained power and prestige as a local and national lobby, politicians wanted to be seen in a good light by its leaders and members. Politicians often asked me about what the IFA was doing because they knew I attended monthly meetings of its county executive and that the 'large farmers' I had come to the county to study were the most influential farmers in the organization. Since 1973 these farmers had become a 'volatile' electorate, i.e., they often abandoned family traditional allegiances and voted for the party at each election whom they perceived better served farmers' interests. By the late 1970s farmers' roles in local politics had become problematic for politicians because many farmers were no longer predictable members of party factions. Who was crossing party lines? In what numbers? For which reasons? were questions that politicians wanted answered. Although a potential supplier of such information, for professional and personal reasons I did not divulge any such information, but this did not deter some of my political friends from trying to get me to exchange confidences, and then needling me when I did not comply.

Some politicians also wanted me to pass along information to those in my networks to whom the politicians wanted to send a confidential message. This occurred most often as 'When you visit _____ you wouldn't mind mentioning _____', or 'Tell _____ I've been working on that matter for him.' These messages invariably involved what the politician had already done, or was working on, or was about to do, for the person in question. The recipient was sometimes a client of the politician, or someone he wanted to woo away from another politician by indirectly approaching the client through me. In some ways my messenger role made me into an information broker too. The act of relaying the message to a person might have been viewed as an implicit validation of the credibility of the politician by me. The longer I stayed in Navan, the more people I came to know. In many ways I had begun to build a network of friends, acquaintances and confidants, among whom were various individuals and groups, such as the newspaper people with whom I worked and lived (I wrote a cinema column for the provincial paper for a year, and my housemates were reporters).

Many professionals in town were also my new friends and acquaintances. I had built up a large network of farmers who were the relatives of a family into which I had been welcomed due to a friendship that had developed between one of its members and me. Above all, I had also constructed the aforementioned networks of farmers and politicians which I had built up over months of observations, interviews, and pints of beer and meals in pubs, hotels and union halls. This became a sizable network for perhaps the only 'political' person in town who was by definition 'non-political,' i.e., I was an observer who belonged to no local party. In a sense, I could cross political borders with impunity, thus enhancing my value as a messenger.

There was one other area that a minority of politicians wished me to exploit for their benefit. On a few occasions, primarily at elections, I was directly questioned about the opposition parties' strategies and weaknesses. In more than one instance, such queries were immediately silenced by other politicians, who rightly pointed out that if I betrayed secrets I would be irreparably damaging my own research, and I would also be indicating my untrustworthiness regarding their own secrets. On other occasions I was asked by politicians when we were alone to comment on their colleagues' behavior, especially that of those in the machine or party. This was a murkier area for me to deal with, but whenever I felt I was being asked to inform rather than analyze public knowledge, I desisted.

As the months I lived in Navan stretched into years, a number of local politicians and I began to engage in increasingly complex political discussions. Like many of my fellow anthropologists, I had experienced a long period of informant and host doubt and incredulity regarding my ability to master the intricacies of local politics and government, including their political geography, electioneering, rhetoric, factions, history and party leadership. By 1979, however, politicians and others began to take my expertise in local affairs more seriously. The degree to which I kept abreast of developments in Navan and Meath politics impressed more than a few local political leaders, cadres and aspirants. Although much of their flattery was clearly part of the network-building gamesmanship detailed above, my long experience in Navan enabled me to discern the real leaders and power-holders in local political circles. These people were invariably in these positions because they had themselves mastered local politics. Their changing reactions to what I did and said were

264

testament to the levels of local political knowledge and acceptance I had attained.

This situation led to my being courted as a political advisor by people inside and outside of the Navan political machine. My skills as an analyst of local and national politics were on a few occasions sought out by aspiring politicians. In one case a local farmer whose family had always been known as Fine Gael opponents of the local machine questioned which direction to go in his new political career. He could go into local politics as a springboard to a parliamentary seat, or he could avoid the county council and gain national political prominence through the IFA. The hypothetical strategies we discussed for a few nights huddled over tea before his sitting room fire proved successful for him in the succeeding decade.

Another prominent citizen, an aristocrat whose name was linked to at least two political parties in the 1980s, knew he would have to take on the remnants of Navan's Fianna Fáil machine in order to gain the Meath seat in parliament he desired. He was using his considerable renown and wealth to develop as good a network of political advisors as possible before he embarked on his quest. This nascent 'think tank' was a good step, in my estimation, but my analytical skills were clearly not to his liking after our one business lunch. Nevertheless, this case illustrates many politicians' need to have concrete advice regarding their aspirations to national office. The elections of 1979 indicated ways some MCCs would use the county council to get to parliament. A good number of these were Fianna Fáil MCCs who knew that the demise of a core machine in Navan gave them potential openings. One young MCC found the town in which he lived to be 'divided up' in terms of party control so that for general elections it would be impossible for him to become a TD. In the late 1970s we had many discussions about the avenues he could take. With no help from me, beyond my role as a sounding board, he soon became a TD, with a strong constituency in Meath which grew to rival the cohesion and strength of the old machine of Navan's Fianna Fáil leadership.

These three examples of local politicians' asking my advice may be seen to both understate and overstate the complexities of my role as an advisor to a transforming political elite. No politician used me as their sole or long-standing advisor, and I have no way to tell whether any of my insights were understood, appreciated or acted upon. I was not there, nor have I ever been there, to act as an advocate or 'action' anthropologist. But the need for information by politicians, hungry for the data and the analysis of the political possibilities, was patent. For the remnants of Fianna Fáil's machine in Navan, shocked by so many changes in local politics, the past resources for information and direction were increasingly suspect, as local politics slowly degenerated into media-warring fiefdoms where everyone knew you could do little to improve your constituents' lives but few were prepared to admit it publicly. Perhaps any ethnographer in Meath, at any time in the past, would have been asked to act as an advisor to local big men. I daresay there are hundreds if not thousands of anthropologists around the world who have been in a similar position. In this particular instance, at the precise historical juncture of the late 1970s in rural Ireland, local politicians were as uninspired and directionless as at any other point in their history. One Navan MCC concluded in an interview with me that this was an extreme identity crisis for politicians because, for the first time since the Civil War of the 1920s, the

266

nationalist debate and pork barrel politics did not together provide the context for their political lives.

Many party supporters began to expect me to represent them in public. As the election of 1979 gathered momentum, a good number of party workers assumed that my presence at so many party meetings meant my allegiances were with them. This was perhaps predictable in any case, but this image of me was also magnified by the absolute number of Fianna Fáil meetings held to nominate, elect and prepare candidates. In the two months before the June election I estimated that I attended twice the number of Fianna Fáil meetings than I did the other two major parties combined. Ironically, my private social life exacerbated the difficulties, because both Fianna Fáil and Fine Gael claimed that the sizable farm family into which everyone expected I was marrying was 'one of theirs.' Thus each party had a number of people who believed I was (secretly, of course) on 'their side.' A great deal of confusion and consternation was therefore caused when a photo of my girlfriend and me at a Labour Party Constituency dinner dance was published in the newspaper. Over the next month I heard from dozens of members of Fianna Fáil and Fine Gael, including two of their TDs, about my fickle political allegiances. It was fruitless to point out to both that I attended all three parties' dinner dances (in the same suit and with the same woman, I might have added), and that I was, after all, as objective an observer of all parties and their operations as I could possibly be.

Into the 1980s in Meath, and up to the days when I moved my principal research to Northern Ireland in the early 1990s, a recurring conversational theme was my 'true' political leanings, i.e., what party would I join if I 'became' a local. In the late 1970s, each major party had leaders who believed I was on their side. As far as I know, this was not due in any way to any accidental or misleading suggestions to this effect on my part. I had conscientiously repeated the mantra that I was examining local politics and government, and that I needed to remain neutral and impartial. But perhaps the conclusions and assumptions about my true political leanings which seemed to surface among some local politicians were predictable for people who believed in the correctness of their actions. I was often surprised about how fervently political leaders and supporters in Meath believed in their parties, and thus expected me to naturally be an ally.

This was particularly true among the politicians I became most associated with in Meath, those of the Navan machine. Over the years of my research, they were, as a group, the most helpful and solicitous in all of my fieldwork. This resulted, in part, in what may be loosely termed a 'special relationship'. No less than three Fianna Fáil MCCs from Navan were quick to point out to other politicians and party members from outside Navan that I had gone to them first to seek advice or help in their professional capacities. This was indicative to them of the machine's efficacy, but also something proudly trumpeted in order to show that they responded first and most efficiently to my requests. Helping a visiting university person, someone of presumed high status (shocking to a PhD candidate, to say the least), was of some symbolic importance. One implied message to locals was that Meath politics, parties, and politicians were worthy of university study. The value of such implied statuses and boasts to politicians should be clear in light of the new era of declining confidence in them which I have outlined above.

Reflexology and codology

Since the 1960s sociocultural anthropology in Ireland has become increasingly reflexive. There has been a growing debate about the roles of ethnography and ethnographer. Some influential research has addressed the role of the anthropologist as both the participant and the observed, rather than the observer. These works have confronted some of the ethical and professional issues of being a scientist and humanist within literate and modernized communities who engage the ethnographer in intellectual dialogue at every stage of research (see, for example, Messenger 1988, 1989; Scheper-Hughes 1979, 2000). Of growing concern has been the responsibility of an anthropologist to both the people s/he lived with and studied, and to the critics of one's published work. Yet little has been written about the role and responsibilities of an ethnographer within the formal institutions and organizations of state politics. Academic gossip aside, there has been little discussion about the ethical and/or professional dilemmas of a social scientist in Ireland, or in Europe for that matter, whose research populations are the leaders of a community, region or nation. The need for such introspection became apparent when the recorded interviews of an Irish presidential candidate conducted years before by a postgraduate student of political science were made public in October 1990, thereby severely damaging the politician's campaign and almost bringing down the government.

As I have suggested, the changing relationship I had with members of Fianna Fáil represented the weakening of political networks which, when stronger, constituted a dynamic political machine. My role as 'objective' ethnographer, which included by own notions of offering reciprocity to all who shared their lives with me while I conducted my fieldwork, was increasingly threatened by my new friends and acquaintances' demands that I act a role with which they were comfortable. These roles were not then, and are not now, mutually exclusive. The ways that I and my friends in Meath came to accept compromise roles with each other were indicative that a zero-sum game of community acceptance in Ireland was rare.

The role many politicians wanted me to play in the late 1970s, however, was symptomatic of the growing and changing traffic in information among all politicians at every level. This vast 'information game' was played in the absence of the goods and services that were supposed to be supplied by political patrons to needy or greedy constituents. Those services that improved the quality of clients' lives were invariably supplied by the public servants of the local and national government. Nonetheless, local residents found it hard not to believe in the political efficacy of local politicians to 'get the job done' and grease the wheels of government to the advantage of loyal voters. The continued insistence on the part of many politicians that I become part of a political machine, or an active member of a political network, pushed me toward a relatively continual re-evaluation of my ethical stance on the politics of doing fieldwork in party politics. At almost every point of fieldwork I had to give myself a research politics-ethics-reality check, to see if in my view I was stepping over a boundary in my research which I ought not. This sort of self-imposed quality control, which every social anthropological field researcher considers if not imposes in long-term research which entails living and working with groups of people for extended periods, intensified once I had learned enough to appreciate the ways I

270

was being asked, perhaps even being recruited, to help political networks, and once I also was aware that I might indeed be able to perform a service for locals.

The politics and ethics of these situations and relationships were intertwined: many postgraduate students of anthropology today are interested in the politics of research, which in some ways refer to interpersonal politics that have been widely theorized in recent years. In other ways though the politics of research really boil down to whether some things are right or wrong, and if they are right or wrong would they be so labeled by human subjects review at universities, and/or would they violate the researcher's own sense of ethics (which in all likelihood do not fit neatly with the reviews of human subject committees, which are often as interested in legal safeguards as they are in the morality and ethics of researchers' interfering in the lives of others).

In my situation in the late 1970s and early 1980s in Meath, and to a decreasing extent in the years that followed after I had returned to a teaching job in the United States, I was asked to provide information, introductions, symbolic validation and other forms of support, at various times and in various ways, to politicians and to others in the county. It was difficult to discern any particular pattern to such requests, beyond the general dimensions I plotted above, but each such request tested my own senses of how the social obligations of sharing community life with others necessitated a give-and-take of general information and cooperation, which some, perhaps in academic circles or perhaps in local community life, would deem inappropriate. After all I was supposed to be an observer, perhaps from the lofty heights usually held by scientists, and despite all I had learned as an apprentice anthropologist in

271

university classes, this observer role is not generally recognized as entailing much participation. But participate we are meant to do! And I was coming up against the simple proposition that to participate in politics, despite all efforts on my part to be fair, equitable, balanced and honest, was seen by many, perhaps the majority of Meath people with whom I came into contact, to mean that I was political, which in local parlance meant that I was taking sides.

My reception in Meath society in general, and in the world of Meath politics in particular, had a great deal to do with local peoples' understanding of social science and social science research. Professional people of all walks of life, who in the main had been university educated at least to a first degree, had a ready awareness of the needs and constraints of research such as I was undertaking. Overall, the professionals of Meath, such as solicitors, accountants, teachers, clergy, local government officers, librarians, journalists, bankers, undertakers, farm consultants, and mine engineers and administrators, were helpful and cooperative. Others, who had never gone to university, but who had been self-taught in new ways of approaching old problems, such as in regard to the changing nature of Irish politics and society due to Europeanization within the EEC, were also aware and supportive of my research. This was particularly true of the vast majority of the large farmers of Meath, including those who served in the IFA and other farm bodies. As must also be clear from the above analysis, the political parties in Meath, as well as their national headquarters and leadership, were also cooperative. Without their approval I could not have done the research among politicians and parties that I did. But other people in Meath often had little idea of what my sort of research entailed, and why it should be conducted at all.

On one occasion, when I was visiting a seaside resort in County Louth with friends and acquaintances from Navan, whom I had then known for two years, one of the wives in the company, whom I had not known long, asked me what exactly I was doing research on, why it was taking so long, and who was paying for it. These direct questions, which were not commonly asked of me in social settings in Ireland, came along naturally enough sitting around the barbecue, over a few drinks, after the group's long day hiking. Once the questions were asked, four others, in a party of eight, quickly followed up with comments along the lines of 'Yes. Tom, what exactly have you been finding out? We/I wanted to know too?' But after my five minute explanation of what anthropology seeks to discover, and my interests in the intersection of politics and culture in everyday life, which in some senses I was relieved to get off my chest within the friendly atmosphere of beach, beer and camaraderie, I was startled to hear from my initial interrogator that it all amounted to 'codology' (her exact words, which I scribbled in my diary later that night out of a sense of exasperation and bewilderment, was 'That all sounds like a load of codology to me').

Codology was a reference to the Hibernian English verb 'to cod', or to fool, to play someone along, as in a tall tale or a practical joke. Her acknowledgment of my (hoped-for) succinct summary of my life and work for over two years was in essence an emotional response that I must be fooling someone, and that this amounted to little that was of worth. She was not angry or aggressive, but simply reacting in a way which displayed her wonder that anyone would be interested in such matters, which

273

to her were distant from the concerns of everyday life, and her greater surprise that someone would pay me to do such work! Not surprisingly, this turned the general banter to a direction that had me, my field research, and universities as the subjects of discussion, and, to be frank, some derision.

Well, the merriment that ensued was not particularly welcome to me, but it showed both that they, as a group, were not too bothered by my answers—in fact the husband of the woman who had asked for and responded first to my summary of my work commented immediately that if he could get paid to cod people for a living then he would gladly change professions. At that point one of his mates in the group pointed out that as a publican he had already been doing just that, codding people, for quite some time! But their responses also indicated that as a university person I was part of a world that was alien to everyday life there, and as such they were all willing to give me the benefit of the doubt regarding my research intentions, plans, and results. But behind it all, among them and often too among the politicians who are the concern of this chapter, I often detected notions of concern tinged with amusement which I put down as their appreciation of my codology. It was as if they saw me as some sort of scientific trickster, who had succeeded in codding many for reasons that were, frankly, beyond their caring.

My own doubts and assessment notwithstanding, Meath politicians were often just as willing as I to play along in my research in order to see what if anything might come back to them that they might be able to use. This sort of political gamesmanship did not end with my doctoral research. When I first returned to the United States, in the early 1980s, my role as network person for a number of politicians continued, but it also slowly dissipated over the following years, due to various reasons. The changing patterns of emigration from Meath had brought many more Meath people to New York and to the rest of the USA. For example, one of the passing acquaintances of mine in Navan moved to New York and bought a pub, after only a few years of bartending in Manhattan. That pub was on the Eastside of Manhattan, and turned into an obligatory stop for all Meath politicians and Gaelic Athletic Association players and supporters who visited or moved to the Big Apple. It also was an example of how Meath people had an expanding network of people upon whom to rely on a global scale. My own research interests turned more to matters pertaining to Northern Ireland and European integration, so I proved to be less informed and connected over the years. Furthermore, some of the social networks in which I had been welcomed and been seen to participate in Meath began to whither as the 1980s wore on, adding to the sense of social and physical distance that develops after field research is conducted.

But for a time I was still a member of politicians' networks when I first moved back to New York. Besides the welcome visits from old friends from Meath who sometimes traveled to New York on holidays, I also received requests to help politicians' relatives, neighbors and friends who were either holidaying or emigrating to America. These requested services included such things as introductions to possible employers (or other brokers) and bed and board. I not only was happy to do such things, out of a sense of friendship, obligation and general reciprocity, but also out of a sense of just doing the right thing, for them and for me. At the same time I was fully aware that by doing so I was behaving in a way that would be expected of me as part of the networks which ultimately

275

compose the informal political machines in Ireland. I was all but stereotypical when I gladly reciprocated the help of my community hosts in Ireland by aiding their clients. In fact, it took my return to New York to make me realize that field research in modern political and economic networks can make an anthropologist a *de facto* member of many of those same networks, and a perceived advocate or enemy of many of the groups studied.

This, of course, raised many questions regarding political ethnography. In political ethnography, to what extent and in what ways do we cross the objective, or objectified, bounds of professional social scientists while utilizing the methods of participant observation? In cases like Meath and its political machine and networks, how far can we go to reciprocate the kindnesses and confidence of our hosts without becoming part of what we seek to study and understand? And when we study the competition and factionalizing of party politics, how can we avoid the perceptions of us as sympathetic supporters or advocates of one side against another? Perhaps most important, to what degree do anthropologists who investigate power in culture adopt positions of power and authority when they slip in and out of political alignments through the creation of networks in the same image as those which we seek to comprehend? In such situations are we not then correctly perceived by our hosts to be manipulating people and situations in the manner of any self-respecting political patron, broker, and big man? I do not suggest that these are new or unique questions in social anthropology, but they are not issues which are often directly addressed in the political anthropology of Europe. This is due, I believe in part, to ethnographers' reluctance to analyze political parties and other aspects of government as social and political institutions, and to investigate party practices and organizations as integral aspects of culture and politics.

In Meath in this period I was never 'needed' by local politicians to maintain their positions or influence. In fact, few individuals were necessary for that because hardly anyone locally could help politicians in this regard. In the 1970s local political actors were increasingly powerless to protect the very bases of what had once been a formidable political apparatus. And yet, Meath politicians worked harder than ever before to be seen by their communities to be necessary to the proper functioning of government. They wished to sustain what was quickly becoming the myth of their role in local politics. Part of that role was to make clients feel that they were vital to party success. Given their intensified efforts, and their inherited roles as information brokers, it was not surprising that many local politicians quickly integrated me into their networks. Because of this, I concluded that they both wanted and needed information regarding their rapidly transforming political system, and that I might be able to help in these regards.

It was also not surprising to me then that many local politicians surmised that I might be able to help in the gathering and use of some politically relevant information. After all I had relatively open access to government functionaries and officers. I participated in many political functions that were not accessible to all politicians, such as party meetings. And I had an aura of someone, trained in the university study of politics, who might have some expertise in these matters to offer. But I rarely had such information and it took me a long time to develop any personal sense of political worth and expertise. It is also fair to say that many Meath politicians did not give a damn about anything I knew. To them and to many others not directly related to party politics and government, I was as much a codologist as I was an anthropologist. But the relationships I developed with the people and parties of Navan, especially within the deteriorating Fianna Fáil machine, were then, and remain today, indicative of the decline in the status of local politicians and their concomitant loss of power and influence in Meath life.

Today, the Navan machine is all but gone. There is at present no Navan-based Fianna Fáil TD. The old Meath parliamentary constituency has been divided into two, into Meath East and Meath West, with three TDs representing each. The Fianna Fáil political clubs from the outlying regions of the county, especially those closest to Dublin, now dominate the party leadership in the county, with two of 'their' TDs having served as government ministers. Party centralization continues to make the national leadership in Dublin more powerful than ever. The government and civil service have tighter control than ever of the basic services. But the politicians carry on. As one chief public servant in Meath local government told me, in the summer of 1987 when we discussed local politicians: 'Let them be as happy in their role as long as they can. They are like dinosaurs, and they haven't sussed out--or more importantly, no one has told them--that the temperature is dropping'.

In the midst of this political climate change, my ethnographic research sought to identify and analyze cause and effect relations in local government and politics, and my original intention was to do this research according to models I had hypothesized back in New York before the research began, which were suitably revised as the research went along. Like

278

many of my peers in social and cultural anthropology at the time, I was not prepared to consider myself as a variable in that research, nor did I expect to be part of what I studied. However, my intention that I would do this research as if I was a fly on the wall slowly dissipated, in direct proportion to my own seasoning as a researcher and as a knowledgeable member of Meath political society. When I conducted this doctoral research I was relatively unaware of the developing turn to reflexive anthropology which was percolating in centers of anthropological thought elsewhere. But the issues raised in the critiques of ethnography which were to follow were in many ways apparent to me as I did my ethnographic turn in Meath. This was especially true in regard to my increasing doubts about my ability to be objective while doing political research, or at the very least my inability, and I grew to conclude any researcher's inability, to maintain a status of observer rather than participant in the middle of ethnographic research on party politics.

Although in the end I did not concur with those in anthropology who concluded that relatively little can be achieved in ethnographic research beyond giving a voice to others, because in this view ethnography is on balance a biased form of writing and interpretation that is fraught with the weaknesses inherent in personalized and idiosyncratic social research, my roles in Meath as visitor, researcher, potential network member and political analyst and pundit helped me to see that I was not in fact codding either the people of Meath or myself. There was much that was happening in Meath politics in the late 1970s and early 1980s that was important locally. These changes were also evidence of national and international forces of change. My ethnographic research provided the data for that historical case study of changing politics and government in Meath, and showed too that a reflexive approach in ethnography is only part of the research experience. But I also became convinced that long-term ethnographic research, perhaps through revisiting field situations, might be the best way for an anthropologist to combine the reflexive with other approaches in the pursuit of party politics and culture.

Chapter 8

Revisiting Political Culture in County Meath

One rainy spring night in 1990, while I was quietly sipping my usual coca cola in my local public house in Navan, my attention was drawn to the back of the establishment by the boisterous activity of two 'half-jarred' local politicians, both of whom I had been friendly with since 1978. Although their gaiety and high spiritedness were not surprising – each was known for a fine sense of humor and an affability that made them among the best liked and most respected politicians in Meath - their conspiratorial air, in each other's company, most decidedly might have been seen by some in the house to be worthier of note, for each, happy in the company, was a local leader of opposing political parties. One, a county councillor, was widely rumored at the time to be preparing a bid for the Dáil in the next general election, to contest the seat of his companion of the evening, a then-serving TD.

Their joking relationship that night might have surprised some, but to most locals this event was not really so out of the ordinary, for reasons which have been examined at some length in the chapters above. The rest of the patrons in the pub in fact had left these two local notables alone, due to what I concluded was a mixture of respect for their rights to privacy and leisure, but also due to a notion that politicians sometimes needed to be let alone to hatch their plans and to suss out their competition.

However, I did not feel so constrained. When they spied me in the front of the lounge I accepted their invitation to join them. They successfully evaded my opening conversational gambit, which was something about whose back was being readied for which knife, when one of the politicos, who was a Navan native, announced to the other that I was 'more of a local than the locals', whereupon his companion, a Kells man, suggested that I was not the property of Navan but 'a citizen of the entire County Meath'. This banter proceeded from 'he almost knows more about County Meath politics than any of us' (a flattering lie when coming from either of them, but not far wrong I thought at the time, since in the greater scheme of things for over two years I had been hard at work painting for myself the bigger picture of local politics and government as working systems of politics) to the playful argument over which of the two main parties I would join if I moved to Meath permanently. Each knew a fair number of people, from both Fianna Fáil and Fine Gael, who claimed I was 'one of theirs'. The discussion moved on when I could not continue apace, that is, when I reiterated my long-standing position that I was a neutral and, as far as possible, an objective observer and analyst.

Upon reflection, of course, and in the best reflexive ethnographic tradition I can muster, I must admit that my implicitly accepted roles that night of political pundit and observer, county resident and citizen, and university specialist, were but versions of my self-projected public identity in Meath, one that had taken years to achieve. Each of those gentlemen was convinced, because of conclusions drawn over the previous months and years, that he was correct in his characterization of my local and political identities. And this was not the first time this subject had arisen in public and private political discussions with me and about me. In fact, discussions of my political affiliations and allegiances had become relatively commonplace in my research in politics, and increasingly so after I had been living in Meath for two years. As a result I had begun to wonder about how common such queries were in anthropological research elsewhere.

Since then I have often speculated as to how often and how many of my colleagues who have done fieldwork in Ireland and Britain have experienced similar pressures to 'become' a local, or to continuously explain why one cannot or will not adopt that identity. The 'identity crisis' I experienced in Meath then, which was in large part a confusion of identifications which others attached to me, has become a facet of normality for me as I continue to live, albeit intermittently, in Meath today. But it definitely went through many stages in the culture shocks of initial fieldwork from 1976 to 1979, when I was known at various times and in various places as 'the Yank student', 'the Yank doing the study', 'the Yank sociologist/anthropologist/archaeologist', or, simply, 'the Yank'. But over the intervening thirty years my local identity has changed according to the ebb and flow of the relationships I have maintained in Meath and to the social statuses which adhere to the academic positions I have held in that time. Today, for example, I am more likely to be referred to as 'the Yank professor'.

During my research and residence in Meath I have played the roles that many ethnographers play in their field sites: cultural adolescent; observer and recorder of public and private behavior; a new link in many social networks; and a symbol, and perhaps at times an agent, of community change. My roles have also reflected my longstanding residence in Navan, a function of the association of person, time and place which I conclude has made much of my life there different, if not in kind then in degree, from most of my ethnographic colleagues who have studied Ireland but who have not lived long there. Simply put, over time I have come to see myself (and I know that others have also come to see me this way too, if their sentiments expressed to me and to others are to be believed) as both 'resident' and 'citizen', both 'local' and 'Yank', more 'friend' than 'stranger'.

Contradictory or multiple identities and identifications are neither new to ethnographers nor to the people we study, but the time factor is a crucial element in the ways these identities are recognized and defined by ourselves and our hosts and neighbors. This is not to say that Meath people made me one of their own, or embraced me as one of theirs, or accepted this outsider in ways no others could be accepted. Frankly, the vast majority of Meath residents have never heard of me, and if they had, the bulk of them would probably not be bothered an iota one way or the other. But through a complicated process, which has gone on a bit longer than most such exercises, of social affiliation and integration, the veritable stuff of the ethnographic experience, I have become a semi-local, a 'blow-in' who never quite blew back out, and at least to some a cultural fact of life of which the communities of the wider Meath are in the main unaware. Over the years I have just seemed to come and go with the seasons.

I hasten to add that all of this fitting in and adapting on my part was not just to blend with the social and cultural background. While friendships and shared experiences have kept me returning to Meath over the last thirty years as much as have my research interests, I have also played some other roles in local society. For example, my facility in local politics has on occasion made me into a political guide and consultant. But the point I seek to make here has more to do with the practice of ethnography and the benefits of doing it repeatedly, over time, in the same places, with the same research personnel. This long process has helped to form identities, identifications and relationships that shape the core of what I have also sought to privilege in this book, which is a historical chronicle and analysis of local social, economic, cultural and political change.

Identity matters

Just as I have undergone identity transformations over the last thirty years, so have the people of Meath. The large farmers I first went to study have gone from a powerful and wealthy interest group to a less vocal and less influential group of businessmen in an increasingly suburban county. Politicians and churchmen have lost a good deal of their social stature and power, the latter not only to the unstoppable force of secularization but also recently due to the tragic unfolding of the evidence of generations of clerical abuse of those entrusted into the Church's care. Many women have redefined their roles at home and in the business world. Young professionals shop at the trendy boutiques of globalized brand-name consumer goods, and holiday in all of the hotspots of the world. Teenagers daily converse with international counterparts while putting down hordes of zombies on their generation X+ boxes. And adults and children sport the global paraphernalia, bling and wardrobe of a Euro-American consumer lifestyle which has transformed the look and feel of all of Ireland.

In fact, so much has happened in Meath over the last generation that it has become extremely difficult to view Meath as anything but a cog in a world culture and economy. It seems to me that Navan has become noisier, dirtier, more crowded and more dangerous, and that Meath's expanding middle class has become more materialistic and less informed than a decade ago. My impression is that this is true for much of Ireland, but in this book I have sought to avoid characterizing the whole of Ireland from a vantage point in one county. While I continue to see, unlike so many of my peers in anthropology, that the strength of social anthropology is in empirical social and cultural comparison, I am aware that the notions of culture, comparison, evidence and analysis are always in contest in scholarly disciplines. But in this book I have offered a portrait of Meath and some of its people which I hope will serve others in their historical and comparative analyses.

One thing is clear to me though, and it is this realization that has also motivated me to write this book. What I choose to write or say about Meath is based on my own data and analysis, and stands and falls on the accuracy of and insight derived from same. The results are as ethnographically accurate and true for me and Meath as any such ethnographic research can be, that is, without reflexively interpreting everything to such a degree that anthropology, culture and ethnography become so idiosyncratic and reductionist as to be meaningless.

Therefore, this motivation also leads me to argue that one of the important roles anthropology can play in social scientific and humanistic scholarship is to construct portraits of local, regional, and national identity. Anthropologists can and should induce from ethnographic studies aspects of national culture which can complement the visions of the other social sciences,

286

as well as those of decision makers in other walks of life. I believe this to be an especially important contribution which ethnographers in particular can make to the understanding of the impact and development of an integrating Europe and globalizing world in places such as Ireland. But working on issues of nation, state, and identity at all levels of social and political integration is not the same thing as characterizing nations, such as the Irish, on the back of ethnographic community studies.

Over the years I have been saddened by my conclusion that the most famous anthropological studies of Ireland in the English-speaking world have earned their reputation because of what they have been seen to say about Ireland and the Irish, about the island, country, nation and culture as a whole. The most quoted and referenced anthropologists of Ireland outside of Ireland have been those who have characterized (or have been seen to characterize) Ireland and the Irish negatively. Without addressing the accuracy of these analyses of Ireland that have become so popular, in American anthropology in particular, and without intending to impugn the intentions of their authors, I would have to conclude, based on the graduate students who have contacted me over the last twenty years and the research proposals I have reviewed for granting agencies over the same period, that in the main Irish people are mentally ill, alcoholic, sexually repressed, clergy dominated, sexist and racist.

While I am certain that much of this rings true to many observers of Irish life, this book in its own small ways has attempted to show that ethnography also offers a window on an Ireland that is different and perhaps more complicated and dynamic. Nonetheless, at least in America, other perspectives on Ireland, such as those that have involved me in my research and in this book, do not seem to spark a great deal of interest on the part of those who seek to further anthropological theorizing today. Ethnography in Ireland rarely seems to be labeled by scholars outside of the country as innovative and creative theorizing and research. One reason for this is that ethnographers of Ireland may view such innovation as trendy and faddish anthropology, geared more to professional anthropological advancement elsewhere than to the understanding of what is happening in social, cultural, political and economic change in historical and everyday Ireland.

This sort of anthropological bipolarism has long been a fact of life in the anthropology of Ireland. For generations after the Arensberg and Kimball threshold, ethnographic practice and academic anthropology in Ireland have been caught between, on the one hand, theoretical concerns and models that were designed and debated in other lands, the most important being the United States and England, and on the other hand the incentives and constraints placed on the development of anthropology in Ireland which tried to isolate and understand the myriad ways in which Irish culture has shaped Irish life, and vice versa. These two often conflicting forces in anthropology in Ireland corresponded roughly to what the sociologist-ethnographer Michael Burawoy (2003) has called constructivist and realist approaches in ethnographic scholarship. But whatever we might want to label these two ways of seeing and doing anthropology, they reflect the simple fact that most anthropological theorizing has its origins elsewhere, outside of Ireland, and unless ethnographers in Ireland are cognizant of this fact, and make efforts to have their research and other scholarly output conform to professional interests beyond Ireland, they run the risk of being seen to be too local and peripheral to ultimately matter in the crafting of a global academic discipline.

Here it would be appropriate to admit that, while there have been conflicting forces at work in the ontology of anthropology in Ireland, there have also been some acknowledged successes and trend-setters. There have been bodies of anthropological research that have been well-received in Ireland, because of their blending of sociological and anthropological theorizing, on the one hand, and finely-grained ethnographic data, on the other hand. This data and analysis were in the main but certainly not universally recognized by many Irish people as being sound portraits of their lives in particular places and at select times. Much of this ethnographic work can be grouped within two research and writing models. The first has been labeled as the 'dying peasant community', mostly found in studies done in the Republic of Ireland from the 1960s to the 1980s, and the second is that of the 'warring tribes' of Northern Ireland, which was based on ethnographic studies done there in the same period.

As Wilson and Donnan (2006) see it, these perspectives in the ethnography of Ireland respectively have served as gate-keeping devices, where the Irish Republic and Northern Ireland have taken on the character of ethnographic and cultural regions, with particular characteristics and features which seem to frame the reasons and methods for ethnographers to research there. These two ethnographic motifs, of the dying communities of traditional Ireland and the warring tribes of the North, i.e., Protestants versus Catholics, Unionists against Nationalists, Loyalists against Republicans, have been especially successful when negotiating with funding agencies, PhD and tenure committees, and publishers, particularly outside of Ireland. The result has been that Ireland continues to be a net importer of anthropological theories and methods, but not entirely so, and there is a great deal of emerging evidence today to suggest that the imbalance is not as steep as it once was (as reviewed in detail in Wilson and Donnan 2006).

The signs of a renewed professional anthropology in Ireland, one that has married an interest in examining and understanding the roles of culture in daily life of Irish people with that of contributing to many forms of global anthropology, are indeed welcome. But they must always be held up to the mirror of professional scholarship, in order to utilize the same methods which have been honed over generations of ethnography to allow us to explore how certain ideas and ideologies in anthropology have become hegemonic. Moreover, current developments in the ethnography of Ireland must also deal with the legacies of past dominant models in the academy which persist and continue to influence the course of global anthropology.

For example, for two generations after the publishing of Arensberg and Kimball's findings, the ethnography of Ireland seemed, at times, to be fated to repeatedly analyze family roles, generational norms, inheritance, marriage patterns, rural and urban social structure, and formal and informal ties within rural and urban landscapes. But I did not engage these many aspects of kinship and social organization, at least not as directly and as principally as did my peers in the ethnographic investigation of Ireland in the 1970s. Rather, I chose to examine the intersections of culture, politics and history, which, as I have argued in this book, not only resulted in a study that diverged considerably from the mainstream at the time in the anthropology of Ireland, but one which also sought to engage other scholars, from political sociology and political science for example, who were also charting new courses for themselves within their own academic disciplines.

These new forms of analysis of the local politics of culture, and the local cultures of politics, were certainly innovative then, but are not particularly novel any longer. On the contrary, in most studies of politics today it is impossible to not encounter a serious attention to culture and identity. All anthropological studies of the contemporary world seem compelled to address the issues of power and politics, even if the overwhelming majority of such studies seem oblivious to the power and politics to be found in government, political parties and factions, and other political and social institutions. That is why in this book I have also sought to demonstrate that ethnographies such as the one I initiated in Meath in the 1970s are also historical case studies of political and cultural change. Ethnography, in its very application, provides long-serving data collection through the longstanding presence of the researcher, who not only stays a fair time in the initial field work, but often returns, and sometimes returns often, to provide greater depth and breadth to the analysis. It is no wonder that anthropology and history not only infuse kindred spirits but also help to fashion equally binding relations of ethnographic and historiographic practice.

History, ethnography, conjuncture and event

In her introduction to a major collection of anthropological essays on history and culture change, Emiko Ohnuki-Tierney (1990: 6) concluded that there are two basic questions in any historical study: in what ways does a culture change or remain

291

stable over time, and how does this change occur? This book has presented a portrait of how political culture in Meath has changed over the course of the twentieth century, and has offered some suggestions as to how and why these changes came about. But what can this tell us of Irish political culture, and of Meath within that wider frame of reference?

While this book has ranged across a great swathe of local and national political history and cultural change, it has not sought to offer an analysis of the *longue durée* of local Irish political change. Rather, it has delved into the forces at work in two other temporal dimensions to local Irish history, dimensions which were suggested by Braudel (1980) as being necessary ones, in addition to long term perspectives, to understand historical change. Besides the more fundamental changes in society, economy and polity that may be best discerned within the long term analysis that is captured in the concept of the *longue durée*, anthropologists and historians must also identify changes which happen in a *conjuncture*, over the course of a decade or two, and in an *event*, a short term happening which may or may not prove significant, depending on how deep-seated that event's social oscillations prove to be.

This book has offered various examples of such conjunctures and events, from the 1930s to the 1980s, that provide purchase on the transforming of local politics and government in County Meath. Events such as those associated with the rise of farmers in political life of the new Irish state in the 1930s, and the workers' and farmers' marches, demonstrations and public resistance in the late 1970s, provided the evidence for my assessment of more fundamental historical conjunctures in local politics and government in County Meath. This longer historical perspective has allowed me to trace the rise and then the beginning of a decline in the influence of large farmers in party politics and local government in the county, but it is a story of a decline that is matched by a local and national rise in prominence of farmer lobbying groups. This new political influence, in turn, has been made possible by the transformation in Ireland that has been framed if not caused by accession to the European Union.

In the course of four decades the role and power of farmers in Irish politics changed significantly, in what I suggest are historical conjunctures that have proved to be tremendously significant, as forces of change which have transformed a rural county into a suburban one, and marginalized large farmers as an elite within local party politics and government. While they still command much prestige and influence in local social, economic and political circles, large farmers as a group no longer dominate Irish politics nationally, and no longer serve as the guiding elite in Meath. This book has also offered some reasons for these transformations, to show that selected events and other historical frames demonstrate remarkably important social oscillations, variations that would not have been so clearly delineated without the benefits of long-term ethnographic research.

The value of ethnographic research for the chronicling and analysis of historical change does not come easily, for ethnography as a methodology has itself experienced major conjuncture and disjuncture since the time of my original fieldwork. This has been due in part to global economic and political change, but also to changes in the academy, where empirical and positivist-orientated research has fallen out of favor in much if not most social science. These forces have conspired to make the lot of an ethnographer, who recognizes that localities must be understood within the contexts of the many national and global landscapes within which they are situated, all that much more difficult when the ethnographer also seeks to come to terms with his or her own entanglement in those same forces. As Clifford Geertz, a pioneer of interpretive anthropology and an ancestor to reflexive anthropologists worldwide, has concluded:

> When everything changes, from the small and immediate to the vast and abstract – the object of study, the world immediately around it, the student, the world immediately around him, and the wider world around them both – there seems to be no place to stand so as to locate just what has altered and how (Geertz 1995: 2; as quoted in Burawoy 2003: 645-646).

Yet the task of ethnography is just this: to locate what has changed and how it has changed, which necessitates that a balance be stuck in all anthropological research into the past and contemporary human condition between reflexivity, where the ethnographer is also a subject of study, and the realist world which surrounds both the investigator and the people and events which are either the subject or the object of critical inquiry.

Striking this balance has proved to be a difficult thing in today's anthropology, principally because, at least in much American anthropology but also increasingly elsewhere, the ethnographer has become the central feature of ethnographic research, the protagonist in the ethnographer's story about others' stories, wherein the internal world of the reflexive anthropologist occludes the worlds external to the researcher. I concur with the conclusion of the sociologist ethnographer Michael Burawoy: 'As they join their subjects in the external world, anthropologists have also all too easily lost sight of the *partiality* of their participation in the world they study. They begin to believe they *are* the world they study or that the world revolves around them' (2003: 673; emphasis in original). As a result of this reflexive turn, that has become the principal course for many ethnographers today, 'ethnography has been slow to emancipate itself from the eternal present' (Burawoy 2003: 646).

This book has championed such emancipation. It has done so with reference to historical events and conjunctures which offer, through an ethnographic lens which also serves as a historical prism, an example of how a reflexive and realist balance in ethnography may be struck. This balance is necessary if anthropologist and sociologist ethnographers persist in the goal of marrying theory to practice in field research, where, as I have argued throughout this book, they may simultaneously serve the interests of both social science and history in the understanding of how the politics and culture of locality and globe intersect. This balance also needs to be struck between the reflexive and the realist in ethnographic practice, between the internal moments necessitated by an ethnographer's wish to understand self in the midst of complex social webs, and the external moments where the ethnographic self must retreat in the face of recognizing and understanding the world outside of the researcher, a world where others have their own internal and external moments.

[R]eflexive ethnography must recognize and build on two dilemmas and the tension between them: there is a world outside of ourselves (realist moment), but ethnographers can only know it through their relation to it (constructivist moment); and ethnographers are part of that world (internal moment), but only *part* of that world (external moment). (Burawoy 2003: 668, emphasis in original).

In attempting to overcome these dilemmas, and to achieve some sort of balance between them, ethnographers, whatever their disciplinary background, should consider this challenge:

The time is nigh for the sociologist-ethnographer to come out of hiding and join the rest of sociology in novel explorations of history and theory. . . . We should not forget that Marx, Weber, and Durkheim grounded their history, as well as their theory, in an ethnographic imagination, whether of the factories of nineteenth-century England, the religious bases of economic behavior, or the rites and beliefs of small-scale societies. (Burawoy 2003: 675).

As one way to emerge from the shadows, to embrace the study of theory in practice in ethnography, Burawoy suggests that ethnographers should revisit their research. His conceptualization of ethnographic revisiting closely approximates the research intentions that provide the bases for my arguments in this book, and is testament too of how far down the road of reflexive anthropology we have gone in the first decade of the twenty-first century when scholars like

Burawoy need to make calls for what many ethnographers, trained in earlier forms of cultural and social anthropology, often assumed to be essential aspects of being an anthropologist: 'An ethnographic revisit occurs when an ethnographer undertakes participant observation, that is, studying others in their space and time, with a view to comparing his or her site with the same one studied at an earlier point in time, whether by him or herself or by someone else' (Burawoy 2003: 646).

Revisiting in ethnographic research must be distinguished from the reanalysis of someone else's data and the replication of someone else's study. Ethnographic revisiting may be viewed as rolling or extended research which is intended to 'explain variation' and 'comprehend difference over time' (Burawoy 2003: 647). In aspiring to do ethnographic revisiting, anthropologists will simultaneously embark on reflexive ethnography, wherein

> ethnography is *reflexive* not only in the sense of recognizing the relation we have to those we study but also the relation we have to a body of theory we share with other scholars. Second, a reflexive ethnography is ethnographic in the sense that it seeks to comprehend an external world both in terms of the social processes we observe and the external forces we discern (Burawoy 2003: 655, Footnote 13, emphasis in original).

It is this sort of continuing and reflexive ethnography that is at the heart of ethnographic history which I have also championed in this book, and I concur with Burawoy (2003:

675) when he concludes that both social theory and historical understanding can be significantly advanced through this sort of ethnographic research.

I have revisited Meath in ethnographic terms on funded research trips three times over the last thirty years, but I have in effect never ended the research that I began in the summer of 1976: Ireland became my home away from New York, and later has become our family home. We have a cottage in the Boyne Valley not far from Navan, and I estimate that since my doctoral ethnographic research began I have lived in Ireland for almost twenty years, never far from the politics and culture which involved me here in this book. Ethnographic revisiting may not be the only way to do reflexive anthropological research, but for me it has been the best way, especially if one seeks to recognize, understand and explain historical change, be it in terms of seemingly unconnected events, longer patterns of change that seem to reflect important cultural conjuncture, or major transformations in the long-term.

Whether viewed as ethnographic revisiting, ethnographic history, historical anthropology, or more simply as the ethnography of the politics of change, anthropologists have a great deal to offer in the explanation of historical continuity and variation. My revisiting has, among other goals, sought to explain transformations in political culture in one Irish county throughout the perturbations of a new Europe in a new supranational continental order.

Revisiting Irish political culture

My research in Meath and much that underpins the analysis I have presented in this book have been informed by what has become a less-favored concept in social science, that of political culture. When I first went to Ireland I was influenced by the writing of Basil Chubb, and particularly by his introduction to the subject that was then and continues to be a major contribution to our collective understanding of Irish government and politics (Chubb 1970). In that text he began his analysis of Irish politics with reference to Ireland's political culture. To Chubb the term referred to

> The general pattern of people's attitudes and beliefs about, and their knowledge of, politics and political phenomena— including matters such as political organization, the government, politicians and public servants, what the state should and should not do, and the extend and effectiveness of their own participation in politics (Chubb 1970: 43).

Borrowing from Pye and Verba (1965: 7), political culture theorists who pioneered this important theme in comparative political sciences, Chubb indicated that he saw political culture as giving 'meaning, predictability and form to the political process'. In Ireland, he noted that national political culture, although part of great social and political change at the end of the 1960s, relied on key ingredients, namely *the British influence* on Irish society, culture and politics; *nationalism*, as it related to the issues of sovereignty, the Irish border with the United Kingdom, anti-Britishness in many aspects of Irish life, and the cultural nationalism associated with the Irish language, arts, and other forms of traditional culture; a *dying peasant society*, where new forms of social and economic life were re-configuring class and other forms of rural and urban Ireland;

Irish Catholicism, which continued to frame Irish social hierarchies, education, social welfare, and conservatism; *authoritarianism*; *loyalty*; and *anti-intellectualism* (Chubb 1970: 44-57). These last three aspects of political culture were the legacy of the Church, colonialism and elites who were inward looking in their efforts to consolidate the new state.

As part of this analysis of Irish political culture, Chubb examined old and new rural and urban classes, and sought to connect class to the old and new political elites of Ireland. In particular he noted the rise of a middle-class bourgeois elite in the cities, replacing the British-oriented and Protestant elites from before independence. There was also a change in elites in the countryside, where the social composition of farming leadership had changed after national independence:

> Although the number of Protestants with large farms did not decline, the social and political leadership of the landed 'West Briton' country gentry was quickly terminated. These had been the leaders of the most significant subculture in the country. Today, it exists mainly as a division based on religious, educational, and, in some respects, social separation—a cleavage in Irish society certainly, but politically of little importance (Chubb 1970: 49).

While the 'today' to which Chubb refers was 1970 or so, two things are of interest to me here, and were planks in my original research platform: the old rural elites had given way to new ones, who had sidelined the Anglo-Irish in national politics; and these elites might be approached as subcultures by social scientists. This was important because the national

300

political culture to which Chubb referred was also local political culture, but the two were not synonymous. This was because there were other aspects of local politics and government which equally gave meaning, predictability and form to local political process. These aspects of local society and culture framed people's general patterns of political attitudes, beliefs, practices, institutions and participation. In other words my self-appointed task as a political ethnographer in County Meath was to recognize and characterize local political culture.

This effort on my part was certainly in keeping with the new paths forged by Paul Sacks and Mart Bax who have been discussed at length above. But local political studies, and particularly ones that focused on political society and culture, were in a decided minority in the 1970s. Up to then, in the vast majority of cases, Irish political studies had concentrated on problems in political structure and organization at the national or state levels. These studies were of the institutions of government and politics (McCracken 1958; Chubb 1974; O'Donnell 1979); Irish party systems in comparative perspective (Moss 1933; Mair 1979); Irish electoral politics, including sociopolitical cleavages as evidenced in voting patterns (Gallagher 1976; Carty 1976, 1981; O'Leary 1979); and the roles and social statuses of parliamentary representatives (Chubb 1963; Whyte 1966; Cohan 1972, 1973, 1974). There had been very few studies of Irish politics from a comparative interdisciplinary perspective, which drew on the models of sociology, anthropology, economics, geography and history in order to deal with macro-political processes (although a notable exception was the excellent history of politics and power by Rumpf and Hepburn 1977), just as there were very few micropolitical studies of individual constituencies, local club electoral behavior or local political culture. One scholar had created an influential body of analysis in regard to the former (Garvin 1974, 1977, 1978, 1981), and as we have seen there had been a few analyses of urban (Garvin 1976; Gallagher 1980; Komito 1984) and rural electoral and machine politics (Bax 1976; Sacks 1976; Carty 1981).

Beyond the national, however, other forms of political culture have taken root in Ireland. Chief among them has been those aspects of culture and identity associated with being and becoming European, processes largely constructed within the frameworks of Europeanization and European integration. Much that affects the Europeans of the EU across the continent relates to new and changing conceptions of territory and place. This book thus has also sought to offer some insight into how ethnography might contribute to our scholarly understanding of the changing nature of localism and regionalism in Europe, both of which have a great deal to do with the realization of the European integration project. In fact, a 'Europe of the Regions' has been an organizing principle in the European Union for at least fifty years, coinciding with the period of Ireland's membership in the EU. And while the term itself still remains a bit fuzzy in practice and in conception, its continuing salience in so much that occurs in European political economy testifies to the significance and the longevity of the concept, even when faced with the daunting task of encompassing the regions of the twenty-seven current EU member states.

In spite of the fact that a Europe of the Regions is a polymorphous and polysemic entity, it is irrefutable that some regions in and across the borders of the EU's member states have successfully used EU development funds and other forms of political and economic intervention to transform their political, economic, social and cultural conditions. These regions have been the beneficiaries of European Commission and national and subnational governmental schemes to right economic inequities within and between member states. Moreover, national and subnational programs of regional development have often been part of regionalization policies which transform nation-states in Europe. Social movements and identity politics have also pushed nations to recognize all sorts of historical and contemporary cultures and identities. All of these policies, programs and practices have given new definition to territorial regions, which in turn, through the types of historical conjunctures reviewed above for Meath and Leinster, have influenced changes in local, regional and national government and governance.

Given these major changes across the landscape of the EU, it is surprising that there has been relatively little ethnographic research in the roles of farmers in politics in Europe. This is surprising on many counts, including the many political changes wrought by the EU in member states, the major transformations in class and other aspects of society in European nations in recent decades, and the continuing importance of farmers and agriculture to all European nations. But it is also surprising because the anthropology of European integration has also been growing (as may be seen in Shore 1993; Bellier and Wilson 2000a, 2000b), but just not in regard to the Europeanization of rural life. This inattention by ethnographers to farmers and politics in the EU mirrors the relative lack of ethnographic research on the lives of European farmers with land, wealth, and power. With the exception of notable works such as those by Greenwood (1976), Newby et al. (1978), Newby (1979), Gröger (1981), Rogers (1991) and Lawrence (2007), the absence of analyses of commercial farmers and agricultural businesses in comparative European research is also indicative of much of recent ethnography worldwide. The failure of ethnographers to deal with the 'haves' as well as the 'have-nots' in European society, economy and polity is a serious problem for the anthropology of Europe, especially if anthropologists will persevere in identifying the social problems related to Europeanization and European integration.

Political culture in Meath over the later decades of the last century clearly was transformed due to many forces internal and external to the county. Globalization in technology and capitalism were enhanced by the twin forces of Europeanization and European integration, giving at the very least a new European dimension to local political culture. But as we have seen in the chapters above, the cultures of local government and politics in particular were transformed. Farmers are no longer the political elite they once were, the county is not the same sort of rural space it once was, local government is being weakened due to forces of national centralization and internationalization, and overall culture and class relations must favor the urban dimensions to Meath life where once rurality predominated. Ethnographic research in Meath over a long period of time has allowed me to conduct the sort of revisiting which Burawoy has proposed, and which seems extremely useful if not ideal in the scholarly pursuit of marrying anthropological theory with ethnographic practice in order to chronicle and apprehend historical change.

Striking balances

The rather curious gaps and imbalances in anthropological approaches to research in local agriculture, government and territorial identities in Europe brings me back to a final consideration of politics and culture, and how their treatment by anthropologists often reflects models, theories and paradigms that have become influential among scholars elsewhere, but increasingly seem devoid of connection to the problems of quotidian life in locales in Europe.

In this vein, I have often wondered if some anthropologists might see it as ironic that the large farmers of Meath were sometimes referred to in local circles as 'big men', because the term itself has a distinct and important pedigree in political and economic anthropology that is far-removed from the Irish context. But I never viewed this as either coincidence or irony. The term 'big man', which derives first and perhaps most importantly from the work of one of the deans of anthropology, Marshall Sahlins (1963), refers to political leaders in tribal Melanesia whose acumen as managers of subsistence goods and of people attains for them a political following, among kin and others who grow to rely on the prestations they receive from their leaders. But these 'big-men', like those of County Meath, are aware that their reputations and following, as prestigious and influential as they might be at any point in time, can only continue if the leader successfully sustains the supply of goods and services that led to his elevated status. Thus the 'big men' of both Melanesia and Meath alike must maintain relations of reciprocity and redistribution of material and political resources, where one's political renown and economic viability equally depend on the ability to balance a reputation as a generous and fair leader with the need to retreat from some aspects of public life, in order to accumulate and ultimately to redistribute economic resources and prestige to oneself and one's kin.

This balance, like other balances that need to be struck in the lives of commercial farmers and politicians in Ireland, and equally by anthropologists who seek to understand historical change reflexively through an ethnographic realization of constructed, realist, internal and external moments, requires the management of many and often continuous transactions. For example, while the specific support a 'big man' receives in Melanesia for his political endeavors and his attempts to build a name and a following is reciprocated by him through a return of bride price wealth and the financing of followers' other ritual obligations, both leader and supporters benefit from the 'big man's' overall increasing political renown. The portrait I have painted above of the Irish farmer-politician is not very different, in that real or imaginary patronage creates social, economic and political relations based on various notions of reciprocity and redistribution, through which over time both politician and supporters may benefit materially and socially. And despite the stereotype that the large farmers of Ireland have property as their source of power and influence, no such farmer can gain or maintain his influence as a big man in local politics and society if he does not use his skills, developed within various dimensions of society such as those of culture and class, to reciprocate and redistribute items of value, whether it be through the provision of such things as roads, fundamental services or information.

Knowing when to act and when to desist, when to project an identity and when to suppress it, when to focus on the private and internal and when to go for public and external goals, are the veritable stuff of politics and culture, whether it be in Melanesia or in Meath. But they are also the stuff of ethnography. Ethnography offers to anthropologists and other scholars the opportunity to immerse themselves within a social and political world of fine cultural difference and differentiation, and of sameness and integration. Chronicling the constructed and real in this effort provides much that can tie together the conjunctures and events of historical change. This book has offered just such a chronicle, of political, social and cultural change in one rural Irish county in the first years when Ireland's membership in the European Union helped to transform the Irish political economy.

It has also offered some insight in how ethnography can facilitate the understanding of such changes at local and regional levels. But it may still be too soon to truly grasp the significance of both the historical change chronicled here and the role of the anthropologist in its examination, because at any one time it may be extremely difficult to determine how fine and how successful a balance has been struck, in the lives of the politician, the farmer and the ethnographer. No matter how hard ethnographers try to balance their exploration of the constructed and the real, in their own research and in the lives of their hosts and informants, the politics and sociality of the moment may upset the effort. In the occasion with which I began this chapter, when time was called in the pub where I met my two political pals, and despite my protestations of neutrality and objectivity, upon taking his leave each asked for my vote at the upcoming local elections.

References

ACOT–Meath 1982. Meath: General Background Information. Unpublished mimeo.

ACOT–Meath.1986 *Agriculture in County Meath: 1986 Report*. Navan: the County Committee on Agriculture.

Aldridge, Alan 1993. Negotiating Status: Social Scientists and Anglican Clergy. *Journal of Contemporary Ethnography* 22(1): 97-112.

Andrilik, Erich 1981 The Farmers and the State: Agricultural Interests in West German Politics. *West European Politics* 4(1): 104-1 19.

Arensberg, Conrad M. 1937. *The Irish Countryman*. Cambridge, MA: Macmillan.

Arensberg, Conrad M. and Solon T. Kimball 1940. Family and Community in Ireland. Cambridge, MA: Harvard University Press.

Arensberg, Conrad M. and Solon T. Kimball 1968. *Family and Community in Ireland*. 2nd edition. Cambridge, MA: Harvard University Press.

Arensberg, Conrad M. and Solon T. Kimball 2001. *Family and Community in Ireland*. 3rd edition. Ennis, Ireland: CLASP Press.

Averyt, William F., Jr. 1977. *Agropolitics in the European Community*. New York: Praeger.

Bailey, F. G. 1969. *Stratagems and Spoils: A Social Anthropology of Politics*. Oxford: Basil Blackwell.

309

Barnes, J. A. 1968. Networks and Political Process. *Local-Level Politics*. Marc J. Swartz, ed. Chicago: Aldine.

Barth, Fredrik 1965. *Political Leadership among Swat Pathans*. London: Athlone.

Bax, Mart 1975. The Political Machine and Its Importance in the Irish Republic. *Political Anthropology* 1: 6-20.

Bax, Mart 1976. *Harpstrings and Confessions: Machine-style Politics in the Irish Republic*. Assen: Van Gorcum.

Bell, Desmond. 1990. *Acts of Union: Youth Culture and Sectarianism in Northern Ireland*. London: Macmillan.

Bellier, Irène and Thomas M. Wilson 2000a. Building, Imagining, and Experiencing Europe: Institutions and Identities in the European Union. *An Anthropology of the European Union: Building, Imagining and Experiencing the New Europe*. Irène Bellier and Thomas M. Wilson, eds. Oxford: Berg.

Bellier, Irène and Thomas M. Wilson, eds. 2000b. *An Anthropology of the European Union: Building, Imagining and Experiencing the New Europe*. Oxford: Berg.

Berger, Suzanne 1972. *Peasants against Politics: Rural Organization in Brittany, 1911-1967*. Cambridge, MA: Harvard University Press.

Birrell, Derek 1983. Local Government Councillors in Northern Ireland and the Republic of Ireland. *Contemporary Irish Studies*. Tom Gallagher and James O'Connell, eds. Manchester: Manchester University Press.

310

Blacking, John, Kieran Byrne and Kate Ingram 1989. Looking for Work in Larne: A Social Anthropological Study. *Social Anthropology and Public Policy in Northern Ireland.* Hastings Donnan and Graham McFarlane, eds. Aldershot, UK: Avebury.

Blackwell, John 1982. Government, Economy and Society. *Unequal Achievement: The Irish Experience, 1957-1982.* Frank Litton, ed. Dublin: Institute of Public Administration.

Blackwell, J and E O'Malley 1984. The Impact of EEC Membership on Irish Industry. *Ireland and the European Community* P. J. Drudy and Dermot McAleese, eds. Cambridge: Cambridge University Press.

Blok, Anton 1974. *The Mafia of a Sicilian Village, 1860-1960.* New York: Harper and Row.

Boissevain, Jeremy 1965. *Saints and Fireworks.* London: Athlone.

Boissevain, Jeremy 1966. Patronage in Sicily. *Man* (n.s.) 1: 18-33.

Boissevain, Jeremy 1974. *Friends of Friends.* Oxford: Oxford University Press.

Boissevain, Jeremy 1975. Introduction: Towards a Social Anthropology of Europe. *Beyond the Community: Social Process in Europe.* J. Boissevain and J. Friedl, eds. The Hague, The Netherlands: Department of Educational Science of the Netherlands.

Boon, James 1982. *Other Tribes, Other Scribes: Symbolic Anthropology in the Comparative Study of Cultures, Histories, Religions and Texts.* Cambridge: Cambridge University Press.

Braudel, Fernand 1980 [1958]. *On History*. Chicago, IL: University of Chicago Press.

Brody, Hugh 1973. *Innishkillane*. London: Allen Lane.

Buckley, Anthony D. 1982. *A Gentle People: A Study of a Peaceful Community in Northern Ireland*. Cultra: Ulster Folk and Transport Museum.

Bufwack, Mary S. 1982. *Village without Violence: An Examination of a Northern Irish Community*. Cambridge, MA: Schenkman.

Buksti, Jacob A.1979. Corporate Structure in Danish EC Policy: Patterns of Organizational Participation and Adaptation. Unpublished paper; European Consortium for Political Research, Brussels.

Bums, Brigid, and Trevor C. Salmon 1977. Policy-Making Coordination in Ireland on European Community Issues. *Journal of Common Market Studies* 15(4):272-287.

Burawoy, Michael 2003. Revisits: An Outline of a Theory of Reflexive Ethnography. *American Sociological Review* 68 (5): 645-679.

Buttel, Frederick H. 1982. The Political Economy of Agriculture in Advanced Industrial Societies: Some Observations on Theory and Method. *Current Perspectives in Social Theory*. S. G. McNall and G. N. Howe, eds. Greenwich, CT: JAI Press.

Buttel, Frederick H. and Howard Newby, eds. 1980. *The Rural Sociology of Advanced Societies: Critical Perspectives*. Montclair. NJ: Allanheld, Osmun and Co.

312

Byrne, Anne, Ricca Edmondson, Tony Varley 2001. Introduction to the Third Edition. Arensberg, Conrad M. and Solon T. Kimball. *Family and Community in Ireland.* 3rd edition. Ennis, Ireland: CLASP Press.

Campbell, J. K. 1964. *Honour, Family and Patronage.* Oxford: Clarendon.

Carey, Siobhan 1986. Role Perceptions among County Councillors. *Administration* 34 (3): 302-316.

Carty, R. K. 1976. Social Cleavages and Party Systems: A Reconsideration of the Irish Case. *European Journal of Political Research* 4: 195-203.

Carty, R. K. 1981. *Parish and Party Pump.* Waterloo, Ontario: Wilfrid Laurier University Press.

Central Statistics Office-Ireland 1928. *Agricultural Statistics Abstract.* Dublin: Stationery Office.

Central Statistics Office-Ireland 1982. *Census of Population of Ireland, 1981.* Dublin: Stationery Office.

Chubb, Basil 1963. Going about Persecuting Civil Servants: The Role of the Irish Parliamentary Representative. *Political Studies* 11: 272-86.

Chubb, Basil 1970. *The Government and Politics of Ireland.* Stanford, CA: Stanford University Press.

Chubb, Basil 1974. *The Government and Politics of Ireland.* Oxford: Oxford University Press.

Chubb, Basil 1982. *The Government and Politics of Ireland.* 2nd ed. London: Longman.

Clifford, James and George E. Marcus, eds. 1986. *Writing Culture: The Poetics and the Politics of Ethnography.* Berkeley, CA: University of California Press.

Cohan, Al 1972. *The Irish Political Elite.* Dublin: Gill and Macmillan.

Cohan, Al 1973. Career Patterns in the Irish Political Elite. *British Journal of Political Studies* 3: 213-28.

Cohan, Al 1974. Continuity and Change in the Irish Political Elite: A Comment on the 1973 Elections. *British Journal of Political Studies* 4: 250-52.

Cohen, Marilyn 1993. Urbanisation and the Milieux of Factory Life: Gilford/Dunbarton, 1825-1914. *Irish Urban Cultures.* Chris Curtin, Hastings Donnan and Thomas M. Wilson, eds. Belfast: Institute of Irish Studies Press.

Cole, Jeffrey 1997. *The New Racism in Europe: A Sicilian Ethnography.* Cambridge: Cambridge University Press.

Cole, John W. 1977. Anthropology Comes Part-Way Home: Community Studies in Europe. *Annual Review of Anthropology* 6: 349-378.

Cole, John W. and Eric R. Wolf 1974. *The Hidden Frontier: Ecology and Ethnicity in an Alpine Valley.* London and New York: The Academic Press.

Collins C. A. 1980. Local Political Leadership in England and Ireland. *Administration* 28 (1): 71-96.

Commins, Patrick 1986. Rural Social Change. *Ireland: A Sociological Profile.* Patrick Clancy, Sheelagh Drudy, Kathleen Lynch, Liam O'Dowd, eds. Dublin: Institute of Public Administration.

Commins, Patrick and Carmel Kelleher 1973. *Farm Inheritance and Succession: A Survey of Present Patterns*. Dublin: Macra na Feirme.

Conway, John J. 1989 The Divergence of Public and Private Development in Two Kilkenny Neighbourhoods. *Ireland from Below: Social Change and Local Communities*. Chris Curtin and Thomas M. Wilson, eds. Galway: Galway University Press.

Conway, Brian 2006. Foreigners, Faith and Fatherland: The Historical Origins, Development and Present Status of Irish Sociology. *Sociological Origins, Special Supplement*. 5 (1): 5-36.

Coulter, Colin 1999. *Contemporary Northern Irish Society: An Introduction*. London: Pluto Press.

Cox, P and B Kearney 1983. The Impact of the Common Agricultural Policy. *Ireland and the European Communities,* David Coombes, ed. Dublin: Gill and MacMillan.

Cresswell, Robert 1969. *Une communante rurale de 'Irlande*. Paris: Institute de Ethnographie.

Crozier, Maurna 1989. 'Powerful Wakes': Perfect Hospitality. *Ireland From Below: Social Change and Local Communities*. Chris Curtin and Thomas M. Wilson, eds. Galway: Galway University Press.

Curtin, Chris and Colm Ryan 1989. Clubs, Pubs, and Private Houses in a Clare Town. *Ireland From Below: Social Change and Local Communities*. Chris Curtin and Thomas M. Wilson, eds. Galway: Galway University Press.

315

Curtin, Chris and Tony Varley 1989. Brown Trout, 'Gentry' and Dutchmen: Tourism and Development in South Mayo. *Ireland From Below: Social Change and Local Communities*. Chris Curtin and Thomas M. Wilson, eds. Galway: Galway University Press.

Curtin, Chris, Hastings Donnan and Thomas M. Wilson, eds. 1993. *Irish Urban Cultures*. Belfast: Institute of Irish Studies Press.

Curtin, Chris and Thomas M. Wilson, eds. 1989. *Ireland From Below: Social Change and Local Communities*. Galway, Ireland: Galway University Press.

Cynical Public Servant 1986. Civil Servant and the Profits of Politics. *Sunday Press* 23 March.

Dempsey, Noel 1986. Councillor Replies to Expenses Attack. *Sunday Press* 13 April.

Department of Agriculture-Ireland 1978. *Review of the Situation in Agriculture, 1978*. Dublin: Department of Agriculture.

Dilley, Roy 1989. Boat Owners, Patrons and State Policy in the Northern Ireland Fishing Industry. *Social Anthropology and Public Policy in Northern Ireland*. Hastings Donnan and Graham McFarlane, eds. Aldershot, UK: Avebury.

Donnan, Hastings 1994. 'New' minorities: South Asians in the North. *The Unheard Voice: Social Anthropology in Ireland*. Pol O Muiri, ed. Belfast: Fortnight Educational Trust.

Donnan, Hastings, and Graham McFarlane 1986. Social Anthropology and the Sectarian Divide in Northern Ireland. *The Sectarian Divide in Northern Ireland Today*. Richard

Jenkins, Hastings Donnan and Graham McFarlane, eds. London: Royal Anthropological Institute.

Donnan, Hastings and Graham McFarlane, eds. 1989. *Social Anthropology and Public Policy in Northern Ireland.* Aldershot, UK: Avebury.

Donnan, Hastings, and Graham McFarlane, eds. 1997. *Culture and Policy in Northern Ireland.* Belfast: Institute of Irish Studies Press.

Drudy, P. J. and Dermot McAleese 1984. Editorial Introduction. *Ireland and the European Community.* P. J. Drudy and Dermot McAleese, eds. Cambridge: Cambridge University Press.

Duchêne, François, Edward Szcyepanik and Wilfrid Legg 1985. *New Limits on European Agriculture.* Totowa, NJ: Rowman and Allanheld.

Eipper, Chris 1986. *The Ruling Trinity: A Community Study of Church, State and Business in Ireland.* Aldershot: Gower.

Eisenstadt, S. N. and René Lemarchand, eds. 1981. *Political Clientelism, Patronage, and Development.* London: Sage.

European Communities - Commission 1982. *Ireland in Europe 1973-1983.* Luxembourg: Office for Official Publications of the European Communities.

Evans-Pritchard, E. E. 1962. *Essays in Social Anthropology.* London: Faber and Faber.

Fahey, Tony 1975. Assessment of Irish Sociology. *Social Studies* 4 (1): 95-98.

Farrell, Brian, and Maurice Manning 1978. The Election. *Ireland at the Polls*. Howard R. Penniman, ed. Washington, DC: American Enterprise Institute.

Feld, Werner 1966. National Economic Interest Groups and Policy Formation in the EC. *Political Science Quarterly* 81 (3):392-411.

Feld, Werner 1974 Subnational Regionalism and the European Community. *Orbis* XVIII: 1176-1192.

Finnegan, Richard B. 1983. *Ireland: The Challenge of Conduct and Change*. Boulder, CO: Westview.

Fischer, M. M. J. 1977. Interpretive Anthropology. *Reviews in Anthropology* 4 (4): 391-404.

Flinn, W. L. 1982. Rural Sociology: Prospects and Dilemmas in the 1930's. *Rural Sociology* 47: 1-16.

Fox, Robin 1963. The Structure of Personal Names on Tory Island. *Man* 63: 153-155.

Fox, Robin 1968. Multilingualism in Two Communities. *Man* (N.S.) 3: 456-464.

Fox, Robin 1978. *The Tory Islanders*. Cambridge: Cambridge University Press.

Fox, Robin 1979. The Visiting Husband on Tory Island. *Journal of Comparative Family Studies* 10: 163-190.

Franklin, S. H. 1973. *The European Peasantry: The Final Phase*. London: Methuen.

Frawley, James 1975. Rural Development in a Regional Context - A Sociological Appraisal. Unpublished paper, An Foras Taluntais, Dublin.

318

Freemen, T. W. 1972. *Ireland: A General and Regional Geography.* London: Methuen.

Friedmann, Harriet 1978. World Market, State, and the Family Farm: Social Bases of Household Production in the Era of Wage Labor. *Comparative Studies in Society and History* 20: 545-586.

Friedrich, Paul 1969. The Legitimacy of a Cacique. *Local Level Politics: Social and Cultural Perspectives.* Marc J. Swartz, ed. Chicago: Aldine.

Gaetz, Stephen 1993. Who Comes First? Teenage Girls, Youth Culture and the Provision of Youth Services in Cork. *Irish Urban Cultures.* Chris Curtin, Hastings Donnan and Thomas M. Wilson, eds. Belfast: Institute of Irish Studies Press.

Gallagher, Michael 1976. *Electoral Support for Irish Political Parties.* London: Sage.

Gallagher, Michael 1980. Candidate Selection in Ireland: The Impact of Localism and the Electoral System. *British Journal of Political Studies* 10: 489-503.

Gallagher, Michael 1985. *Political Parties in the Republic of Ireland.* Dublin: Gill and MacMillan.

Gallagher, Michael 1988. The Outcome. *How Ireland Voted.* Michael Laver, Peter Mair and Richard Sinnott, eds. Dublin: Poolbeg Press.

Garvin, Tom 1974. Political Cleavages, Party Politics, and Urbanization in Ireland: The Case of the Periphery-Dominated Centre. *European Journal of Political Research* 2: 307-27.

Garvin, Tom 1976. Local Party Activists in Dublin: Socialization, Recruitment, and Incentives. *British Journal of Political Studies* 6: 369-80.

Garvin, Tom 1977. Nationalist Elites, Irish Voters, and Irish Political Development: A Comparative Perspective. *Economic and Social Review* 8: 161-86.

Garvin, Tom 1978. The Destiny of the Soldiers: Tradition and Modernity in the Politics of de Valera's Ireland. *Political Studies* 26: 328-47.

Garvin, Tom 1981. *The Evolution of Irish Nationalist Politics.* Dublin: Gill and MacMillan.

Garvin, Tom 1982. Change and the Political System. *Unequal Achievement: The Irish Experience, 1957-1982.* Frank Litton, ed. Dublin: Institute of Public Administration.

Geertz, Clifford 1995. *After the Fact: Two Countries, Four Decades, One Anthropologist.* Cambridge, MA: Harvard University Press.

Gibbon, Peter 1973. Arensberg and Kimball Revisited. *Economy and Society* 2: 479-98.

Gibbon, Peter and Chris Curtin 1978. The Stem Family in Ireland. *Comparative Studies in Society and History* 20 (3): 429-453.

Gibbon, Peter and Chris Curtin 1983a. Irish Farm Families: Facts and Fantasies. *Comparative Studies in Society and History* 25 (2): 375-380.

Gibbon, Peter and Chris Curtin 1983b. Some observations on 'The stem family in Ireland reconsidered.' *Comparative Studies in Society and History* 25 (2): 393-395.

Gibbon, Peter and Michael D. Higgins 1974. Patronage, Tradition, and Modernization: The Case of the Irish Gombeenman. *Economic and Social Review* 6: 27-44.

Gillmor, Desmond A. 1977. *Agriculture in the Republic of Ireland.* Budapest: Akademiai Kiado.

Gilmore, David 1991. Subjectivity and Subjugation: Fieldwork in the Stratified Community. *Human Organization* 50 (3): 215-224.

Giordano, Christian 1987. The 'Wine War' Between France and Italy: Ethno-anthropological Aspects of the European Community. *Sociologia Ruralis* 27: 56-66.

Gmelch, George 1977. *The Irish Tinkers*. Menlo Park, CA: Cummings.

Gmelch, George 1986. Return migration to rural Ireland. *Return Migration and Regional Economic Problems*. R. L. King, ed. London: Croom Helm.

Gmelch, George and Sharon Bohn Gmelch 1985. The Cross-channel Migration of Irish Travellers. *The Economic and Social Review* 16 (4): 287-296.

Gmelch, Sharon Bohn 1989. From Poverty Subculture to Political Lobby: The Traveller Rights Movement in Ireland. *Ireland From Below: Social Change and Local Communities*. Chris Curtin and Thomas M. Wilson, eds. Galway: Galway University Press.

Government Information Service-Ireland 1979. *Financial Statement of the Tanaiste*. Dublin: The Stationery Office.

Greenwood, Davydd 1976. *Unrewarding Wealth*. Cambridge: Cambridge University Press.

Grillo, R. D. 1980. Introduction. *'Nation' and 'State' in Europe: Anthropological Perspectives*. R. D. Grillo, ed. London: Academic Press.

Groger, B. Lisa 1981. Of Men and Machines: Co-operation Among French Family Farmers. *Ethnology* 20: 163-176.

Gulliver, Phillip 1989. Doing Anthropological Research in Rural Ireland: Methods and Sources for Linking the Past and the Present. *Ireland From Below: Social Change and Local Communities*. Chris Curtin and Thomas M. Wilson, eds. Galway: Galway University Press.

Hannan, Damian 1970. *Rural Exodus*. London: Geoffrey Chapman.

Hannan, Damian 1972. Kinship, Neighbourhood and Social Change in Irish Rural Communities. *Economic and Social Review* 3: 163-188.

Hannan, Damian 1979. *Displacement and Development: Class, Kinship and Social Change in Irish Rural Communities*. Dublin: Economic and Social Research Institute.

Hannan, Damian 1982. Peasant Models and the Understanding of Social and Cultural Change in Rural Ireland. *Ireland: Land, Politics and People*. P. I. Drudy, ed. Cambridge: Cambridge University Press.

Handler, Richard 1988. *Nationalism and the Politics of Culture in Quebec*. Madison: University of Wisconsin Press.

Hansen, Edward C. 1977. *Rural Catalonia under the Franco Regime*. Cambridge: Cambridge University Press.

Havens, A. E., and H. Newby 1983. Agriculture and the State: An Analytical Approach. *State and Agriculture*. P.

Ehrensoft, W. H. Friedland, and F. H. Buttel, eds. Amsterdam: Amsterdam University Press.

Harris, Rosemary 1961. The Selection of Leaders in Ballybeg, Northern Ireland. *Sociological Review* (N S.) 9: 137-149.

Harris, Rosemary 1972. Prejudice and Tolerance in Ulster. Manchester: Manchester University Press.

Harris, Rosemary 1988. Theory and Evidence: The 'Irish Stem Family' and Field Data. *Man (N. S.)* 23 (3): 417-434.

Hart, J 1985. The European Regional Development Fund and the Republic of Ireland. *Regions in the European Community.* Michael Keating and J. Barry Jones, eds. Oxford: Clarendon Press.

Hastrup, Kirsten, and Peter Elsass 1990. Anthropological Advocacy: A Contradiction in Terms? *Current Anthropology* 31 (3): 301-311.

Hazelkorn, Ellen 1986. Class, Clientelism and the Political Process in the Republic of Ireland. *Ireland: A Sociological Profile.* Patrick Clancy, Sheelagh Drudy, Kathleen Lynch, Liam O'Dowd, eds. Dublin: Institute of Public Administration.

Helleiner, Jane 1993. Traveller Settlement in Galway City: Politics, Class and Culture. *Irish Urban Cultures.* Chris Curtin, Hastings Donnan and Thomas M. Wilson, eds. Belfast: Institute of Irish Studies Press.

Hertz, Rosanna and Jonathan B. Imber 1993. Introduction: Fieldwork in Elite Settings. *Journal of Contemporary Ethnography* 22(1): 3-6.

Herzfeld, Michael 1982. *Ours Once More: Folklore, Ideology, and the Making of Modern Greece*. Austin: University of Texas Press.

Herzfeld, Michael 1987. *Anthropology through the Looking Glass: Critical Ethnography in the Margins of Europe*. Cambridge: Cambridge University Press.

Higgins, Michael D. 1982. The Limits of Clientelism: Towards an Assessment of Irish Politics. *Private Patronage and Public Power: Political Clientelism in the Modem State*. Christopher Clapham, ed. London: Frances Pinter.

Hirsch, Eric and Charles Stewart 2005. Introduction: Ethnographies of Historicity. *History and Anthropology* 16 (3): 261-74.

Hogan, James 1945. *Election and Representation*. Cork: Cork University Press.

Howe, Leo 1989a. Unemployment, Doing the Double and Labour Markets in Belfast. *Ireland From Below: Social Change and Local Communities*. Chris Curtin and Thomas M. Wilson, eds. Galway: Galway University Press.

Howe, Leo 1989b. Social Anthropology and Public Policy: Aspects of Unemployment and Social Security in Northern Ireland. *Social Anthropology and Public policy in Northern Ireland*. Hastings Donnan and Graham McFarlane, eds. Aldershot, UK: Avebury.

Howe, Leo 1990. *Being Unemployed in Northern Ireland*. Cambridge: Cambridge University Press.

Humphreys, Alexander J. 1966. *New Dubliners: Urbanization and the Irish Family*. London: Routledge and Kegan Paul.

Hunter, Albert 1993. Local Knowledge and Local Power: Notes on the Ethnography of Local Community Elites. *Journal of Contemporary Ethnography* 22(1): 36-58.

Jenkins, Richard. 1983. *Lads, Citizens, and Ordinary Kids*. London: Routledge and Kegan Paul.

Jenkins, Richard 1986. Northern Ireland: In What Sense 'Religions' in Conflict? *The Sectarian Divide in Northern Ireland Today*. Richard Jenkins, Hastings Donnan and Graham McFarlane, eds. Royal Anthropological Institute of Great Britain and Ireland. Occasional Paper no. 41.

Jenkins, Richard 2008. *Rethinking Ethnicity: Arguments and Explorations*. 2nd ed. London: Sage.

Kane, Eileen 1968. Man and Kin in Donegal. *Ethnology* 7: 245-258.

Kane, Eileen 1978. *The Last Place God Made*. New Haven: HRA Flex Books.

Kane, Eileen 1979. The Changing Role of the Family in the Rural Irish Community. *Journal of Comparative Family Studies* 10: 141-162.

Kane, Eileen, John Blacking, Hastings Donnan, and Graham McFarlane 1988. A Review of Anthropological Research, North and South. *The State of Social Science Research in Ireland*. Liam O'Dowd, ed. Dublin: Royal Irish Academy.

Kelly, John 1986. How Councillors Make £160 a Week Expenses. *Sunday Press S2* March.

Kelly, Rose S. 1936. *Ireland's Bloodless Revolution, 1932-1936*. Chicago: Joyce and Smith.

Kenny, Michael 1961. *A Spanish Tapestry*. New York: Harper and Row.

Kertzer, David 1980. *Comrades and Christians*. Cambridge: Cambridge University Press.

Kockel, Ullrich 1991. *Regions, Borders, and European Integration*. Liverpool: Institute of Irish Studies, University of Liverpool.

Komito, Lee 1984. Irish Clientelism: a Reappraisal. *The Economic and Social Review* 15: 173-194.

Laver, Michael 1986a. Ireland: Politics with Some Social Bases: An Interpretation Based on Aggregate Data. *The Economic and Social Review* 17: 107-131.

Laver, Michael 1986b. Ireland: Politics with Some Social Bases: An Interpretation Based on Survey Data. *The Economic and Social Review* 17: 193-213.

Lawrence, Christopher M. 2007. *Blood and Oranges: Immigrant Labor and European Markets in Rural Greece*. Oxford: Berghahn.

Layne, Linda 1989. The Dialogics of Tribal Self-Representation in Jordan. *American Ethnologist* 16: 24-39.

Lee, Joseph 1982. Society and Culture. *Unequal Achievement*. Frank Litton, ed. Dublin: Institute of Public Administration.

LeMaster, Barbara 1993. When Women and Men Talk Differently: Language and Policy in the Dublin Deaf Community. *Irish Urban Cultures*. Chris Curtin, Hastings Donnan, and Thomas M. Wilson, eds. Belfast: Institute of Irish Studies Press.

326

Lévi-Strauss, Claude 1963 [1949]. History and Anthropology. *Structural Anthropology.* New York: Basic Books.

Leyton, Elliott 1966. Conscious Models and Dispute Regulation in an Ulster Village. *Man* (N. S.). 1: 534-542.

Leyton, Elliot 1970. Sphere of Inheritance in Aughnaboy. *American Anthropologist* 72: 1378-1388.

Leyton, Elliot 1974. Opposition and Integration in Ulster. *Man* (N. S.) 9: 185-198.

Leyton, Elliot 1975. *The One Blood: Kinship and Class in an Irish Village.* St John's: Institute of Social and Economic Research, Memorial University of Newfoundland.

McCall, Cathal and Thomas M. Wilson, eds. 2010. *Europeanisation and Hibernicisation: Ireland and Europe.* Amsterdam and New York: Rodopi B. V.

McCann, May 1994. A Woman's Voice: A Feminist Looks at Irish Anthropology. *The Unheard Voice: Social Anthropology in Ireland.* Pol O Muiri, ed. Belfast: Fortnight Educational Trust.

McCracken, J. L. 1958. *Representative Government in Ireland.* Oxford: Oxford University Press.

McFarlane, Graham 1979. Mixed marriages in Ballycuan, Northern Ireland. *Journal of Comparative Family Studies* 10: 191-205.

McFarlane, Graham 1989. Dimensions of Protestantism: The Working of Protestant Identity in a Northern Irish Village. *Ireland From Below: Social Change and Local Communities.* Chris Curtin and Thomas M. Wilson, eds. Galway: Galway University Press.

327

McFarlane, Graham 1994. A Soft Voice: The Anthropology of Religion in Ireland. *The Unheard Voice: Social Anthropology in Ireland.* Pol O Muiri, ed. Belfast: Fortnight Educational Trust. January.

McLaughlin, Eithne. 1989. In Search of the Female Breadwinner: Gender and Unemployment in Derry City. *Social Anthropology and Public Policy in Northern Ireland.* Hastings Donnan and Graham McFarlane, eds. Aldershot, UK: Avebury.

McNabb, Patrick 1964. Demography and Social Structure. *The Limerick Rural Survey 1958-1964.* J. Newman, ed. Tipperary, Ireland: Muintir na Tire.

Mair, Peter 1979. The Autonomy of the Political: The Development of the Irish Party System. *Comparative Politics* 11 (4): 445-65.

Mann, Susan A. and James M. Dickinson 1980. State and Agriculture in Two Eras of American Capitalism. *The Rural Sociology of the Advanced Societies.* F. H. Buttel and H. Newby, eds. Montclair, NJ: Allanheld, Osmun and Co.

Manning, Maurice 1971. *The Blueshirts.* Toronto: University of Toronto Press.

Manning, Maurice 1979. The Farmers. *Ireland 1945-70.* J. J. Lee, ed. Dublin: Gill and Macmillan.

Marcus, George E. and M. M. J. Fischer 1986. *Anthropology as Cultural Critique: An Experimental Moment in the Human Sciences.* Chicago: University of Chicago Press.

Matthews, Alan 1983. The Economic Consequences of EEC Membership for Ireland. *Ireland and the European*

——— *Communities*. David Coombes, ed. Dublin: Gill and MacMillan.

Meghen, P. J. 1961. Community Studies in America and Ireland. *Rural Ireland* 1961: 48-67.

Messenger, Betty. 1975. *Picking up the Linen Threads*. Austin: University of Texas.

Messenger, John 1964. Literacy vs. Scientific Interpretation of Cultural 'Reality' in the Aran Islands of Eire. *Ethnohistory* 11: 41-55.

Messenger, John 1968. Types and Causes of Disputes in an Irish Folk Community. *Eire-Ireland.* 3: 27-37.

Messenger, John 1969. *Inis Beag.* New York: Holt, Rinehart and Winston.

Messenger, John 1978. Anthropology: Present and Future. Unpublished paper, presented to the American Committee for Irish Studies, SUNY Cortland.

Messenger, John 1983. *An Anthropologist at Play: Balladmongering in Ireland and Its Consequences for Research.* Lanham, MD: University Press of America.

Messenger, John 1988. Islanders Who Read. *Anthropology Today* 4: 17-19.

Messenger, John 1989. *Inis Beag Revisited: The Anthropologist as Observant Participator.* Salem, WI: Sheffield Publishing.

Milton, Kay 1993. Belfast: Whose City? *Irish Urban Cultures.* Chris Curtin, Hastings Donnan and Thomas M. Wilson, eds. Belfast: Institute of Irish Studies Press.

Milton, Kay 1994. An Environmentalist's Science: An Examination of Social Science and Social Change. *The Unheard Voice: Social Anthropology in Ireland.* Pol O Muiri, ed. Belfast: Fortnight Educational Trust.

Mogey, John 1947. *Rural Life in Northern Ireland.* Oxford: Oxford University Press.

Moss, Warner 1933. *Political Parties in the Irish Free State.* New York: Columbia University Press.

Murray, Stephen O. and Keelung Hong 1988. Taiwan, China, and the 'Objectivity' of Dictatorial Elites. *American Anthropologist* 90: 976-978.

Neville-Rolfe. Edmund 1984. *The Politics of Agriculture in the European Community.* London: European Centre for Policy Studies.

Newby, Howard 1979. *Social Change in Rural England.* Madison: University of Wisconsin Press.

Newby, Howard 1980a. Rural Sociology-A Trend Report. *Current Sociology* 28(1):1-141.

Newby, Howard 1980b. State Intervention in British Agriculture: Social and Political Consequences. Unpublished paper, presented to the Council for European Studies, Washington, D.C.

Newby, Howard 1983. The Sociology of Agriculture. *Annual Review of Sociology* 9:67-81.

Newby, Howard, and Frederick H. Buttel 1980. Towards a Critical Rural Sociology. *The Rural Sociology of the Advanced Societies: Critical Perspectives.* F. H. Buttel and H. Newby, eds. Montclair, NJ: Allanheld, Osmun and Co.

Newby, Howard, Colin Bell, David Rose and Peter Saunders 1978. *Property, Paternalism and Power*. Madison: University of Wisconsin Press.

O'Brien, K. 1978. Ireland Has EEC's Fastest Growth Rate. *Irish Times,* 11 October.

O'Donnell, James D. 1979. *How Ireland Is Governed*. Dublin: Institute of Public Administration.

O'Leary, Cornelius 1979. *Irish Elections, 1918-1977.* Dublin: Gill and Macmillan.

O'Leary, Olivia 1981. TDs as Patrons and Brokers Have Replaced the Landlords and Gombeen Men. *Irish Times*, 7 April.

Orridge, Andrew W. 1981.The Political Economy of Irish Fascism. Unpublished paper, presented to the Political Studies Association, University of Hull.

O'Sullivan, Eoin 1993. Identity and Survival in a Hostile Environment: Homeless Men in Galway. *Irish Urban Cultures*. Chris Curtin, Hastings Donnan and Thomas M. Wilson, eds. Belfast: Institute of Irish Studies Press.

Ohnuki-Tierney, Emiko 1990. Introduction: The Historicization of Anthropology. *Culture Through Time: Anthropological Approaches*. Emiko Ohnuki-Tierney, ed. Stanford, CA: Stanford University Press.

Paine, Robert, ed. 1985. *Advocacy and Anthropology: First Encounters*. St. John's, Newfoundland: Institute of Social and Economic Research, Memorial University.

Peace, Adrian 1989. From Arcadia to Anomie: Critical Notes on the Constitution of Irish Society as an Anthropological Subject. *Critique of Anthropology* 9(1): 89-111.

Peace, Adrian 1993. Environmental Protest, Bureaucratic Closure: The Politics of Discourse in Rural Ireland. *Environmentalism: The View from Anthropology*. Kay Milton, ed. London: Routledge.

Peace, Adrian 1997. *A Time of Reckoning: The Politics of Discourse in Rural Ireland*. St. John's, Newfoundland: Institute of Social and Economic Research, Memorial University.

Peillon, Michel 1982. *Contemporary Irish Society: An Introduction*. Dublin: Gill and Macmillan.

Peillon, Michel 1986. Stratification and Class. *Ireland: A Sociological Profile*. Patrick Clancy, Sheelagh Drudy, Kathleen Lynch, Liam O'Dowd, eds. Dublin: Institute of Public Administration.

Pitt-Rivers, Julian A. 1961. *The People of the Sierra*. Chicago: University of Chicago Press.

Pye, Lucian. W. and Sidney Verba, eds. 1965. *Political Culture and Political Development*. Princeton, NJ: Princeton University Press.

Roche, Desmond 1982. *Local Government in Ireland*. Dublin: Institute of Public Administration.

Rogers, Susan Carol 1987. Good to Think: The 'Peasant' in Contemporary France. *Anthropological Quarterly* 60:56-63.

Rogers, Susan Carol 1991. *Shaping Modern Times Rural France*. Princeton: Princeton University Press.

Roth, Paul A. 1989. Ethnography Without Tears. *Current Anthropology* 30 (5): 555-569.

Rottman, David B. and Philip I. O'Connell 1982. The Changing Social Structure. *Unequal Achievement*. Frank Litton, ed. Dublin: Institute of Public Administration.

Rottman, David B., Damian F. Hannan, Niamh Hardiman, and Miriam M. Wiley 1982. *The Distribution of Income in the Republic of Ireland: a Study in Social Class and Family-cycle Inequalities*. Dublin: Economic and Social Research Institute.

Ruane, Joseph 1989. Success and Failure in a West of Ireland Factory. *Ireland From Below: Social Change and Local Communities*. Chris Curtin and Thomas M. Wilson, eds. Galway: Galway University Press.

Rumpf, E., and A. C. Hepburn 1977. *Nationalism and Socialism in Twentieth-Century Ireland*. Liverpool: Liverpool University Press.

Sacks, Paul 1976. *The Donegal Mafia*. New Haven, CT: Yale University Press.

Sahlins, Marshall 1963. Poor Man, Rich Man, Big Man, Chief: Political Types in Melanesia and Polynesia. *Comparative Studies in Society and History* 5: 285-303.

Sahlins, Marshall 1985. *Islands of History*. Chicago, IL: University of Chicago Press.

Schapera, Isaac 1962. Should Anthropologists Be Historians? *Journal of the Royal Anthropological Institute* 92: 143-56.

Scheper-Hughes, Nancy 1979. *Saints, Scholars, and Schizophrenics: Mental Illness in Rural Ireland.* Berkeley, CA: The University of California Press.

Scheper-Hughes, Nancy 2000. Ire in Ireland. *Ethnography* 1 (1): 117-140.

Schmidt, Steffen W., James C. Scott, Carl Landé and Laura Guasti, eds. 1977. *Friends, Followers, and Factions.* Berkeley, CA: University of California Press.

Schneider, Jane, and Peter Schneider 1976. *Culture and Political Economy in Western Sicily.* New York: Academic Press.

Schneider, Jane, Peter Schneider and Edward Hansen 1972. Modernization and Development: The Role of Regional Elites and Noncorporate Groups in the European Mediterranean. *Comparative Studies in Society and History* 14: 328-350.

Scully, John J. 1971. *Agriculture in the West of Ireland.* Dublin: The Stationery Office.

Shanahan, Ella 1981. Fitting the CAP to Irish Farming. *Irish Times*, 14 April.

Shanklin, Eugenia 1980. The Irish Go-between. *Anthropological Quarterly* 53: 162-172.

Shanklin, Eugenia 1982. *Donegal's Changing Traditions: An Ethnographic Study.* New York: Gordon and Breach.

Shanks, Amanda. 1994. Cultural Divergence and Durability: The Border, Symbolic Boundaries and the Irish Gentry. *Border Approaches: Anthropological Perspectives on*

334

Frontiers. Hastings Donnan and Thomas M. Wilson, eds. Lanham, MD: University Press of America.

Sheehan, Elizabeth A. 1991. Political and Cultural Resistance to European Community Europe: Ireland and the Single European Act. *Socialism and Democracy* 13: 101-118.

Sheehan, Elizabeth A. 1993. The Academic as Informant: Methodological and Theoretical Issues in the Ethnography of Intellectuals. *Human Organization* 52 (3): 252-259.

Sheehy, S. J. 1978. Ireland and the CAP. *Community Report* 5(2):4-5.

Sheehy, S. J. 1980. The Impact of EEC Membership on Irish Agriculture. *Journal of Agricultural Economics* 31(3):297-308.

Sheehy, S. J. 1984. The Common Agricultural Policy and Ireland. *Ireland and the European Community*. P. J. Drudy and Dermot McAleese, eds. Cambridge: Cambridge University Press

Sheehy, S. J. and R. O'Connor 1985. *Economics of Irish Agriculture*. Dublin: Institute of Public Administration.

Shore, Cris 1993. Inventing the 'People's Europe': Critical Approaches to European Community 'Cultural Policy'. *Man* 28: 779-800.

Shutes, Mark 1991. Kerry Farmers and the European Community: Capital Transitions in a Rural Irish Parish. *Irish Journal of Sociology* 1: 1-17.

Shutes, Mark 1993. Rural Communities Without Family Farms? Family Dairy Farming in the Post-1993 EC.

Cultural Change and the New Europe. Thomas M. Wilson and M. Estellie Smith, eds. Boulder, CO: Westview Press.

Silverman, Marilyn 1989. 'A Labouring Man's Daughter': Constructing 'Respectability' in South Kilkenny. *Ireland From Below: Social Change and Local Communities*. Chris Curtin and Thomas M. Wilson, eds. Galway: Galway University Press.

Silverman, Marilyn and P. H. Gulliver 1992a. Historical Anthropology and the Ethnographic Tradition: A Personal, Historical, and Intellectual Account. *Approaching the Past: Historical Anthropology Through Irish Case Studies*. Marilyn Silverman and P. H. Gulliver, eds. New York: Columbia University Press.

Silverman, Marilyn and P. H. Gulliver, eds. 1992b. *Approaching the Past: Historical Anthropology Through Irish Case Studies*. New York: Columbia University Press.

Silverman, Sydel 1965. Patronage and Community-Nation Relationships in Central Italy. *Ethnology* 4:172-89.

Sinclair, Peter R. 1980. Agricultural Policy and the Decline of Commercial Family Farming: A Comparative Analysis of the U.S., Sweden, and the Netherlands. *The Rural Sociology of the Advanced Societies*. F. H. Buttel and H. Newby, eds. Montclair, NJ: Allanheld, Osmun and Co.

Stacul, Jaro 2003. *The Bounded Field: Localism and Local Identity in an Italian Alpine Valley*. Oxford: Berghahn.

Szuchewycz, Bodhan. 1989. The Meanings of Silence in the Irish Catholic Charismatic Movement. *Ireland From Below: Social Change and Local Communities*. Chris

Curtin and Thomas M. Wilson, eds. Galway: Galway University Press.

Taylor, Lawrence 1980a. Colonialism and Community Structure in Western Ireland. *Ethnohistory* 27: 169-181.

Taylor, Lawrence 1980b. The Merchant in Peripheral Ireland: A Case from Donegal. *Anthropology* 4: 63-76.

Taylor, Lawrence 1981. 'Man the Fisher': Salmon Fishing and the Expression of Community in a Rural Irish Settlement. *American Ethnologist* 8: 774-788.

Taylor, Lawrence 1989a. Bas i-nEirinn: Cultural Constructions of Death in Ireland. *Anthropological Quarterly* 62 (4): 175-187.

Taylor, Lawrence 1989b. The Mission: An Anthropological View of an Irish Religious Occasion. *Ireland From Below: Social Change and Local Communities*. Chris Curtin and Thomas M. Wilson, eds. Galway: Galway University Press.

Taylor, Lawrence J. 1995. *Occasions of Faith: An Anthropology of Irish Catholics*. Philadelphia: University of Pennsylvania Press.

Varenne, Hervé. 1993. Dublin 16: Accounts of Suburban Lives. *Irish Urban Cultures*. Chris Curtin, Hastings Donnan and Thomas M. Wilson, eds. Belfast: Institute of Irish Studies Press.

Vincent, Joan 1983. Marriage, Religion and Class in South Fermanagh, 1846-1920. *Emergent Structures and the Family*. Owen Lynch, ed. Delhi: Hindustan Publishing.

Vincent, Joan 1989. Local Knowledge and Political Violence in County Fermanagh. *Ireland From Below: Social Change and Local Communities*. Chris Curtin and Thomas M. Wilson, eds. Galway: Galway University Press.

Vincent, Joan 1992. A Political Orchestration of the Irish Famine: County Fermanagh, May 1847. *Approaching the Past*. Marilyn Silverman and P. H. Gulliver, eds. New York: Columbia University Press.

Vincent, Joan 1993. Ethnicity and the State in Northern Ireland. *Ethnicity and the State*. Judith D. Toland, ed. New Brunswick, NJ: Transaction Publishers.

Vincent, Joan 1994. *Anthropology and Politics: Visions, Traditions, and Trends*. Tucson: University of Arizona Press.

Weingrod, Alex 1968. Patrons, Patronage, and Political Parties. *Comparative Studies in Society and History* 10: 377-401.

Whyte, John 1966. *Dail Deputies*. Dublin: Tuarim.

Whyte, John 1974. Ireland: Politics without Social Bases. *Electoral Behaviour: A Comparative Handbook*. Richard Rose, ed. New York: Free Press.

Wilson, Thomas M. 1984. From Clare to the Common Market: Perspectives in Irish Ethnography. *Anthropological Quarterly* 57 (1): 1-15.

Wilson, Thomas M. 1987. Mythic Images of the Irish Family in the Works of Flaherty, deValera, and Arensberg and Kimball. *Working Papers in Irish Studies*, Northeastern University 87 (2/3): 14-31.

Wilson, Thomas M. 1988. Culture and Class Among The 'Large' Farmers of Eastern Ireland. *American Ethnologist* 15 (4): 680-695.

Wilson, Thomas M. 1989a. Large Farms, Local Politics, and the International Arena: The Irish Tax Dispute of 1979. *Human Organization* 48 (1): 60-70.

Wilson, Thomas M. 1989b. Broker's Broker: The Chairman of the Meath County Council. *Ireland From Below: Social Change and Local Communities*. Chris Curtin and Thomas M. Wilson, eds. Galway: Galway University Press.

Wilson, Thomas M. 1990. From Patronage to Brokerage in the Local Politics of Eastern Ireland. *Ethnohistory* 37: 158-187.

Wilson, Thomas M. 1991. On Characterisation and Identity: Further Reflections on Long Term Field Research in Ireland. *Anthropology Ireland* 1 (1-2): 6-10.

Wilson, Thomas M. 1993a. An Anthropology of the European Community. *Cultural Change and the New Europe*. Thomas M. Wilson and M. Estellie Smith, eds. Boulder and Oxford: Westview Press.

Wilson, Thomas M. 1993b. Frontiers Go But Boundaries Remain: The Irish Border as a Cultural Divide. *Cultural Change and the New Europe*. Thomas M. Wilson and M. Estellie Smith, eds. Boulder and Oxford: Westview Press.

Wilson, Thomas M. 1993c. Consumer Culture and European Integration at the Northern Irish Border. *European Advances in Consumer Research, Volume 1*. W. Fred van Raaij and Gary J. Bamossy, eds. Provo, UT: Association for Consumer Research.

Wilson, Thomas M. 1994a. A Question of Identity: Problems of Social Anthropology in Ireland. *The Unheard Voice: Social Anthropology in Ireland.* Pol O Muiri, ed. Belfast: Fortnight Educational Trust.

Wilson, Thomas M. 1994b. Symbolic Dimensions to the Irish Border. *Border Approaches: Anthropological Perspectives on Frontiers.* Hastings Donnan and Thomas M. Wilson, eds. Lanham, MD: University Press of America.

Wilson, Thomas M. 1998. An Anthropology of the European Union, From Above and Below. *Europe in the Anthropological Imagination.* Susan Parman, ed. Upper Saddle River, NJ: Prentice-Hall.

Wilson, Thomas M. and Hastings Donnan 2006. *The Anthropology of Ireland.* Oxford: Berg.

Wolf, Eric R. 1956. Aspects of Group Relations in a Complex Society: Mexico. *American Anthropologist* 58: 1065-78.

Wolf, Eric R. 1966. Kinship, Friendship, and Patron-client Relations in Complex Societies. *The Social Anthropology of Complex Societies.* Michael Banton, ed. London: Tavistock.

Worsley, Peter 1968. *The Trumpet Shall Sound.* 2nd ed. New York: Schocken.

Wren, M. 1987. Governments May Change But Not the Realities. *Irish Times,* 20 February.

Zimmerman, Joseph F. 1976. Role Perceptions of Irish City and County Councillors. *Administration* 24 (4): 482-500.

Zimmerman, Joseph F. 1978. Role Perceptions of Dual Office Holders in Ireland. *Administration* 26 (1): 25-47.

Index

Cavan, County, 52
Celtic Tiger, 2, 43, 50, 117, 170
census, 96
centralization, 32, 173, 176,
    248, 278, 304
Chicago, 34
Christianity, 49
Chubb, Basil, 299-301
church, 23, 70, 81, 147
Church of Ireland, 101, 104,
    112
citizen, 5, 37, 42, 50, 133, 136,
    137-138, 153, 159, 282
citizenship, 6
Civil War, Irish, 40, 113, 127,
    132, 133, 138, 140, 145,
    152-153, 166, 170, 225,
    258, 266
civil servants, 173-208, 216
civil service, 148, 278
Clann na Talmhan Party, 144
Clare, County, 18-23, 33, 53-
    81, 94, 121-122, 231
class, 20, 21, 22, 25, 33, 37, 44-
    46, 60, 62-63, 67, 75, 81,
    83-125, 245, 248, 300, 306
    middle, 90-91, 105-110,
    119, 123
client, 33, 35, 69, 127-170,
    248, 257, 261
clientage, 183
clientelism, 135-147, 165
clinics, 187
codology, 243, 269-280
Cole, John W., 24-25
colonialism, 49, 300

Combined Purchasing Act
    (1925), 140
commerce, 147
Committee of Agriculture,
    Meath, 151, 196, 227
Common Agricultural Policy
    (CAP), 2, 7, 49, 84, 214,
    217-220, 230
Common Market, 1, 66, 212,
    239, 241
community, 18, 23-25, 31, 41,
    48, 55, 61, 68, 72-73, 75,
    77, 89, 104, 107, 245, 249,
    258, 269, 271
Community study, 19, 43, 54-
    73, 75, 91, 129
Connaught, Province, 80
Connynghams, 102
conservatism, 132
conspicuous consumption, 44
constituency, 33, 36-37, 39, 72-
    73, 88, 186, 256, 267
constituents, 6, 32, 37, 87, 160,
    174, 186, 270
Cork, County, 35, 72-73, 132,
    163, 194, 230
county councillors, 141, 175,
    216, 249
county councils, 132
County Electoral Area (CEA),
    39, 141, 143, 149-156, 166,
    170, 181, 185, 198
county families, 44, 100-103
County Management Act
    (1940), 128, 134, 164, 201,
    252

labor force, 7

laborers, 144

Labour Party, Ireland, 143, 157, 159, 162, 178, 205, 222, 236, 267

Land Acts, 103

Land Wars, 105

Lane, Paddy, 226, 228-229, 235

Laois, County, 234

Latin America, 24

Lawrence, Christopher M., 304

leadership, 135, 163-164, 168, 173-208, 250-280, 300

Leddy, Anthony, 235

Leinster, Province, 27, 38, 40, 42-43, 75, 80, 88, 95, 124, 148, 157, 222, 303

Lévi-Strauss, Claude, 14

levy, 85, 220, 225-236

Leyton, Elliott, 23, 62, 67

Limerick, County, 61

lobby, 5, 40, 47, 240
environmental, 28

lobbying, 85

Local Appointments Commission, 140, 164

Local Government Act (1925), 139

Local Government (Extension of Franchise) Bill (1933), 155

Local Government (Ireland) Act (1898), 208

localism, 132, 160-161, 165, 302

Louth, County, 52, 273

loyalty, 132, 146, 300

Luxembourg, 2, 97

Lynch, Jack, 231-233, 236

McFarlane, Graham, 67

McNabb, Patrick, 61

Maher, T. J., 229

Maitland, L. M., 15

Manhattan, 275

markets, 7, 70, 168
British, 3, 43, 150
Dublin, 43

marriage, 55, 59, 69, 290

Marx, Karl, 296

Mayo, County, 35

meat mountain, 84

Meath Chronicle, 185, 204

Meath, County, 4-5, 8, 14-18, 22, 25, 34-36, 39-51, 80, 83-125, 127-170, 173-208, 212-242, 243-280, 281-307
life, 18
people, 18

Meath County Council, 40, 52, 139-147, 173-208, 251-280
chairman, 141, 157, 176-208, 251-253
committees, 141, 145, 162, 177, 193, 195-198, 227, 253

Meath County Councillors (MCCs), 38, 134, 147-171. 178-208, 252, 260, 265-266, 281-307

Mediterranean, 115

Melanesia, 305-308

members, county council, 38,
134, 147-171. 178-208,
252, 260, 265-266, 281-307
Member of the European
Parliament (MEP), 40, 162,
171
merchants, 144
Messenger, John, 23, 61, 64
methodology, 19, 56, 79
methods, 28
Middletown, 56
migration, 75, 76, 81
milk lake, 84, 219
mines, 96
modernization, 2, 22, 60, 64,
66, 70, 83, 90, 94
Monaghan, County, 52
Munster, Province, 80

nation, 24, 25, 26, 43, 71, 72,
287
nation-state, 51, 80, 303
National University of Ireland-
Maynooth, 63
nationalism, 26, 67, 132, 299
Navan, 39, 80, 88, 108, 116,
119, 124, 161-165, 173-
208, 226, 237, 243-281,
283, 286, 298
Urban District Council
(UDC), 171, 251
Netherlands, The, 2
networks, 23, 36, 39, 73, 128,
130, 147, 161, 168-169,
175, 217, 245, 255, 257,
259, 261, 265, 274-279
political, 33, 246, 270

social, 245-246
New York, 34, 275-276, 278,
298
Newburyport, 20
Newby, Howard, 303-304
newspapers, 143, 170, 185,
202-204, 263
North America, 54, 69, 72
Northern Ireland, 27, 34, 47,
50-52, 60, 62, 63, 66, 67,
70, 79, 80, 81, 90, 100, 113,
170, 267, 275, 289

Offaly, County, 52
Ohnuki-Tierney, Emiko, 291

Pale, The, 100
paradigm, 54, 75, 79, 305
participant observation, 28, 31,
52, 77
patron, 33, 35, 69, 127-170,
200, 276
patron-client, 35-36, 170
patronage, 50, 128-170, 183,
247, 249, 258
imaginary, 36, 135, 173,
175, 181, 306
Peillon, Michel, 91
personalism, 132, 161, 165
Pitt Rivers, Julian, 128
policy, 5, 27, 29-30, 31, 36, 46-
51, 67, 68, 76, 84-89, 100,
200, 211, 215, 228, 236,
238, 255
political culture, 8, 34, 51, 53,
88, 125, 131-135, 137, 169,
175, 257, 281-307

349

Thomas M. Wilson

Dr. Thomas Wilson received his Ph.D. in Anthropology from the City University of New York. Dr. Wilson is currently completing research projects in both Canada and the Republic of Ireland.